D0128298

Just the Facts!
Close Reading
and Comprehension
of Informational Text

Author

Lori Oczkus, M.A.

Foreword

Pam Allyn, M.A.

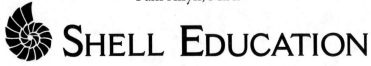

SHELL EDUCATION

Image Credits
p.14, 16, 22, 39, 43, 45, 50, 64, 71, 87, Lori Oczkus; All other images Shutterstock

Shell Education

5301 Oceanus Drive
Huntington Beach, CA 92649-1030
http://www.shelleducation.com

ISBN 978-1-4258-1316-1

© 2014 Shell Educational Publishing, Inc.

The classroom teacher may reproduce copies of materials in this book for classroom use only. The reproduction of any part for an entire school or school system is strictly prohibited. No part of this publication may be transmitted, stored, or recorded in any form without written permission from the publisher.

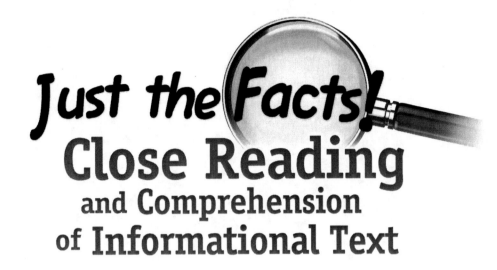

Table of Contents

© Shell Education

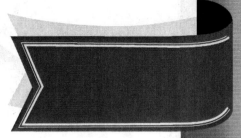

Foreword

This book is an invaluable tool for teachers to realize a great hope for every student: to become a close reader of text and of the world through the power of knowing, reading, and responding to informational text. Informational text is a powerful genre, surrounding us and illuminating our worlds every day, and yet is also one that can overwhelm and confound our student readers at times, and us as teachers, too. Lori's wise voice guides us through the thicket of the texts that matter, giving us strategies to share with our students that will indeed change their reading lives.

In many cities here in the United States, and in communities around the world, understanding how to read informational text well is a life raft. I have been teaching and innovating in education reform and advocacy for over 15 years and writing about my discoveries. As a literacy educator, I have spent decades working alongside teachers and students and the area of struggle for many is how we address informational reading with our children. The child who has hopes and dreams for her college- and career-ready future must be able to not only comprehend informational text but to master it. And indeed, that is what this one-of-a-kind book does: it provides practical and inspirational strategies for how we can be sure every child has the tool kit for success in an information-based world, and how that child not only manages it, but masters it.

In these times of great change, of transformation for our society through the ever-growing power of communication and speed of how information is shared, more than ever we as educators need to know how to navigate this world with our students. We live in an era of collaboration, communication, and community. But in order to best prepare our students for this kind of world, we have to be the kind of teachers who can boldly, rigorously, and compassionately share with our students the best practices for close reading and how we do that can give them ownership over an ever-changing landscape of text and ideas. What Lori has done here is to create a remarkable combination of research, best practices, and ready-to-use lesson plans that illuminate children's natural curiosity and love of informational text. In an approachable manner, she makes it possible for us to teach strategies for close reading of informational text in a way that our students can both understand and love. But beyond all those very important foundations, she gives us a road map for how we can guide children through the maze of information and help them to become the kinds of lifelong readers who know text, read text critically, and understand it so deeply that they can build their own new ideas from it.

Lori values the child's voice and the teacher's heart. She has created practical lessons, tips, techniques, and recommendations that both seek the highest level of standards for all children, and are also joyful, practical, and user friendly. What a rare and wonderful combination! From ample project-based learning suggestions to kid-tested activities, she has seamlessly given us close-reading procedures and guides that can and should be implemented instantly and tend to all children: from our most reluctant readers to our children already reading beyond grade level. At a time when we all worry about the preciousness of those teaching moments and how to make the most of them, a book comes along, this one, that will make that time matter most.

—Pam Allyn, M.A.
Author and Executive Director of LitLife and LitWorld

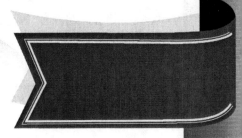

Acknowledgments

I am very pleased to present to you *Just the Facts! Close Reading and Comprehension of Informational Text* as a desk top resource that I hope you will return to often for lessons and ideas to reach all of your students and improve literacy and student engagement in your classroom. I feel blessed to have the opportunity to share this exciting collection with you and would like to thank some special folks who made this book possible.

Special thanks to the variety of schools around the country who sign on to become "project schools" with me each year. Our hard work together in classroom demonstration lessons, coaching, and grade level meetings helped shape the lessons in this book. I am especially thankful for the opportunity to work with the teachers and students this past year at Salvador Elementary School in Napa. (They are the stars in the photos!)

The team of special readers who reviewed and gave feedback to drafts of this text range from district administrators, classroom teachers and reading specialists, to university professors. This distinguished group represents a variety of school districts in New York, Florida, Indiana, California, Missouri, and Kansas. A warm and heartfelt thanks goes to reviewers Mary Jo Barker, Mary Charles, Amanda Cleary, Mary Jo Fox, Audrey Fong, Kathy Langham, Tarie Lewis, and Ellen Osmundson.

Thanks to Sara Johnson, Editorial Director, and Lori Nash, Editor, along with all of the the talented staff at Teacher Created Materials and Shell Education for their love of children, close ties to the classroom, knowledge of current research and trends, and ability to listen and create books teachers love!

Love and a thousand thanks to my wonderful husband, Mark, and our young adult and teen children Bryan, Rachael, and Rebecca for their support even when I stuck my head in my lap top a few hours each day last summer to work on this manuscript while on our family mountain and beach vacations!

To the readers of this text, thanks for joining me in sharing informational text strategies that will engage and improve literacy in you classroom and across your school!

© Shell Education

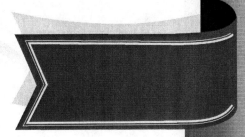

Introduction

Informational text bombards us every day in our fast-paced world. Now more than ever our students need powerful strategies and skills to help them as they navigate their way through informational texts. In a culture where critical thinking, collaboration, and creativity matter, our classrooms need to grow students who are, college and career ready. The Common Core States Standards call for more rigor, complex materials, and lots of time spent on informational texts. The good news is students actually like reading informational text. Watch eyes light up as you show the cover of *Mummies and Their Mysteries* (Wilcox 1999) to sixth graders, or flip through the pages studying the size of the pyramid at Giza or a python in *How Big Is It?* (Hillman 2007) with a third-grade guided-reading group. Ask first graders gathered on the rug what they know about dinosaurs and watch hands shoot up. Many of our students are already naturally drawn to informational texts and topics. For some of our boys, informational texts are the only texts they willingly read (Gurian, Smith, and Wilhelm 2001).

Teachers in schools around the county, share some of the same concerns about meeting the rigor of the Common Core State Standards, increasing the volume and complexity of informational text, and keeping students motivated.

The following are some common concerns and questions teachers share:

- What does this mean for my students everyday in the classroom?

- Which strategies and lessons are most important to teach?

- What is close reading and how do I teach it?

- How will I meet the needs of my English language learners and struggling readers as they read complex texts?

- How do I teach students to ask and answer text-dependent questions?

- What are some ways to help my students navigate through the unique structures and features of informational text?

- What does instruction with informational text look like in different settings, such as whole class, guided-reading groups, literature circles, and with text sets?

- How can I adjust my comprehension strategy lessons to fit informational text?

- What do lessons for teaching text evidence look like?

- How can I motivate my students to read more challenging texts with improved comprehension?

This book seeks to answer the questions and concerns previously raised and is specifically designed for busy teachers like you! You can choose to read the text in order, soaking it in one chapter at a time or flip around and pick and choose lessons to use on the fly! The professional development guides found on the Digital Resource CD are loaded with discussion topics and ideas ideal for staff meetings. Whether you read this book by yourself, in a small group, or with your entire school, you'll find interesting questions for reflection, helpful tips and suggestions, and compelling lesson ideas to lead you down the pathway of success!

Chapter Overviews

Throughout every chapter you will find:

- effective lessons that you can use time and time again with different texts;

- ideas that make learning fun for you and your students so everyone will be engaged;

- lessons built on what we know works from solid research in reading;

- ideas that require very little preparation;

- lots of options for meeting the needs of struggling readers and English language learners; and

- practical lessons that are scaffolded with teacher modeling, guided practice, and independent practice with informal assessment suggestions.

Chapter 1—Informational Texts Move to the Front of the Class

Why are informational texts so important now? Many students experience problems reading informational text. The challenges of reading this type of text continue to contribute to the "fourth-grade slump" (Chall 1983)—a researched trend where third-grade students suddenly experience a drop in reading scores when they hit the increase of informational text found in fourth grade. Now, with the Common Core requirements for more informational text, there is an immediate need to focus on strategies that work at all grade levels. This chapter covers everything from dealing with the shifts in the Common Core, to text complexity and critical thinking. The *because* lesson and hand gesture help your students find evidence in the text. We examine everyday text complexity and classroom examples of key ideas and details, craft and structure, and the integration of knowledge and ideas. Ways to sprinkle in peppy think alouds using your informational text reading help students understand the purposes for reading nonfiction texts.

Chapter 2—How Informational Texts Are Different: Text Features, Structures, and Strategies

How do people use informational texts in the "real" world? Through interviews and examples, students learn more about why informational texts are so important to read well. The creative *Pillowcase Lesson* brings into focus text types and purposes for reading. Project based learning puts students' reading and writing skills to work by doing activities for a purpose or audience such as making dog biscuits for an animal shelter or making recycling posters for a local mall. Interactive lessons for teaching students text features include a *Text Feature Hunt, Find the Feature, Text Feature Bingo* and more! Teaching text structures is easier and practical with mentor texts and graphic organizers. Did you know readers even look a little different when they are reading informational text? Try modeling how to flip around, reread, and other nonfiction reading behaviors to help students learn to fully engage with texts.

Chapter 3—Motivating Students to Read Informational Texts: Practical Classroom Routines

How can you promote informational text reading all day long in your classroom? This chapter is loaded with explanations of routines you can rely on including:

- informational text think-alouds that really work;
- practical close reading strategies and text dependent questions;
- teacher-led guided reading ideas;
- ways to incorporate reciprocal teaching for a comprehension boost; and
- practical ways to build and teach with the magic of text sets.

Chapter 4—Promoting Comprehension with Engaging Text Feature Lessons

Text features are what distinguish informational text from fiction. They are the key road signs along the way that signal the reader to stay on track. Teach students to pay attention to these important reading features with lessons dedicated to the table of contents, headings, visuals (photos, maps, charts, graphs, diagrams), glossary, and index. Students will enjoy anticipating what they will learn with *Guess My Prediction* using the table of contents. Students will stump one another with the lesson *What's My Heading?* as they summarize the text. Never again will students overlook the glossary or index when you teach the lessons *Thumbs Up, Thumbs On* with the *Glossary* or *Index Hunt* to strengthen their index skills. These lessons also build important academic vocabulary!

Chapter 5—Interactive Strategy Lessons for Informational Text

In Chapter 5, we examine what comprehension strategies should look like in today's classroom. This chapter includes an updated set of comprehension strategy lessons designed to meet the Common Core State Standards while at the same time, revisiting the familiar research-based comprehension strategies such as making connections, asking questions, clarifying, and synthesizing across texts.

I hope you enjoy this resource that will hopefully give you student-centered, practical research-based options for engaging your students as you increase the complexity and amount of informational text in your classroom.

Chapter 1

Informational Texts Move to the Front of the Class

When asked to define nonfiction or informational texts, students often respond with some variation on the following:

> *"Nonfiction texts are real."*
>
> —Lupe, 4th grade
>
> *"Nonfiction is any piece of real life you want to know about like oil rigs, ships, planes, sports, animals, and trains."*
>
> —Jason, 1st grade
>
> *"The more nonfiction you read, the smarter you'll get."*
>
> —Bryan, 3rd grade

One of my all-time favorites is the response that Carlyn, a second grader, thoughtfully crafted. She shared, *"Nonfiction books don't start with 'Once upon a time.'"*

What Do We Mean by Informational Texts?

Whether you refer to them as nonfiction or informational texts, this genre is here to stay thanks to the new demands of the Common Core State Standards that require informational texts to fill at least 50 percent of the elementary reading curriculum over the course of the day. The Common Core State Standards refer to informational texts as a broad category that includes various types of texts including procedural books, maps, how-to books, history, social studies, primary source documents, and even nonfiction literary works such as biographies and first-hand accounts. For example, an informational text on dolphins could include facts about dolphins or it could outline an individual's encounter or story involving a dolphin (Shanahan 2012). The good news is that with the Common Core State Standards our students need to know how to read, synthesize, and evaluate information about a wide variety of topics from an array of sources and text types.

Fortunately, elementary students naturally gravitate to informational texts to learn about sports, animals, historical events, or scientific wonders. Many English language learners and struggling readers prefer and enjoy informational texts to fiction because it helps them understand the world around them (Vasquez, Hansen, and Smith 2013). Teachers observe many students consistently choose informational text over fiction as they enjoy

reading about "real" topics (Jobe and Dayton-Sakari 2002). Informational texts appeal to students' interests in the world around them including animals, gadgets, inventions, nature, famous peoples' lives, sports, and countless other topics. If we take advantage of children's natural curiosity in the classrooms and couple that with some important strategy instruction and meaningful learning projects, we will have readers who become college- and career-ready as well as lifelong learners!

Classroom Connection

Primary Example: The Great Snake Debate

"Would a snake make a good pet? Why or why not?" asks Nim, a second grader, as she circulates the playground with her clipboard, surveying students from other classrooms. Each of the 31 students in Mr. Johnson's second grade are busy interviewing at least two students from another grade level for their input on the great snake debate. The students are reading a variety of texts on snakes and compiling their information into a class book to share facts about snakes. They are also tallying and analyzing the results from their surveys for a "Snakes as Pets" debate to share over the morning announcements on the school's speaker system at the end of the week. Mr. Johnson began the snake study by reading aloud to the class a page on the cobra from Seymour Simon's *Animals Nobody Loves* (2001), and asked the students to think about reasons some people do not like snakes. During guided-reading, the class also read *Snakes Up Close* by Christopher Blazeman (2012) to begin gathering facts about snakes.

Students touched and observed snakes when the local wildlife museum curator visited with her traveling snake collection. Swapping book titles during reader's workshop is a popular activity. Mr. Johnson offers 25 different titles of books about snakes from the school and local library and invites students to read several articles on snakes that he downloaded from the Internet. The students dive into their important work as they choose their arguments for or against the idea of housing a pet snake.

Intermediate Example: Colonial America Unit

The fifth graders grimace and shake their heads in disbelief as they listen to their teacher read aloud from *The Dreadful Smelly Colonies: The Disgusting Details About Life in Colonial America* by Elizabeth Raum (2010). The chapter titled, "No Privacy in the Privy," grabs the students' attention as the author describes the outdoor toilet conditions of the early colonies. The students join in a chorus of reactions on the toilet conditions of the colonists that include: "Gross!" "Smelly!" Their teacher, Mrs. Ramos, focuses the students' attention back on the text and more broadly the theme of the unit, by repeatedly asking the central question, "How did the American colonies change during the two centuries following their founding?" When reading about the early cave-like homes of the colonists, students search the text for answers to the questions, "Why did the author describe the bugs skittering onto their beds through the roof?" and "Why did the author choose this word and not another?" lively discussion ensues as students read on, discuss, and explore the bleak living conditions in the colonies. In the afternoon during writer's workshop, the students write first-person diary entries of typical colonists and prepare to dramatize and videotape their entries. The unit on the colonies will continue as the students participate in the close reading of a wide variety of texts including primary sources and a reader's theater about Jamestown.

Why Informational Texts Are So Important Now

Our students live in a fast-paced digital world where they need to develop sophisticated strategies for reading informational texts. David P. Pearson tells us that it is competency with expository reading, not narrative, that matters most to our students' future employers (2004). In our adult lives much of our literacy depends on gleaning information for a variety of purposes from non-narrative texts. Besides reading for work in our everyday lives, we read recipes,

It is competency with expository reading, not narrative, that matters most to our students' future employers.

—David P. Pearson 2004

directions, news articles, maps, charts, product reviews, and promotional materials. It is estimated that 85–90 percent of our adult daily reading material is informational (Smith 2000). Around 95 percent of the sites online contain informational text (Kamil and Lane 1998).

Students must learn to read informational text so they will gain the critical-thinking and reading skills they need to be truly college-and career-ready (CCSS 2010). Reading informational text well *is* the key to success in school (Duke 2000). Informational text builds background knowledge and vocabulary as students learn about the world around them (Duke and Hays 1998; Duke, Bennett-Armistead 2004, and Roberts 2002, 2003).

Acccording to research, informational text:

- **is the key to success in school** (Duke 2000; Chall 1983). By sixth grade most of what students are expected to read in school is informational text. Success with such text is critical for overall success in school. Students need to be introduced to informational text long before the intermediate grades so that students will become comfortable "reading to learn." In order to prepare our students to be truly college- and career-ready in today's world, students must leave our schools armed with tools to read and write and evaluate informational texts proficiently.

- **surrounds us as adult readers** (Venezsky 1982). Literacy tasks in the adult world focus on obtaining information from informational texts. Since 90 to 95 percent of our daily reading material is informational, it makes sense to prepare our students to become strong consumers of informational text (Smith 2000; Kamil and Lane 1998). From work-related articles, memos, and briefs, to following the news, or researching topics for career and home, we are bombarded daily with loads of informational text. With our fast-paced changing world, students need to be prepared to sift through vast amounts of texts for a variety of purposes.

- **is the favorite reading material for some children** (Caswell and Duke 1988). Fortunately, many children gravitate to the real-world topics found in informational texts. Boys especially often prefer reading about topics such as sports, historical events or people, and scientific topics like space travel or animals (Gurian, Smith, and Wilhelm 2001). Research suggests that for some girls and boys in the middle grades and older, informational text is preferred over fiction (Monson and Sebesta 1991). Other researchers have found that for many of our more gifted students, informational text is the genre of choice (Swanton 1984).

- **includes topics and questions of interest for children** (Schiefele, Drapp, and Winteler 1992; Guthrie et al. 1996). Children are naturally curious about the world around them and enjoy wondering about many nonfiction topics. If you've ever spent time with a four-year-old, you know the favorite question is, "Why?" Using informational texts to answer students' questions is a great way to build on their interests and to promote motivation for reading. Through the grades, informational text topics such as animals or the environment bring out our students' inquisitive natures.

- **builds background knowledge about the world and ultimately fosters comprehension** (Anderson and Guthrie 1999; Duke and Hays 1998; Wilson and Anderson 1986). Informational text plays a role in building background about the world around us. Strong readers pick up information about history, science, and a myriad of topics that prove useful as they read other texts including fiction. The knowledge gained from wide reading provides essential background information for our students. For example, when a student enjoys reading about World War II and then reads a novel, such as *Number the Stars* (Lowry 1989) which takes place during that era, the student uses the background information from the nonfiction text to aid his or her understanding of the novel. Primary students reading informational texts about caterpillars will comprehend Eric Carle's *The Very Hungry Caterpillar* (1991) in a deeper way by connecting the nonfiction text information about caterpillars to the picture book. Reading informational text provides students with essential background information they need to comprehend a wide variety of texts.

- **builds vocabulary and literacy** (Dreher 2000). The very nature of informational text requires and prompts discussion of new concepts and challenging vocabulary. Researchers have found that teachers and parents alike pause more often when reading informational text with children. Adults stop to explain and discuss unknown words and challenging ideas, as well as text features unique to informational text (e.g., maps, sidebars, and charts). This means that students benefit from reading informational texts with adults by learning vocabulary as well as learning informational text reading skills such as using text features (Duke, Bennett-Armistead, and Roberts 2002).

Keep Track of Your Informational Reading

Try keeping track of your own informational text reading and the various purposes for your reading. For an entire day, I kept track of my informational text consumption, and documented reading the following variety of informational texts for a myriad of purposes including:

- books and Internet searches on dog training advice, *because* our little dog barks too much in the evenings

- books and Internet searches on Jacksonville, Florida, area hotels and maps *because* I was preparing a visit to an ailing relative and the area

- brochures and Internet searches on the universities and colleges my son is accepted to, *because* he is making a decision based on majors

- cookbooks, to find a healthy, easy crock-pot recipe, *because* I had no time to cook dinner on a busy work day

- the newspaper, *because* I want to know what is going on in the world and my local area

- the *Daily Beast* online news source, *because* I want to make sure I get all the important news of the day.

Key Questions for Evaluating a Text

- Who wrote this? Is this a trusted source?

- What purpose or gain does this author have in writing the information and posting or publishing the work?

- How does the information in this text compare/contrast with other texts on the same topic?

- How would I rate the text? Explain.

Evaluating My Reading of the Text

- How closely did I read each piece of information? Did I reread? Why or why not?

- What is my purpose for reading this? How will I use the information gained?

- Was it too easy, just right, or too difficult for me to understand?

- How helpful was the text in helping me understand the content? Did I enjoy reading it? Why or why not?

Share my list of daily informational text reading with students, and discuss unique and different purposes for reading each text. It is great to see the students perk up and enjoy hearing about the real-world reasons for reading informational text. Also explain the importance of evaluating the sources that one is reading. Students need to be able to read closely for a purpose, synthesize the information, and then evaluate the authenticity and value of the sources read.

Problems Students Encounter When Reading Informational Text

Reading informational text presents an enormous challenge for many students. The following are challenges students face when reading informational text:

- text complexity
- challenging content/ideas
- incomplete or limited background information/knowledge
- high academic vocabulary load
- text format, including structures and features
- determining importance/main ideas
- finding text-based evidence/drawing conclusions
- inferring

Informational text is loaded with facts on every page. Students are bombarded with text structures and features that fiction books may not have such as headings, tables, charts, graphs, maps, captions, and more. When asked to share "main ideas," students are overwhelmed and throw their hands up in frustration as they admit they can't separate the main ideas from details. "It all looks important!" they say. Students also struggle with reading informational texts due to the lack of background knowledge necessary to understand the text. Additionally, the vocabulary load that permeates informational texts presents serious challenges. According to 2009 NAEP results, American nine-year-olds are still more proficient at reading literary text than they are at reading informational text (Park 2010). Therefore, students need strategies for unlocking the meaning of informational texts that will arm them with the tools necessary to understand what they read.

All Students Need to Read Informational Texts

In the past there was a misconception that primary students were not "ready" for informational texts. Researchers suggest that young children with their natural curiosity about the world around them need exposure to informational text beginning in preschool or even earlier (Duke 2000). Perhaps you've seen firsthand how very young children do indeed have an appetite for informational texts. When my husband and I read to our three children (even as babies), they begged for nonfiction books about insects, gardens, stars, and transportation. My son's books about tractors and trucks became worn and tattered from literally hundreds of rereadings.

When my neighbor's little boy entered the first-grade classroom on the very first day of school, the teacher invited her students into the classroom library to select books for independent reading. Jason tugged on his teacher's skirt and pleaded in a worried tone, *Mrs. Sanchez, where are the nonfiction books? Don't you have any nonfiction books?* Of course his teacher scrambled to the library and gathered up a variety of nonfiction to offer up the very next day. Today our classroom libraries have improved to include about one third informational texts, but we still need more if students are to reach 50 percent of their classroom reading time spent on such texts (Ness 2011).

In her landmark study, Nell Duke (2000) found that many primary students at that time were only exposed to 3.6 minutes per day of informational text. Since that time, our professional development efforts coupled with a positive response from publishers have helped schools fill their book rooms with inviting informational texts for grades K–6. Still, many schools need even more nonfiction texts, especially with the requirement of the Common Core State Standards to immerse students for 50 percent of their reading day in a variety of informational texts. Our students also need to be armed with strategies they can use to comprehend this wide variety of texts for different purposes. Just think how ready our intermediate students will be for more content-area reading when we begin teaching students from kindergarten to access information from a variety of nonfiction texts.

Three Major Shifts in the Common Core

The Common Core State Standards shifts require teachers to create meaningful opportunities for students to learn content though experiences with informational text.

1. Build knowledge through content-rich nonfiction.

Students need exposure to informational text that is interesting and has depth and strong text features. Informational texts encompass a broad assortment of genres that include biographies, autobiographies, essays, speeches, primary sources, directions, forms, and digital sources. Students will often read more than one text on a topic to gain content knowledge for their grade-level objectives, to be able to ask and answer questions during research, and to complete research necessary for hands-on projects. Therefore, students need explicit instruction in reading material strategies specifically designed for comprehending informational texts.

What this means for your classroom:

- Provide lots of different reading materials on the same topic, not just textbooks.

- Bring in a wide variety of resources including trade books, leveled texts, letters, maps, primary sources, and other rich reading to build content.

- Build text sets or collections of different texts for students to read and research.

2. Create opportunities for communication (reading, writing, speaking) based on evidence from the text.

When reading informational text, students need to first study the text at hand rather than moving too quickly to respond or make connections. By returning to the text first for answers to questions and evidence to support opinions and arguments, students build life-long behaviors that make them stronger readers. Yet our students also need opportunities to do something meaningful in the real-world with the information they've gained from texts. As they research, they will dive in deeper if they know what the end product involves. Students might do research to write a letter, make a brochure or presentation, or share what they've learned with a partner class across town or across the world. Research suggests that students develop their literacy skills more quickly when they need to use them for a purpose (Purcell-Gates, Duke, and Marineau 2007). Gathering evidence and arguments from the reading becomes central to communicating with others.

What this means for your classroom:

- Create opportunities for students to share what they have learned. Even just presenting the information to a buddy class or younger class gives students a real reason to learn the material. Posting photos and videos of projects online on the school or class website is another way for students to share what they've learned with others.

- Discuss television competition shows or courtroom programs, where judges must offer up evidence for their thinking. Evidence-based arguments permeate competition shows where contestants sing, dance, and cook their way to the top. The plethora of "expert judges" shares reasons and evidence for their scoring. When we relate our evidence-based instruction to these shows, students remember what it means to provide evidence for arguments.

- Post evidence-based language starters on charts to guide student discussions.

Evidence-Based Starters

- Because…
- For example…
- The author stated…
- According to the text…
- From the text I know that… because…
- A reason for… is found on page…
- The text says… on page…

Evidence-Based Instruction with the "Big Because"

In my various project schools around the country we emphasize the word "because." I ask students to pound their fists on their hands like a judge's gavel whenever they say "because" and then back it with evidence from the text. Any time students make a statement such as, *"I like this book,"* they need to back it up with a "because" statement. By adding the because statement to opinions and arguments and by featuring the

fist-pound gesture, students remember more often to provide reasons for their ideas and arguments. In Mr. Sim's first-grade class during their partner discussions, they prompt one another's thinking with the "because" hand signal. Recently, Juan commented that he thought Gila monsters are just as dangerous as rattlesnakes. His partner, Jenny, fist pounded and prompted him to add a "because." Juan added proudly, "Because we read about it on page 26." In Mrs. Purty's sixth-grade class, the students take sides to an issue in history: "Was Moctezuma a hero or villain?" Students back each claim with a "because" fist and evidence for their opinion drawn from the texts they've read.

3. Conduct regular practice with complex text and vocabulary.

The more students read complex text the better they will get at it. Across the day, they need exposure to informational texts during interactive read alouds, reading block, content-area instruction, guided reading, and independent reading times. Explicit instruction in vocabulary as well as strategies for figuring out vocabulary during reading provide foundations for the vocabulary exposure students need to internalize new words and relate it to content (Graves 2006; Graves and Watts-Taffe 2002).

What this means for your classroom:

- Provide opportunities throughout the day, not just during reading or content-area instruction, for students to read informational text. The classroom library should hold 50 percent informational texts to provide ample interesting practice for students.

- Conduct teacher demonstrations on "close reading" strategies such as rereading, marking text, and discussing complex texts and deeper meanings with others.

- Use word walls, instructional games, and activities to provide students with opportunities to practice academic vocabulary.

Classroom Connection

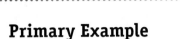

Primary Example

Third graders in a Florida school read and study two different books on desert habitats as well as an article from an Internet site. The class builds a chart comparing the information collected from each of the texts. Then, classes videoconference so that the students in Florida can interview students in Arizona about their local desert habitat. Both groups share photos, reports, and interview questions, and then become pen pals to extend the learning all year long.

Intermediate Example

Sixth graders in California study Rome using a variety of rich informational texts along with their district-adopted history text. They also study travel guides and brochures to compare and contrast how information on Rome is presented to tourists. The students create both paper and online brochures for a local travel agency that puts together trips to Rome for senior citizens. A group of senior citizens communicates with the students from Rome on the class blog.

Everyday Examples of Text Complexity

Competent readers consume a wide variety of informational texts from a range of reading levels (Smith 2000). For our students to be college- and career-ready we need to expose them to increasingly difficult informational texts. To introduce the concept of text complexity, let's consider how good readers use informal text complexity criteria such as concept load, length of the text, ease of readability, amount of unfamiliar vocabulary, number and appeal of visual supports, or size of font to select their own texts. Whether you are reading a voter information ballot, a chapter for a test in your graduate-level educational psychology course, or online articles about a particular medical condition, you are navigating your way through complex text.

> "The book to read is not the one that thinks for you, but the one that makes you think."
> —James McCosh (1901)

> "How is reading complex text like lifting weights? Just as it's impossible to build muscle without weight or resistance, it's impossible to build robust reading skills without reading challenging text."
> —Shanahan, Fisher, and Frey (2012, 68)

Another example where text complexity comes into play is in recreational reading. Have you ever selected the wrong book for a weekend trip or to take on summer vacation? For example, you decide to finally catch up on your classics and read *War and Peace* by Leo Tolstoy on a beach vacation. Once you arrive to your sandy destination, the lapping waves, balmy air, and sun's luscious warm rays cast a spell, stealing your concentration. You soon realize the heavy text in your beach bag doesn't fit your reading mood after all. Instead, you find yourself craving a juicy romance or best-selling mystery page-turner. You decide to abandon the more challenging complex classic and pick up a quick, easier read. However, the complicated camera text from your photography course that you also tossed in your tote turns out to be handy. This time, your purpose for reading trumps text difficulty and drives your need to plow through the technical manual so you can capture some gorgeous beach sunsets on camera.

When you flip through texts in a bookstore or library, or shop for eBooks online, you most likely size up texts using quantitative measures such as the length of the book or the print font size or number of illustrations. You might also use your qualitative tools by checking out the table of contents, back cover, and introduction, as well as sampling a page of text to sample the author's style and voice. Your own background knowledge, interest in the topic, and reason or purpose for reading the text also drives motivation to select the text. Recently, I read a review in a women's magazine promoting a new cookbook written by Jerry Seinfeld's wife called *The Can't Cookbook: 100+ Recipes for the Absolutely Terrified* (Atria 2013). Since I am not a great cook, this title caught my eye. I hunted around online until I found a few reviews and a way to peek inside at the text at some of the pages. My criteria for a cookbook includes recipes with just a few ingredients, visual supports, and vocabulary I understand or at least an explanation of the specialized cooking words such as "blanch." I decided that the humor infused in this book would help keep me interested. I also read an interview with the author who I thought might also be a timid cook. Instead, I learned that her non-cooking buddies relied on her for constant cooking advice, which prompted writing a text for people like me, the not-so-confident-in-the-kitchen crowd! The book passed muster with my cookbook text complexity criteria and moved onto my holiday wish list.

Text Complexity is Critical to the Common Core State Standards

The idea of text complexity lies at the center of the Common Core State Standards. The standards call for students to "read widely and deeply from among a broad range of high-quality, increasingly challenging, literary and informational texts" (2010, 10). What exactly do we mean by "complex texts"? The dictionary definition defines the adjective *complex* as "characterized by a very complicated or involved arrangement of parts," and "so complicated or intricate as to be hard to understand or deal with." What exactly makes a text challenging to understand?

© *Shell Education*

Readers may find a text difficult due to challenging vocabulary, or a topic they lack sufficient background to understand, or to complex sentence structure that demands multiple readings to grasp the meaning.

Three tools that the CCSS suggests using together to measure text complexity include (NGA and CCSO 2010):

- **Quantitative measures:** technical measures of word length, word frequency, and text cohesion often measured by software.

- **Qualitative measures:** levels of meaning based on text structure and features, and knowledge demand best measured by a human.

- **Reader and task:** the background of the reader along with his or her interests and motivation and the complexity of the task best measured by professional teacher judgment.

Quantitative Measures

Quantitative measures for determining text complexity can be calculated manually or by computers and include measuring word length, word frequency, and text cohesion. Quantitative measures are useful because they identify which grade-level band or reading level a text falls into. Many textbook publishers today provide the "level" of their texts by indicating the grade-level range and number for one or more of the most commonly used quantitative readability tools.

Quantitative measures are calculated by using readability formulas. These formulas identify how complex a text is by assigning a numerical rating to the text. Readability formulas may be used manually and some may be computer-generated by analyzing all of or a selection of a text.

There are many readability formulas and tools to assist with analyzing quantitative measures of text complexity, including the following:

- Flesch-Kincaid (1975) calculates text difficulty using sentence length and number of syllables in words.

- Dale-Chall Readability Formula (1948) measures sentence length and percentage of difficult words (words that are not found on the familiar word list).

- Lexile® Framework for Reading (2014) calculates sentence and word length as well as word frequency.

Using quantitative information about text levels helps us match students to texts that are appropriate for them to read. When students are placed in the appropriate level, they practice reading and develop decoding, fluency, and vocabulary (Allington and Gabriel 2012). Students also need to stretch their reading ability by reading complex texts with support in order to grow as readers. Relying on quantitative measures alone is not enough to determine text complexity and appropriate texts for students. For example, a text such as *Charlotte's Web* by E.B. White demonstrates a Lexile® level of 680L, which technically falls in the second- and third-grade range of 420–820. Yet, the beloved classic text with its rich nuances in language and theme often lands on fourth-grade reading lists in school districts. While quantitative measures prove helpful in placing students in texts that give them practice in valuable reading skills, other factors including qualitative features of text should be considered as well.

Qualitative Measures

Qualitative measures include levels of meaning, figurative language, organization and structure, text features, register (formal or informal), clarity, and knowledge demands. Even though a particular text may be sized quantitatively and determined "easy," the concepts behind it and background required to comprehend the words are much deeper and require the understanding of more advanced ideas. Qualitative measures help us to define what makes a text challenging for students. Doug Fisher, Nancy Frey, and Diane Lapp in their book *Text Complexity: Raising Rigor in Reading* (2012), share a very clear example of the limitations of only employing quantitative measures. The following simple six-word sentence, supposedly written by Hemingway, is not complex in terms of readability, as it figures in at second-grade level. Yet, from a qualitative standpoint, one must use mature background knowledge to more deeply understand the sentence, "For sale: baby shoes, never worn."

Hemingway's masterpiece, *The Sun Also Rises* (1926), when analyzed using quantitative measures, is technically written at about a third-grade reading level. Of course, this text is much more challenging when considering the author's style, language, content, and the context. Qualitative considerations that take into account the nuances of language and more challenging topics must be incorporated into the text complexity puzzle.

Pam Allyn (2012) suggests asking key questions when considering the qualitative measures of text complexity of informational texts, including questions about meaning and purpose as well as structural considerations:

- What is the purpose of this piece?
- Is the purpose obvious to the reader?
- Who is the intended audience?
- What is the structure of the text?
- Are multiple structures included?
- Are the graphics easy to understand?

- Is the language formal or informal?
- Is figurative language included?
- Is the text straightforward or does it rely on analytical thinking and inferring?

Reader and Task

The reader brings special and worthy considerations to text complexity. The prior knowledge and motivation of the reader significantly impact his or her ability and stamina to comprehend a text. Many of our students will tackle reading a text that challenges them if they are passionate about the content.

Passion and interest often lead students to dig in and study books above their level. As a child, I can remember borrowing one volume at a time from our neighbor's encyclopedia set and pouring over the letter J for hours, pausing on selected subjects of interest such as Jupiter or Andrew Jackson. I loved the inviting illustrations, the dark blue heavy books, and even recall the musty smell of the slick pages. Reading the encyclopedia made me feel "smart" and "grown up." I recently experienced a first-grader named Jason dive into a challenging book on railroads during reader's workshop because it was his passion and hobby. And down the hall in fourth grade, Juana hungrily scoured Internet articles on coyotes after one visited her backyard. These examples show how a reader's background knowledge, motivation for understanding, and purpose for reading play a significant role when considering text complexity.

The following questions should be asked when considering the reader and the task:

- What is the purpose or motivation the reader has for reading the text?
- What will the reader "do" with the information?
- What is the interest level of the reader regarding the text?
- Is the reader familiar with the topic? What does he/she know about it?
- Does the reader possess the stamina and strategies to deeply read and comprehend the text?
- How will the reader be supported by the teacher, peers, or if working independently during the reading process?

Making Critical Thinking Part of Every Lesson

In the content-rich classroom where students read challenging texts for a variety of purposes, the role of critical thinking becomes more important than ever before as our students develop the skills to become truly college and career ready. Next generation assessments, such as PARCC (2011) and Smarter Balanced Assessment Consortium (2014), focus on evaluating students' higher-level thinking skills. This means critical thinking needs to permeate the way we teach all day long. The good news is that our lessons become more engaging for students as they think more deeply about the content.

What does critical thinking look like in the classroom? Teachers lead lessons by challenging students to evaluate, compare, and investigate topics and ideas. Students move away from taking a passive role and instead more actively participate in lessons while synthesizing and evaluating what they have learned. For example, instead of learning just the facts about the early colonies, students could write a letter posing as a colonist and post it in an online blog. Or students could learn about the environment by reading online articles, listening to read-alouds, and by making posters for a trash cleanup day of the grounds around the school. After reading a variety of books about whales, students could also work in teams to pose their questions about whales, then dig deeper to answer questions and compose multimedia reports and presentations that they post online. Finally, the students could write persuasive letters to the local newspaper to promote the Save the Whales Foundation.

One way to promote critical thinking is to ask high-quality questions. "To question well, is to teach well" (Ross 1860). Researchers find that we get the results we ask for. When teachers rely more on low-level questioning, such as recall and memorization, students respond accordingly. If teachers ask higher-level thinking questions, then deeper thinking is fostered (Wilen 1991). In today's fast-paced world we want our students to ask and answer higher-level questions while providing arguments, reasons, and evidence from the text.

Some helpful tools that assist in providing the anchor vocabulary for getting at critical thinking, and shaping our questioning and learning experiences for students include Webb's Depth of Knowledge (DOK) (2002) and Bloom's Revised Taxonomy (Bloom 1956; Anderson and Krathwohl 2001). Bloom's Revised Taxonomy identifies the level of thinking required to complete a task and Webb's Depth of Knowledge takes into consideration the task and the difficulty of the content. You can use DOK, Bloom's, or even combined language from both models to guide cognition in your lessons even though they each serve slightly different purposes. It is also helpful to post the vocabulary that promotes critical thinking in the classroom so you and your students can refer often to the path that leads to more challenging levels of thinking. Figure 1.1 and 1.2 are two tools that combine the labels for thinking for both Bloom's Revised Taxonomy (1956) and Webb's Depth of Knowledge (2002; Hess 2006).

© Shell Education

Figure 1.1 Thinking Deeply Template

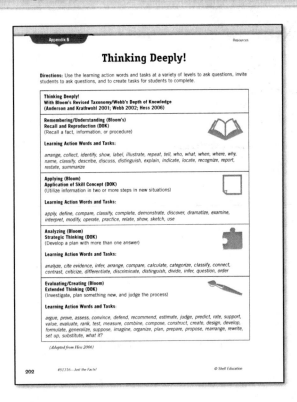

Figure 1.2 Digging Deeper Thinking Bookmark

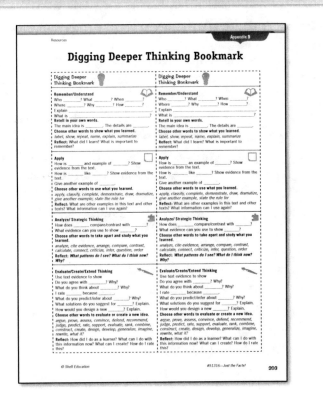

The Pillars of the Common Core for Informational Text

Four essential pillars serve as the organizing structures for the specific standards for informational texts for each grade level. These foundational organizers include:

- key ideas and details
- craft and structure
- integration of knowledge and ideas
- range of reading and level of text complexity

Each of these four pillars serves as an organizer for the standards and becomes more sophisticated and complex through the grade levels.

Key Ideas and Details

Key ideas and details require students to remember and sort main ideas from details, draw conclusions and make inferences, as well as to make claims and arguments with evidence from texts. Students may ask and answer questions and fill in graphic organizers to learn about main ideas and details in texts.

Classroom Connection

Primary Example: Question Back to the Text

The second graders take turns passing around a colorful plastic play microphone at the guided reading table as they take turns role playing as the "questioner," asking questions that lead their peers back to the text. To provide scaffolding for the questioning, Mrs. Heintz offers question starters on paper strips on the table so students may refer to them or pick them up to use. Danny, the current questioner, glances at the starters: "What can we learn about _____ on page _____? Why do you think the author said _____?" Danny thinks a moment, flips through the text then asks, "What can we learn about tadpoles on page nine in *A Frog's Life* by Dona Rice (2012)? Why do you think the author said the tadpole looks like a little fish?" When students raise their hands, Mrs. Heintz prompts them to refer back to the text by making the hand gesture which includes a question mark in the air, and then pointing to the book and chanting "question and back to the text."

Mrs. Heintz continues guiding the students as they pass the microphone and take turns asking text-dependent questions.

Classroom Connection

Intermediate Example: Interview Questions

"Why did you radio that your fuel was running low? What happened to your plane?" Mr. Shuey modeled a question for Missy who took a turn role-playing as Amelia Earhart. Missy and the class silently reread the text for a moment, then Missy responds, "I was in trouble as my plane started slowing down and making weird noises. I ended up crashing into the sea because I didn't have enough fuel to land on the nearby island." Mr. Shuey's sixth graders continue to reread silently *Histories Mysteries* by Dona Herweck Rice (2012). Mr. Shuey encourages students to work in pairs to take turns role-playing as interviewers and the famous mysterious persons on each page. He circulates to listen in and offers support as students ask and answer text-based questions. Students create text-based questions as they interview the "pretend" Elvis, Jimmy Hoffa, and Jack the Ripper.

Craft and Structure

Craft and structure becomes the foundational pillar for standards that focus on the nuances of vocabulary and figurative language, as well as how and why the author organized the piece. Point of view and the purpose bring deeper meaning to the reading as students consider bias and the author's viewpoint. Craft and structure include teaching students strategies to clarify ideas, words, and academic language that they do not understand in their reading. It also includes identifying the text structure and using graphic organizers to organize information from the reading.

Classroom Connection

Primary Example: Looking In and Around Tricky Words

"Let's review the hand signal for how we figure out tricky words with our partners," directs Miss Johnson. The first graders eagerly turn and point with their index fingers for clues inside the word and then make circles with their fingers to represent looking outside the word for clues. Miss Johnson tells the class that there may be some tricky words in this text they are reading aloud today and to be ready to look in and around for clues to figure them out. She introduces the text *Oceans Counting* (2013) by Janet Lawler by first reading the title, back cover, and flipping through the text. Next, Miss Johnson guides the discussion to include the text features: a "did you know?" question on every page, an animal facts chart, a map, the author's bio, and a glossary.

Throughout the reading, Miss Johnson pauses every few pages on a tricky word or invites students to briefly turn to partners to identify a word they found tricky. She chooses the word *icy* on page 8 and demonstrates how to look in the word for ice and around the word at the word Arctic as well as to check the picture where the seals are clearly perched on the ice. The students listen to the page again and turn to partners to identify another tricky word and use their hand gestures as they share their words.

Intermediate Example: Picture This!

"Listen to this one," starts Savannah, "The spittlebug is an insect that makes bubbles that look like spit. First, it makes a big glob of froth. Then, it sits inside it." She reads on to describe how the spittlebug hides from predators inside the bad tasting froth. The other students at the table sketch the spittlebug in its froth in their reader's notebooks. Savannah shares that the author's choice of words that helps her to see this scene in her mind were *froth, glob,* and *hides.* Each of the five students at the table share a passage or sentence from the text their book club selected, called *Bug Builders* (2012) by Timothy Bradley. In the end, the group votes on their favorite example of a well-done mind-movie passage or sentence to share with the class. The class is making a PowerPoint™ presentation to show their second-grade buddies on Friday.

Integration of Knowledge and Ideas

Integration of knowledge and ideas prompts students to rise to higher levels of thinking as they argue claims in a text and synthesize and evaluate information across texts. Students study and analyze how information is presented in a text and consider the author's craft, text features, and use of visuals to evaluate whether the text was useful to the reader. They also compare and contrast the way different texts treat the same information. Students also use the information, including arguments and claims from several different texts, to write, act out, or produce a product that they share online or in a creative way. Students then become "reading judges," deciding what score to grant a text (Oczkus 2004, 2009). Readers answer the following in their judging process:

- Does this text hold the information I am looking for?

- Is this text useful to help me with my goal?

- Do I agree with the information found in the text?

- Are the ideas supported with evidence that makes sense to me?

- How is the information presented?

- What was helpful about this text and each of the following: the content, text features, and visuals?

- How does this text compare/contrast to the other texts I've read on the topic?

Classroom Connection

Primary Example: Walk to Show What You Know!

The discussion becomes lively as the first graders discuss the two texts their class read about Susan B. Anthony and Abraham Lincoln. Mr. James posts the names of the two famous Americans on opposite sides of the classroom so students may demonstrate their understanding by walking across to stand by each name. Mr. James also posts a sign that reads, "Both Susan B. Anthony and Abraham Lincoln." Students take turns reading their riddles. Reina begins with "I believed that all people were equal because I was a Quaker." Students hesitate but migrate to the Susan B. Anthony sign. They travel with their two texts and open them up to share with partners the page number or evidence for Reina's statement. She then shares her riddle "I believed in the rights of African Americans." Students move to the "both" sign to share the pages that prove her claim. After the students share more of their ideas, Mr. James guides the class in creating a list of ideas that both Lincoln and Anthony share. Students write a compare and contrast class book for the class library as they share facts about the two famous Americans.

Intermediate Example: Compare It! Contrast It!

Fifth graders finish studying about whales by reading two books and a series of articles from the Internet. They work in teams of four to complete a chart that helps them list facts they learned from each book. They read *Whales* by Lesley A. Du Temple (1999) and *Whales* by Seymour Simon (1989). Students in Petra's group speak out as they share what they learned from each text and compare and evaluate the author's treatment of the topic. "I think Seymour Simon's book has more interesting sentences like where he says, 'Just the tongue of the blue whale weighs as much as an elephant.' on page 6." Other students in the group chime in to share their specific examples of Simon's metaphors and style. Erik interjects that he prefers the other book by Du Temple because the author uses headings to guide the reader. The discussion continues as students compare the way both authors treat the topic of whale endangerment. The students are surprised to find that Simon does not include much information about the future of whales. The group agrees that the Du Temple text includes more reasons why whales are endangered and includes discussions on whaling and pollution. The students use information from the reading and choose to either write letters to the Pacific Whale Foundation or to the editor of the local newspaper to express their views on saving whales.

Range of Reading and Level of Text Complexity

The Common Core State Standards require students to read a range of complex informational texts independently with success. Students should read difficult texts supported by the teacher and peers, but should also attempt over the school year to grow into more challenging independent texts as well. Research suggests that students also need to practice with texts at their appropriate instructional level (Allington and Gabriel 2012). When reading widely, students consider their purposes for reading texts. What will they need to know? What will they do with the information—take a test, give a report, participate in an activity, learn a new skill, or share information with others using technology? Students also need a toolbox of strategies for reading closely or skimming, depending upon their purpose.

Classroom Connection

Primary Example: Reader's Workshop

During reader's workshop, Mr. Feldman meets to conference individually with his third-grade students. Jamal shares his book log which lists several titles from an adventure series of chapter books, but nowhere on Jamal's log is there evidence of recent informational text reading. Mr. Feldman begins to probe: "So I noticed you've read lots of great fiction so far, but I wonder if you might try some informational texts that are on topics of interest for you." The two look at Jamal's interest inventory and see that his interest is in marine mammals and baseball. Jamal decides he wants to read about marine mammals next, so he heads to the classroom library. Mr. Feldman guides his students to read increasingly more difficult texts on informational topics in his individual and group conferences.

Classroom Connection

Intermediate Example: Read Aloud to Build Background and Interest

To build background for the next chapter in the sixth-grade history text, Mrs. Cooper reads portions of the book, *You Wouldn't Want to Be A Mayan Soothsayer!* (2007) by Rupert Matthews and David Salariya. The creators' humorous tone and cartoon art grabs the students' attention as they learn interesting facts about Mayan culture. Students write in their readers' notebooks after each read-aloud session to record facts to remember and their reactions to learning. When they read the history book chapter on the Mayans, Mrs. Cooper models how to closely read the portions of text that are confusing. Students work in teams to relate and discuss what they learned from the high interest read aloud to the more complex text in the book. Later, when they each select topics to research, they rate the reading difficulty giving each of their sources a score from 1–5 for easy to more challenging texts. Students discuss the merits of reading a range of both challenging and easier materials on a given topic.

Wrap-Up and Reflection

The demands of the modern information age require our students to read informational text well in order to be ready for college and the career-world. In our adult lives it is estimated that 85–95 percent of our daily reading load is informational text (Smith 2000; Kamil and Lane 1998). Fortunately, many of our students enjoy and even prefer reading about real-world topics such as animals, planets, sports, and inventions (Jobe and Dayton-Sakari 2002). Yet many students experience difficulties reading informational text due to concept, challenging vocabulary, and the text structures and features that are unique to informational texts. To capitalize on students' interest in informational topics and the need for strong instruction with informational texts, we can employ a variety of strategies to help students deeply understand and utilize the "real" genre!

Here are some key ideas to think about from this chapter:

- By keeping track of your adult informational text reading and sharing not only what you read, but your purposes for reading, it helps students to see the relevance of reading informational text.

- Students from all grades, including primary, need instruction to strengthen reading informational texts.

- Using the word "because" (and an optional gesture) helps students return to the text for text-based evidence as they read complex texts.

- Understanding what makes a text difficult for students helps us to design instruction that targets text complexity. Text complexity may be calculated by looking at a variety of factors including quantitative and qualitative measures as well as considering the reader and the task.

- The tools for promoting critical thinking include asking higher-level questions and designing instruction using models such as Bloom's Revised Taxonomy (Anderson and Krathwohl 2002) and Webb's Depth of Knowledge (2002).

- The essential pillars of the Common Core provide organization for instruction and include key ideas and details, craft and structure, integration of knowledge and ideas, and the range of reading and level of text complexity.

Reflect and Discuss

1. What challenges do your students experience when reading informational texts?

2. How do text complexity and critical thinking impact student comprehension of informational text? What can you do to help students tackle challenging texts and think more deeply about the content?

3. Discuss how text complexity impacts your reading. Select an article or book of interest to use as an example.

How Informational Texts Are Different: Text Features, Structures, and Strategies

It is estimated that nonfiction reading constitutes 85 to 95 percent of adults' reading. For our students to succeed in the 21st century, they need to learn not only *how to read* informational texts but also *how to use* the information gained for a variety of purposes. Many careers in our busy world today require reading informational texts well in order to perform on-the-job tasks. Here are some examples of on-the-job literacy in action:

- The doctor *weighs* information about drug reactions before administering a shot to a patient.

- The attorney and legal assistant *pore* over court cases and documents before a trial.

- The reporter *studies* the facts about a controversial new water plant for a featured spot on the nightly news.

- The science teacher *skims* online to find out about current volcanic activity around the world to prepare a lesson.

- The marketing executive *prepares* for an ad campaign for a new healthy cereal by *taking* in the merits of the ingredients and *comparing* them to other cereals.

- The antique store owner *learns* online about the historical significance of some antiques he acquired for his store.

- The cook at the local diner *peruses* recipes for different ways to make lasagna to help him whip up his own innovative, spicy, unique creation for the weekly special.

In each of these examples, notice how the action-oriented synonyms for the word *read* help to convey reading for a purpose: *weigh, pore (over), study, skim, find, prepare, take in, compare, peruse,* and *learn*. We read informational text to take action in the real-world. Students dive into texts with more motivation when we incorporate meaningful purposes for reading. Just imagine students engaged in hands-on learning with informational texts as they share reports online, write letters to pen-pals, interview seniors about historical events, or make brochures and posters for local museums. Students need to see the endless purposes and relevant roles informational texts play in our world today. Here are two lesson ideas that help students understand the relevance and importance of informational text.

Real-World Interviews: Reading Informational Text on the Job

Students interview adults to find out how they use informational text in their jobs and careers. Interviews might be done at home or by inviting a professional into the classroom, or by a conference call or videoconference.

Questions to ask might include:

- What kinds of materials do you read on the job?

- What tasks do you need to accomplish with the information you gain from the reading?

- What do you do to help you understand the material you are reading?

- What is your most favorite/least favorite reading you have to do for your job? Why?

- What reading advice do you have for students?

Compile the interview information from one or more individuals into a presentation to share live, online, in a video, or in a student-created class book. Or students may role-play as various career people and participate in mock interviews.

Figure 2.1 Informational Text Reading Interviews Template

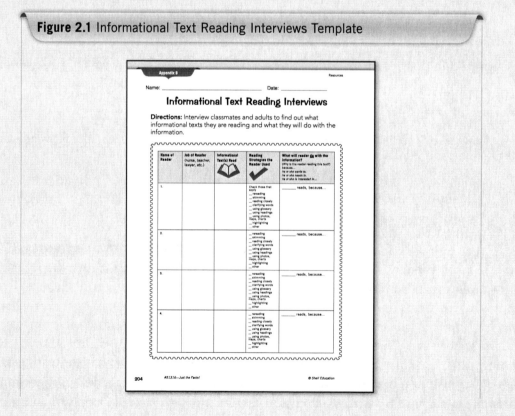

The Pillowcase: Purposes of Informational Text

This lesson helps students understand the importance of and purposes for informational text in our everyday lives at work, school, and home. This lesson is adapted from Kathy Au, former president of the International Reading Association (Au 2013).

Objectives

Students will identify informational texts and reasons for reading them by observing and discussing the teacher's pillowcase full of reading material.

Students will also discuss reading strategies used when reading informational text.

Materials

- pillowcase
- variety of informational text

Teacher Model

In preparation for the lesson, gather texts from all around the house and car to bring to school, such as maps, recipe books, history books, manuals, magazines, guides, and catalogs. Put the texts inside of a pillowcase. Figure 2.3 shows a list of Mrs. Oczkus' texts read at home.

1. Tell students that you gathered just a sampling of your own informational texts to use to demonstrate how informational texts are used in everyday life. Tell students that informational text makes up 85 to 90 percent of an adult's daily "diet" of reading.

2. Hold up your pillowcase and ask students to turn to a partner and guess what several of the texts might be.

3. Pull the texts out one at a time. Before you show each one, you might give a riddle such as, "This text helped me find the directions to the lake." Or, "This text kept my kids' tummies from growling." Share your reasons for reading each text.

4. Share and model reading strategies by giving examples of how you used rereading, close reading, skimming, clarifying words, inferring, considering author's purpose, etc., when reading the text.

Technology Option: If you mostly read on an electronic device, you can still run this lesson—but do so on an interactive whiteboard or other projection device. To make this electronic lesson more memorable, you might also display a quick "selfie" photo or quick phone video to show where you were as you read your device (e.g., show a phone picture of you in your kitchen flipping through recipe books and sharing your purpose for doing so.)

Guided Practice

5. Have students engage in a guided practice activity. Here are a few different options:

Stick it: Have students work in teams and use sticky notes to list informational texts they find at home. Instruct students to sketch drawings to go with the lists and stick their notes on a class chart. When students have all posted their ideas, work together to sort the sticky notes into categories such as guides, magazines, etc.

Look Away and Remember: Play a game where you show all of your texts for a short length of time, then cover the texts. In pairs, have students try to remember all of the texts displayed by naming them and discussing purposes for reading each one.

This Day in Informational Reading: Several students might take seats at a table in the front of the room while holding their informational books to share. Another student role-plays as the "host" and asks questions of students who are on the "show". Questions might include: What informational text are you reading now?; What is it about?; Why did you select it?; What are you learning that is new and exciting?; Would you recommend this text to others; why or why not?

Roving Reporters: Have students interview other students in class, the school, on the playground, or adults at home as they share their purposes for informational reading.

Independent Practice

6. Distribute copies of the *Informational Text Recording Sheet* to students. Have students work independently, in pairs, or in small groups to complete the chart.

Figure 2.2 Informational Text Recording Sheet

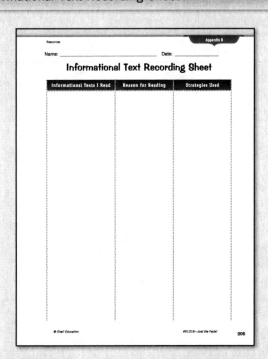

7. As a class, have students share what reading strategies they used, such as rereading, looking up words, or skimming.

Wrap-Up

8. Ask students to reflect on the lesson. What did they learn about informational texts in everyday life? Why do people read informational texts?

Assessment

Observe students as they participate in the various phases of the lesson. Can students explain the purposes for reading various informational texts or strategies for doing so?

Figure 2.3 Sample of Mrs. Oczkus' Informational Text Reading from Home

Informational Texts I Read	Reason for Reading	Strategies Used
newspaper	• to learn about the local transportation subway strike • to read the garden section for ideas • to read the world news • to see who won the local high school sports competitions this week	• skimming and scanning • studying headings, captions
online driving directions	• to study the best directions to the school to avoid traffic	• reading a map • taking notes, highlighting
camera manual	• to figure out how to operate the sports action mode during my daughter's dance recital	• reviewing index • rereading
book about hikes in the Bay Area	• to compare hikes and decide which one to do with my friends	• skimming and scanning • reading on • rereading
autobiographies	• to learn more about the life of a country western musician whose music I enjoy, Rosanne Cash. (*Composed: A Memoir* by Roseanne Cash) • to listen in the car to a recorded version of a favorite book because I enjoy books from WWII (*The Diary of Anne Frank*)	• reading captions with photos • making connections to other books/sources
National Geographic magazine	• to look at the photos in the photo issue because I am interested in photography • to read articles of interest	• studying photos • previewing table of contents • skimming/scanning • reading on • rereading
cookbook	• to choose recipes and interesting stories to tell at dinner parties	• previewing table of contents • index • glossary • marking text • rereading
dog training books	• to see how to get the dog to sleep in its crate again	• previewing table of contents • marking text • rereading • using photos, headings • glossary
The Reading Teacher journal	• to read about research-based methods for teaching reading and new research and lessons	• previewing table of contents • skimming and scanning • questioning/summarizing • highlighting
driver's license manual	• To help my 15-year-old study for the driver's test to get her permit	• questioning • rereading • summarizing • headings
books about "how things work"	• To quench my son's interest in how things work (This is his children's book collection; He is in college now and these are from his childhood!)	• studying visuals, maps, diagrams, charts • skimming • rereading

© Shell Education

Project-Based Learning: Authentic Reading and Writing of Informational Text

Another way for students to understand the importance and relevance of informational text is through the use of authentic project-based learning opportunities. Imagine a school where first graders cruise the playground with clipboards interviewing students about their pets for a class book. Down the hall, third-grade students videoconference with a buddy class in London as they share book reviews. Fifth-graders passionately hunch over their desks to write letters to the city council on new ways to involve students in recycling volunteer opportunities. These students are all actively engaged in hands-on projects that require them to question, research, think critically, collaborate, and communicate in diverse formats.

Providing opportunities for students to become aware of real-world purposes for reading and writing using informational texts helps make learning more meaningful in the classroom. Researcher Nell Duke (2000) reminds us that, "We want to make sure that we have students reading informational text because they want or need information. And we want to have students writing informational text because they actually want to convey information to someone who wants or needs it" (Oczkus 2012, 74). Research suggests that students will develop as informational readers and writers more quickly in those situations (Purcell-Gates, Duke, and Martineau 2007). Project-based learning requires students to actively participate in literacy projects that extend beyond the classroom walls, using reading and writing of informational text to its full potential. To be college and career ready, students need to actively engage in meaningful learning that emphasizes creativity, collaboration, critical thinking, and problem solving, as well as the ability to produce a variety of presentations. There is a myriad of exciting ways to involve students in meaningful projects to inform or persuade audiences about informational topics including:

- writing a letter
- creating a classroom museum
- producing class books
- producing slideshows for an assembly
- conducting interviews
- publishing articles about local places for the newspaper or school website
- creating posters for local businesses or doctors offices
- writing procedural texts such as cookbooks or how-to guides
- designing board games
- sharing book reviews to display in the library or local bookstore
- producing videos or plays

The possibilities for project-based learning are endless. The good news is that as students become more engaged, the stage is set for teaching explicit lessons in literacy that students put to use in a meaningful context. It isn't necessary to make every project a huge month-long endeavor, either. When students write a quick postcard or post a drawing or report online, they benefit as well.

Here are some examples of hands-on projects that utilize literacy skills in a meaningful way. The student-centered projects involve inquiry and help pique curiosity throughout with questioning driving the learning along every step of the process.

- Students write letters sharing what they've learned about their local history, state history, or U.S. history, with pen pals in another country who also share their history units about their city or country.

- Students create class books about the history of their local region and allow local merchants to display and/or sell the books at their shops.

- Students conduct a live video interview with an author or illustrator which allows them to ask questions that they have about the author/illustrator's work. The students then write an article for the school newsletter that goes out to parents and the community.

- Students read a variety of cookbooks and online recipes and then they create a class e-cookbook that is posted online for parents and families to access. Families are able to respond to the exciting healthy offerings on a comment page.

- Students study the school's recycling procedures and make suggestions for improvement in a letter they write to the principal or school board. Next, they embark on action steps and document their involvement with a slideshow that they present at an assembly or school board meeting.

- Students study a particular endangered animal by reading multiple texts about it and write to a conservation organization for information. The class adopts an animal and writes about their experience. They create posters for local shops and the mall to encourage others to support saving the chosen animal.

- Students read books and collect quarters for a charity organization such as the International Heifer Project's *Read to Feed*. Students help families in third-world countries become self-sufficient by purchasing animals such as chickens to donate. The class reads books and online articles from the charity organization about how the work they do is helping their cause. They write articles for the school website and lobby families for donations at an assembly.

Students will enjoy helping others, sharing important information, and solving problems for the classroom, school, or community, as they dive into reading and writing about real-world issues.

Project-Based Learning Books for Students

Each of these compact student books stand alone or may be used together to provide many exciting, practical ways for students to get involved in community service. These visually appealing student texts include project ideas as well as websites, books, and other resources to turn to.

Hand to Paw: Protecting Animals by Jessica Cohn (2013)

Some of the projects include: Making homemade dog biscuits for a dog shelter, writing letters or reporting on endangered species, collecting pet food and other donations for a shelter, putting on a pet show and donating earnings to a local shelter, researching animals, and searching suggested websites for project ideas.

Hand to Earth: Saving the Environment by Jessica Cohn (2013)

Some of the projects include: Cutting down on water while brushing teeth, reusing plastic cups, unplugging appliances, recycling, and repairing broken items instead of buying new ones. Students may measure their carbon footprint by going to http://myfootprint. org. The book also contains suggestions for websites with ideas for recycling, protecting water resources, and making crafts from recyclables.

Hand to Heart: Improving Communities by Jessica Cohn (2013)

Some projects include: Writing letters of thanks to firefighters, holding fundraisers for charity, selling handmade items or collecting canned food, sending care packages to soldiers, writing to newspapers or politicians, making bookmarks to sell or donate, babysitting, donating blankets, planting a garden, and checking out five wonderful websites full of ideas for kids to volunteer.

Resources for Teachers

- *Reading and Writing Genre with Purpose in K–8 Classrooms* by Nell Duke, Samantha Caughlan, Mary Juzwik, and Nicole Martin (2012). The authors outline many exciting ways to help scaffold the learning and teach foundational literacy skills as students embark on project-based learning including writing letters, sharing procedural texts, putting together informational texts and presentations, putting on dramatic performances, writing persuasive texts with arguments, and more!

- Edutopia (http:// www.edutopia.org). Edutopia includes a multitude of free online resources for teachers including videos, lesson plans, articles, blogs, and more! Search "project based learning."

Reading Informational Text Is Different Than Reading Fiction

In addition to having students understand the significance of informational text and its prevalence in today's society, it is also important for them to understand that good readers move through fiction and informational texts quite differently. Picture how a reader looks when he is lost in a fiction book with eyes moving quickly across the text, concentrating, pages turning. Now, picture a reader lost in a nonfiction book. They may look randomly around the page pausing for a moment to study a visual that caught their eye. Or they may flip to a page already read to reference a chart. Perhaps they will turn to the glossary or flip ahead to skim the next portion of text. Their brow may furrow in puzzlement as they reread a page several times, pausing to make notes on a page, to highlight, or write on a sticky note.

In my home, we had our own resident informational text specialist. From a very young age my son, Bryan, mostly preferred informational text. I'd peek into his room and see him slowly pausing on pages for long periods of time when pouring over his collection of texts on dinosaurs or the solar system. He always looked more pensive when lost in his nonfiction favorites. I tell students about my son's reading behaviors. Then I grab a fiction book and make myself comfortable and read away (silently) asking them what they notice. Then, I do the same with informational text and model flipping about, looking around the page, looking puzzled, shaking my head for confirmation, and rereading. I ask students to discuss the difference. This is my lead-in to a discussion on informational text behaviors and strategies. Students need to understand that it is okay to poke around, pause and study, go back, reread, peek ahead, and flip through an informational text to get the most out of it.

© Shell Education

Model the following behaviors for informational text. Be dramatic by making faces or small gestures like head nodding since you are doing this silently!

- flip through for a text-to-text walk or briefly glance at illustrations and/or headings before reading
- jump to a chapter you are interested in to read it first
- pause on text to study a feature
- reread portions of the text you didn't understand
- look puzzled
- turn to the glossary
- nod for confirmation when you "get" something
- look surprised, delighted, or amazed by the information

The following is a lesson idea to support the explicit modeling of informational text reading behaviors with students.

Lesson Idea

Acting and Thinking Like A Reader!

Objective

To help students understand how reading informational text is different than reading fiction.

Materials

- chart paper or interactive whiteboard
- *Informational Text Checklist* (See Appendix B)

Teacher Model

Fiction Model

1. Ask students to watch as you first model silent reading of a fictional text. Turn the pages quickly and look engaged or "lost" in the text. Invite partners to discuss what they noticed.

2. Model the same text by reading it aloud and sharing what you are thinking as you read. Say things like, "I wonder what will happen next. I can't believe the character did that!" Ask students to turn to a partner and share what they noticed.

Informational Text Model

3. Model silent reading of an informational text. Be dramatic as you reread portions of the text, flip through the text, and pause on visuals. Ask students to turn to a partner and share what they noticed.

4. Model the same text by reading it aloud. Share your thoughts such as, "I want to look at this really cool picture of ____. I wonder ____. Oh, this is interesting! I need to reread this part. I want to study this map because… I need to flip back to… I need the glossary to see what…"

Discussion

5. Pose the following questions for discussion:

- What did you notice when I read the two books?

- Is reading informational text the same as reading fiction? Discuss.

6. Create a chart of informational text reading behaviors titled, *When I Read Informational Texts I….*

7. Have the class help you list the behaviors and strategies you used in your demonstration or that they use when reading informational texts. Possible suggestions should include:

- Reread parts I do not understand

- Use text features such as headings and visuals

- Stop on confusing words and try _____

- Stop to think when I see something interesting

8. Leave the chart up somewhere in the classroom for easy reference and add to it in subsequent discussions.

Guided Practice

9. Distribute a copy of *Informational Text Checklist* to each student. As students read with partners, ask them to pause every two pages and have each student share one informational text reading strategy that they used to help them understand the text. Invite students to refer to the class chart or their *Informational Text Checklist*.

Independent Practice

10. Have students keep track of their informational text reading behaviors using their *Informational Text Checklist*.

Wrap-Up

11. Invite students to summarize the differences they noticed good readers use when reading informational text vs. fiction text.

Assessment

Conference with students and ask them to show you which informational text reading behaviors they are using and cite specific examples.

Figure 2.4 Informational Text Checklist

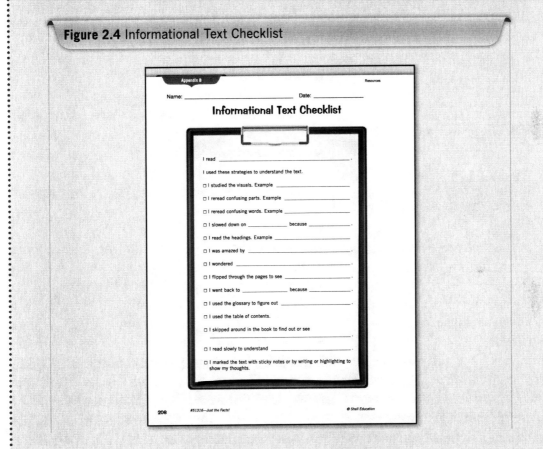

Special Features Unique to Informational Texts

In second grade, during guided reading, Robbie sighed as he made an important discovery not only about the leveled book on whales that we were reading, but in general about informational text features. "Mrs. Oczkus, I didn't realize we were supposed to read the map, too! I didn't think it was important!"

Unfortunately, Robbie is not alone. Many of our students skip over or do not spend enough time with the text features because they don't fully grasp the importance or purpose of text features as an integral part of the informational reading experience. Nonfiction, or informational text, looks quite different than fiction. Fiction may include illustrations in a picture book or even a chapter book where running text prevails. Although informational text may also include running text, it often includes special visual stopping points along the way. Even with a quick flip through a nonfiction book, we find unique text features sprinkled throughout including photos, captions, diagrams, headings, maps, charts, tables, graphs, and more. On the reading "road," text features are sure examples of "road signs" that signal us to yield, stop, or turn as they tell us what lies ahead.

Text features are the hallmark of informational text. They serve a variety of important purposes that ultimately aide the reader in comprehending the text. Text features such as photos, sketches, cross sections and cutaways, maps, diagrams, sidebars, charts, and the glossary convey information that either enhances the content or adds new and additional ideas and details about the topic. Other text features such as the table of contents, headings, subheadings, and the index help label the information in the text and guide the reader through the reading experience. Students often ignore or skip these text features, only paying attention to the text itself (Kelley and Clausen-Grace 2007). Teaching lessons that show students the purpose of each of these features in informational text and how to use them builds comprehension. Discussing text features helps students to anticipate what the text is about, set purposes for reading, and make a mental "map" or outline of the content (Lubliner 2001; Recht and Leslie 1988).

Practical Ideas for Teaching Text Features

When you make learning text features interactive and meaningful, students remember to use them to deepen their comprehension. The following are some hands-on lessons and game-like ideas for teaching the different purposes of informational text features and the value they each bring to the reading experience.

Text Feature Hunt

A quick and easy lesson idea for introducing students to informational text features comes from the work of Stephanie Harvey (1998) in her book, *Nonfiction Matters*. Have teams or partners casually flip through informational texts and list each text feature that they find. Instruct students to number their text features as they page through the text hunting for as many text features as possible in a limited time frame. You may also ask students to take turns being "in charge" of a particular page as they take a turn pointing out the text features (Kelley and Clausen-Grace 2007). Each team may use the same text or different texts.

A Text Feature Hunt may include:

- headings
- subheadings
- photos and captions
- drawings
- maps

- graphs
- diagrams
- charts and graphs
- cutaways and cross-sections
- sidebars

- different fonts
- highlighted words
- tables of contents
- indices
- glossaries

Find the Feature

When teaching younger students, try using an informational text read-aloud and then pause on each page for students to turn to a partner to share the text features they see. Then, have students raise their hands when they think they've spotted the feature you have in mind. It is fun to make up riddles or play guessing games for each feature. For example say, "I am thinking of a text feature that shows where _____ is" (map) or "I am thinking of a text feature that shows me what page each chapter is on _____" (table of contents)."

You may choose to label the features with sticky notes in a big book or electronically on an interactive whiteboard. Another way to conduct the lesson is to provide a checklist of text features and have students check them off and list a page number as they find each feature.

Find the Text Feature!

Objectives

Students will identify one or more informational text features and label them in a text.

Materials

- *Text Feature Organizer* (See Appendix B)
- fiction text
- informational text
- chart paper or interactive whiteboard
- sticky notes
- cards
- large construction paper for signs

Teacher Model

1. Hold up a fiction text and an informational text. Ask students what they know about each type of text—how they are the same and how they are different.

2. Open both texts and hold them side by side. Ask what students notice.

3. Tell students that text features are like road signs during reading, guiding the reader through the book and telling the reader what is up ahead and when to pause.

4. Flip through each page of the informational text, thinking aloud as you focus on each text feature with a portion of text. Create a chart of text features as you encounter each one. As you create the chart, ask students what the purpose of each feature is and what it does for the reader. Add that information to the chart. Additionally, you may wish to place a sticky note next to each text feature in the text.

Guided Practice

Stick it: Provide teams or pairs of students with sticky notes to use to label text features in a selected text appropriate for their reading level.

You're in Charge: Assign each group or pair of students a text feature to be "in charge of" during the reading by writing the name of the text feature on a large paper or card. As you read aloud a selected text, students are on the lookout for their assigned feature. They raise their hands if they see their feature on the page as it is being read. Then, discuss with students why some features appear more than once in a text.

Partner Text Feature Walk: Have students work in teams or pairs to preview a text and use the *Text Feature Organizer* to record all of the text features they see. After reading the text, invite students to return to the organizer to write the purpose of each text feature and what they learned from it.

Text Feature Cruise Around: Post signs for each of the text features around the room at various stations. Have students travel with a partner or team of four to each sign and look for the text feature either in a text they travel with or one you provide at the station. Have students fill in their *Text Feature Organizer* as they move through the stations. Signal with music or another sign when it is time for students to move clockwise to a different station. Continue until students have rotated around to all the text features.

Independent Practice

5. Have students use either an informational text of their choice or one you've designated to complete the *Text Feature Organizer*. Students should think about what information the author was trying to convey using each feature.

Wrap-Up

Ask students to reflect on the lesson. What did they learn about informational text features? How do they help the reader? Which text features were most helpful?

Assessment

Observe students as they participate in the various phases of the lesson. Can students identify text features and their purposes?

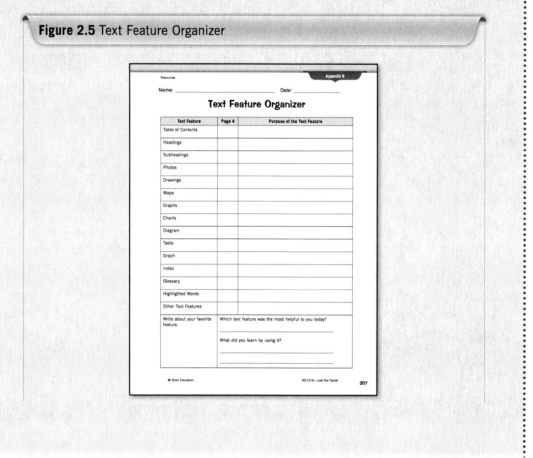

Figure 2.5 Text Feature Organizer

Text Feature Wall

A text feature wall is a wonderful tool to get your students involved in a hands-on way to find examples of text features (Kelly and Clausen-Grace 2008). After brainstorming a list of text features, create a large butcher paper backdrop for students to use as they cut, paste, and display examples of text features from magazines and newspapers. Draw lines and label sections of the chart for each text feature. You may wish to ask students how much space to block off for each feature and let them decide how to organize the chart, or simply block off an equal amount of space for each feature. Another option is to cut out features and lay them out to see how much space is needed for each. The Text Feature Wall can be an ongoing project all year long. See Kelly and Clausen Grace's sample of a text feature wall on their website at www.teachingcomprehension.org.

Here are some more hands-on practical ideas for teaching text features.

- Students cut, paste, and label examples of text features in their notebooks.

- Students use colored highlighters or colored pencils to mark text features in articles or pages copied from the textbook.

- Students cut and paste examples of each of the text features on an 8.5 x 11 sheet of paper labeled with that feature, then three-hole punch or staple for a text feature book. The same cut-and-paste book can be made into a flip deck using large index cards hole punched and hooked together with a ring.

- Play Text-Tac-Toe: Have students use nine text feature cards (Figure 2.6) and place them in any order they like on the text-tac-toe board (Figure 2.7) face up. When the leader shows an example of one of the text features, if a student has that feature they flip it over face down. Three in a row is a "Text-Tac-Toe."

Figure 2.6 Text Feature Game Cards

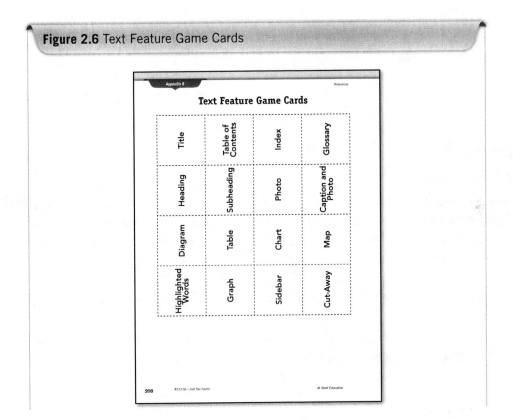

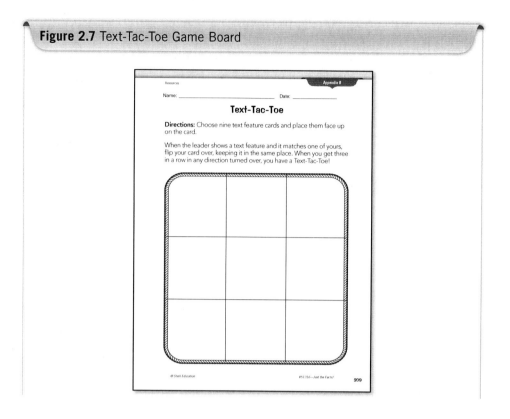

Figure 2.7 Text-Tac-Toe Game Board

Teaching Text Structures

While text features, such as photos, maps, and headings are easily recognizable, text structures require some training for students to be able to identify on their own. Informational texts are written to inform, describe, persuade, or report. The topic or content and author's purpose determines the text structure. For example, a first-grade science text about the life cycle of a butterfly is written to inform and fits neatly into a time order sequence pattern. The Revolutionary War chapter in a history text may contain different organizational structures within the chapter, such as time order for sequence of the events in a particular event or cause and effect when discussing the causes of the war. Understanding text structure strengthens overall comprehension and provides models for organizing writing (Lipson 1996). The most common text structures in informational text are as follows:

- Descriptive

- Problem/solution

- Time order sequence

- Compare and contrast

- Cause and effect

How do we help our students to recognize informational text structures? One effective way to help students understand how different text structures work is to show what one topic would look like if we wrote about it using different text structures (Hoyt and Stead 2011). Try choosing a topic appropriate to your grade level and plugging it into the different text structures for a few sentences, similar to the example in Figure 2.8 on frogs. You could work together with your students to try writing a few sentences about a simple topic using the different organizers. Teams of students may then take another topic and rewrite it to fit one of the organizers. This writing exercise will help students recognize and understand different informational text structures.

Figure 2.8 Text Structures Chart with Sample Frogs Text

Description Descriptive adjectives, in, appears to be, under, over, beyond	Frogs are cold-blooded amphibians. There are more than 4,800 species of frogs found all over the world. Frogs' skin varies in color from brown to grey, yellow, green, black, or even red. They may live in fresh water, on land, underground or in trees.
Problem/Solution Reason, conclude, problem, solution, an idea, result	Frog populations are declining due to a fungus called Chytrid. Scientists are working hard to solve the frog problem by encouraging zoos, botanical gardens, and universities to choose at least one species to study. The idea is to control the fungus and release the amphibians back into their homes.
Time Order Sequence First, second, now, later, then, finally, tomorrow, eventually	First, the mother frog lays her cluster of eggs in the pond water. After 21 days the eggs hatch and out come tadpoles. The tadpoles start out with gills, tails, and two legs, and look like fish. Then, after six to nine weeks, the tadpoles grow small legs and start to look more like frogs.
Compare Contrast Like, as, different, similarly, same, both, although, yet, while	Frogs and toads are in the same family but are from different species. Frogs have smooth skin while toads are bumpy. They both eat worms and insects.
Cause and Effect Because, since, in order to, caused by, reason	Frog populations are declining because pesticides cause frogs to become ill or die. Since frogs breathe through their skin, they become ill or die when exposed to various pesticides. Pesticides also weaken the frogs' ability to ward off diseases and infection.

(adapted from Hoyt and Stead 2011)

Graphic Organizers to Support Understanding of Text Structures

Good readers use their knowledge of how a text is organized to help them summarize (Lipson 1996). Using graphic organizers throughout reading lessons improves comprehension (Heimlich and Pittelman 1986). Help students understand and visualize the structures of informational texts by using a unique concept map or web to support it. After modeling how the graphic organizer supports the text structure, post it in the classroom and use it to fill in information from informational texts read throughout the year. Some texts will be based entirely on just one organizer, while others may incorporate topics under different headings that require a different organizer. Here are some ways to use those graphic organizers to support the understanding of text structures with before, during, and after reading activities.

Before reading, when your class or small group is predicting and inferring what the text will be about, try skimming the text and anticipating which type of organizer should be used based on clue words and the topic (Oczkus 2009).

During reading, fill in the graphic organizer to monitor and keep track of the learning so far and to anticipate what will be covered next.

After reading, complete the organizer as a way to summarize the material. Use the organizer to guide students as they produce brief verbal or written summaries.

Mentor Texts to Support Understanding of Text Structures

When you show students straightforward examples of informational text structures from books and other published texts, the experience becomes an anchor that you can refer to in subsequent lessons. We often call these "mentor texts" because they become our teachers or models for that type of text. Dorfman and Cappelli (2013) suggest returning to mentor texts many times with students to reread for different purposes. For example, when reading a cause and effect leveled reader that is a science text about earthquakes with small groups you might refer back to the read-aloud book about volcanoes that you shared with the whole class to teach the cause and effect structure. You might say, "What do you remember about the way the volcano book was organized around cause and effect? Let's see how this book about earthquakes is organized. How can you tell if it is a cause and effect text?" The mentor text becomes a model we return to time and time again as our anchor for the ways each type of text is organized.

Here are some examples of mentor texts that help students to recognize each text structure in the materials they read and to use the structures in their own writing.

Figure 2.9 Mentor Texts to Support Text Structure

Text Structure	Mentor Text (Primary)
Description	*Yucky Worms* by Vivian French *Senses at the Seashore* by Shelley Rotner
Sequence	*From Wax to Crayon* by Robin Nelson *A Day in Our Lives* by Dawson J. Hunt
Problem/Solution	*Seeds of Change* by Jen Cu Johnson *Can We Save the Tiger?* by Martin Jenkins
Cause/Effect	*Staying Healthy* by Dona Herwick Rice *How Toys Work* by Lisa Greathouse
Compare/Contrast	*Do I Need It? Or Do I Want It?: Making Budget Choices* by Jennifer Larson *Is It Transparent or Opaque?* By Susan Hughes

Text Structure	Mentor Text (Intermediate)
Description	*Straight Talk: The Truth About Food* by Stephanie Paris *The Great Fire* by Jim Murphy
Sequence	*River of Dreams* by Hudson Talbott *Jane Goodall* by William Rice
Problem/Solution	*Hit It! History of Tools* by Dona Herweck Rice *Kids' Solar Energy Book* by Tilly Spetgang
Cause/Effect	*Titanic: Disaster at Sea* by Martin Jenkins *Unsolved! Mysterious Events* by Lisa Greathouse
Compare/Contrast	*Games Around the World* by Casey Petersen *Women's Suffrage* by Hariet Isecke

 © *Shell Education*

Mentor Text for Text Structure Lesson

Objective

Students will recognize and learn one of the informational text structures by listening to a read aloud.

Materials

- Informational text
- graphic organizer

Teacher Model

1. Explain to students that when good readers read informational text, they often use the text structure to help them comprehend the material better. Tell students today they will use the structure _____ (choose one of the five) as they read to help understand the text. Or, if students are familiar with text structures, have them guess which structure goes with the text by previewing it.

2. Display the graphic organizer that goes with the type of text.

3. Model for students how to text-walk before reading to anticipate the structure of the text. Say, "I think the author organized this text by _____ (choose one of the five structures), because I see _____ (visuals, headings, other clues)." Pause often during reading to think aloud and share with students how the information "fits" into the text structure.

Guided Practice

Partners Share: Have students work in pairs to discuss and complete the graphic organizer that goes with the selected text.

Same-o Structure Hunt: Give teams of students different texts to "hunt" for the text structure you just modeled in the mentor text read-aloud. Texts for the hunt could include textbooks, classroom magazines, nonfiction picture books, encyclopedias, and other texts.

Independent Practice

4. Give students a new text or have students complete the graphic organizer with key words from the mentor text or other texts.

Wrap-Up

Discuss how understanding text structure helps with both reading and writing.

Assessment

As students are working, look to see whether they can recognize and explain the text structure organizer and complete the organizer correctly for the selected text structure.

Figure 2.10 Graphic Organizers for Informational Text Structures

Text Structure	Mentor Text (Primary)
Description	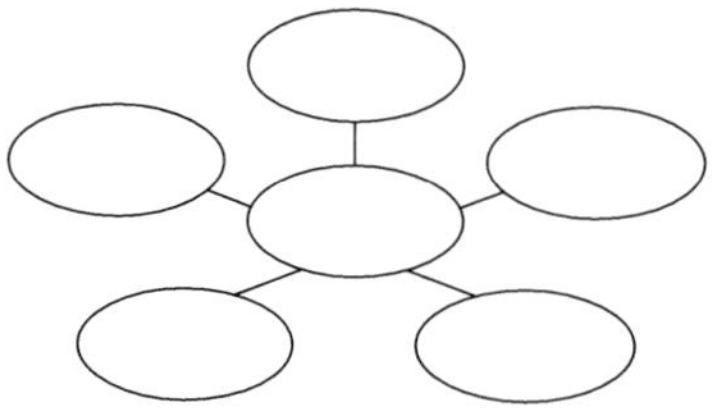
Sequence	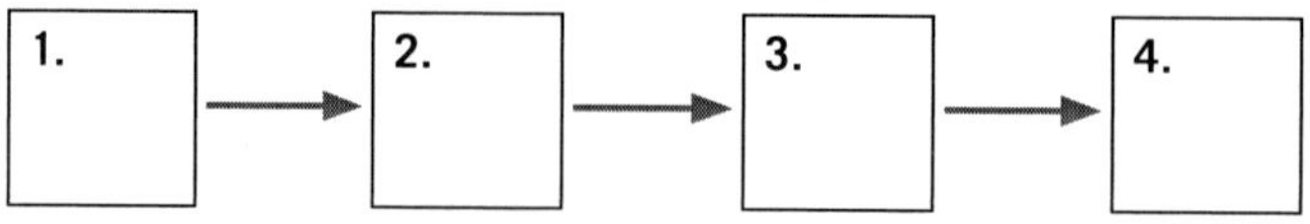 1. → 2. → 3. → 4.
Problem/Solution	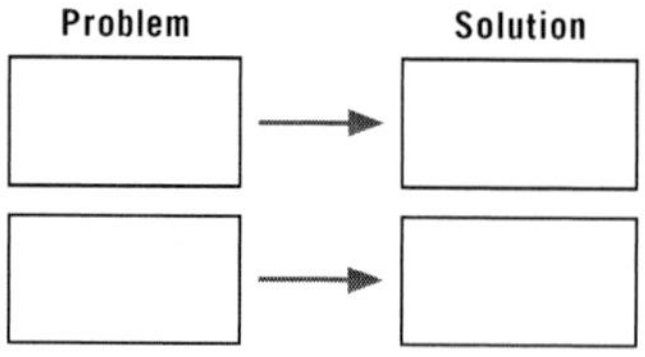 Problem → Solution
Cause/Effect	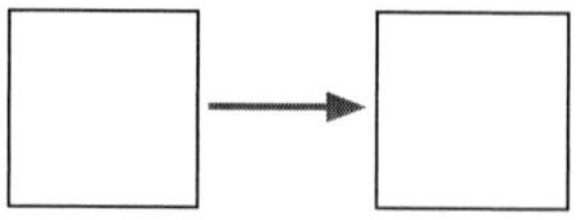 □ → □
Compare/Contrast	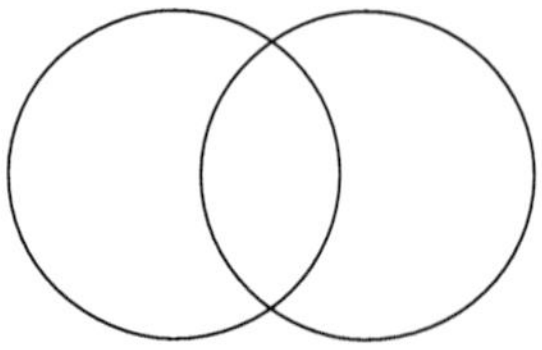

#51316—*Just the Facts!* © *Shell Education*

Wrap-Up and Reflection

Informational text is vastly different from fiction, just as the many reasons we read are different from one another. To succeed in the 21st century, students not only need to learn how to *read* informational text but they also need to learn how to *use* the information gained for a variety of purposes. By encouraging students to peek into the real-world uses of informational texts, they begin to understand that people read such texts for various reasons and with different degrees of intensity. Informational texts are vastly different in the ways they are organized, using text structures that range from main idea and details, to cause and effect, to problem/solution. Text features are used throughout informational text to support the reader and give it a different look with headings, captions, diagrams, charts, and cutaways.

Here are some key ideas to think about from this chapter:

- In the career world, people read nonfiction texts in many different ways.

- Lessons should focus on helping students to understand the purposes for reading informational texts as well as the strategies readers use such as rereading, skimming, summarizing, and using text features.

- Project-based learning requires students to actively participate in literacy projects that extend beyond the classroom walls, thereby using reading and writing of informational text to its full potential. Research suggests that students will develop as informational readers and writers more quickly in those situations (Purcell-Gates, Duke, and Martineau 2007). Some project-based learning includes writing letters, creating a museum, producing class books and online projects, performing, and more.

- Good readers move through informational texts differently than fiction, by skipping around, lingering on certain pages, and reading at different paces, depending upon the difficulty of the text and purpose for reading.

- Teaching text features such as bold words, headings, captions, maps, charts, and visuals helps students to anticipate content and pause to summarize as they read.

- Informational text structures include description, problem/solution, sequence, compare/contrast, and cause and effect. Mentor texts are useful in helping students recognize different text structures.

Reflect and Discuss

1. Why is important for students to know about how adults read informational text on the job and in their lives? What role does "purpose" for reading play in selecting informational texts?

2. What is project-based learning and how is it beneficial for students at your grade level? What are ways to get started? How does informational text relate to project-based learning?

3. In what ways are informational texts different from fiction? How can you teach text features and structures?

4. What are mentor texts and how can they help you teach and reinforce informational text structures and features?s

Motivating Students to Read Informational Texts: Practical Classroom Routines

For some of our students, the only informational texts they will ever encounter are the content-area textbooks they read in school (Moss 2013). If we want to truly equip students with 21st century reading skills, then part of our challenge is to inspire students to read widely from a range of informational texts *all day long*! The Common Core State Standards (2010) call for us to go beyond just arming students with the strategies to "read and comprehend complex literary and informational texts." In this chapter you will find many practical ways to teach from informational texts throughout the school day. From participating in informational text read-alouds to small-group lessons, to independent reader's workshop, the opportunities to inspire students with rich content and strategies for comprehending informational text abound.

Using Informational Text All Day Long

Classroom Connection

Primary Example

Mrs. Sanchez invites the first graders to the rug for an informational text read aloud. When she holds up the cover of *Bugs A to Z* by Caroline Lawton (2011), the students quietly study the title and photo anticipating how the author organized the text. Hands shoot up and Will explains, "Some authors like to use the A, B, C's for their books." Jenna adds," We read *Into the A, B, Sea* (Rose 2000) about ocean animals." Javier interjects, "I think this is about bugs. *A* will be for *ant*!"

After the lively read aloud, the students move into their stations to read more about insects using a variety of texts for independent and partner reading and research-writing activities including writing mini fact books to share in the classroom library. During guided reading, the insect study continues as the groups read *A Bee's Life* by Dona Herweck Rice (2012). Later in the day the students study about the insects found in the local botanical garden so they can make posters that the garden will put on display for the public to view.

Intermediate Example

During reader's workshop, fourth graders hunch over their books, working in teams on the floor and at tables, taking notes and gathering the facts and information about California's Hetch-Hetchy Dam. The students read newspaper articles, online resources, and their history text as they record the facts and controversies surrounding the dam. The class is preparing a mock interview of the important "characters" from California history in 1913, including members of congress who were both for and against the dam, and naturalist John Muir, who was opposed. After lunch, Mr. Gertz helps students conduct a close reading of an essay written by John Muir by providing copies for them and projecting a copy to model from. Students use their colored markers to mark confusing parts and questions to ask. During science, the students work in teams of four to read about the water cycle by studying *Water Scientists* (2007) and *Inside the Water Cycle* (2007) by William Rice. The students build a chart and compare and contrast what they learned from both texts. The students then prepare to interview a local water treatment scientist via videoconference and begin to write up their water facts in picture books that they will read aloud to their first-grade buddies.

Using Informational Text with Reciprocal Teaching

Good readers often use comprehension strategies as a "package." Rarely do readers use strategies in isolation. Reciprocal teaching (Palincsar and Brown 1986) is a scaffolded discussion technique that guides the reader to employ four of the most critical strategies good readers use:

- predict
- question
- clarify
- summarize

Reciprocal teaching is an ideal technique to use to strengthen comprehension with any text but especially for informational texts. Research has found that students who engage in reciprocal teaching, a multiple strategy approach, not only improve in their reading level, but they also retain the content better (Reutzel, Smith, and Fawson 2005). Research has shown that in as little as 15 days, students will raise their hands with more confidence and after three months they may grow one to two years in their reading levels (Cooper et al. 2000; Rosenshine and Meister 1994; Hattie 2008). I nicknamed reciprocal teaching, "The Fab Four," to make it more student-friendly and thousands of teachers now use that term with students (Oczkus 2010). In my work in schools, when reciprocal teaching is incorporated in any setting, including intervention groups, content-area lessons, small guided-reading groups, and close reading, we see one to two year gains for many students, especially struggling readers and English languge learners. In my project, where reciprocal teaching strategies were used, students made gains within the first few months when these strategies are used during small-group intervention lessons. When we incorporate the strategies throughout the day, the scores rose even more. Most schools were impacted with English language learners and struggling readers who are two or more years below grade level. Reciprocal teaching with its discussion scaffolds is perfect for guiding students with special needs through discussions.

Each of the Fab Four strategies is valuable, research-based, and worthy of standing on its own. Together the four are a package that works to strengthen comprehension through discussion and their consistent use together. Figure 3.1 provides more detail about each of the strategies in the instructional model. A student-friendly bookmark version of this figure is available in Appendix B.

Figure 3.1 Reciprocal Teaching Strategies

Predict *I think I will learn ____ because ____.*	Students make inferences and use text evidence throughout the reading process to predict what they will learn next. They use text features and structure to help make predictions.
Question *Who, what, when, where, why, how?*	Students ask and answer text-dependent questions and wonderings.
Clarify *The confusing word or idea was ____. I ____ to figure it out.*	Students know and apply grade-level phonics and word analysis skills in decoding words. They also learn to reread, self-correct and use the senses to visualize.
Summarize *This was about ____.*	Students identify main ideas and details, compare and contrast the content and structure of texts. They use text features to guide their summaries.

Figure 3.2 Reciprocal Teaching Bookmark

Appendix B   Resources

Reciprocal Teaching Bookmark

Reciprocal Teaching Bookmark (adapted from Oczkus 2010)	Reciprocal Teaching Bookmark (adapted from Oczkus 2010)
Predict Look at the headings, illustrations, and text. What do you think you will learn? Talk to your partner or team. **I think I will learn _____ because _____.**	**Predict** Look at the headings, illustrations, and text. What do you think you will learn? Talk to your partner or team. **I think I will learn _____ because _____.**
Question Ask questions before, during, and after reading. Use who, what, when, where, why, and how. Share with partners or your team. **My question before reading** _____ **My question during reading** _____ **My question after reading** _____	**Question** Ask questions before, during, and after reading. Use who, what, when, where, why, and how. Share with partners or your team. **My question before reading** _____ **My question during reading** _____ **My question after reading** _____
Clarify Be on the lookout for difficult words or ideas. How did you figure them out? Talk to partners/team. **Difficult words** _____ **Confusing ideas** _____ I used the following strategies __reread __sounded words out __read on __used syllables, prefixes, word parts __talked to a friend __looked up the word	**Clarify** Be on the lookout for difficult words or ideas. How did you figure them out? Talk to partners/team. **Difficult words** _____ **Confusing ideas** _____ I used the following strategies __reread __sounded words out __read on __used syllables, prefixes, word parts __talked to a friend __looked up the word
Summarize In your own words, tell the main ideas from the text. **Sketch your summary.** **This text is about** _____	**Summarize** In your own words, tell the main ideas from the text. **Sketch your summary.** **This text is about** _____

210   #51316—Just the Facts!   © Shell Education

What Reciprocal Teaching Looks Like in the Classroom

The Fab Four may be used in any order and are first modeled by the teacher, then practiced by the students in collaborative partners or teams, and finally individually applied. The key to yielding such positive results with reciprocal teaching is to include all four strategies in one lesson. It is also important to make sure students witness teacher modeling and participate in discussions with peers throughout the lesson. When reciprocal teaching lessons are offered at least twice a week, students make gains. You can choose to use reciprocal teaching effectively in a variety of settings from whole class to guided reading to literature circles (Oczkus 2010). Here are some classroom scenarios to further reinforce what reciprocal teaching looks like in implementation.

Reciprocal Teaching and Content-Area Reading: During a history lesson in a sixth-grade class, the teacher asks students to work in teams of four to take on the roles of predictor, clarifier, questioner, and summarizer. Teams read the chapter from the textbook together and discuss using their roles or jobs to guide the discussion. They mark the text along the way with sticky notes to identify main ideas, questions, and words or concepts to clarify. Groups then fill in a graphic organizer and discuss text structure, main ideas, and key details from the text.

Reciprocal Teaching and Close Reading: Fifth-graders take out pencils for a close reading of a page from a science text. The teacher reviews the four strategies with the students and tells them that today they will use the strategies to closely read one of the most challenging pages from the science book. Their teacher distributes a copy of the text for each student to mark up and displays a copy using the document camera. The first reading of the text is silent while students underline words to clarify. For the second read, the teacher reads it aloud and models words to clarify. Partners discuss and share their challenging words. The teacher then asks some text-dependent questions and the students reread with a partner to answer the questions using evidence from the text. Lastly, the pairs read the text once more and highlight three important points and two details. The class creates a shared summary and students illustrate.

Reciprocal Teaching and Small-Group Instruction: Third-graders in a reading intervention group gather around the table to read leveled informational texts using reciprocal teaching. The students begin the lesson sharing what they know about volcanoes, the topic they will read about. Then, the teacher asks students to study the headings and share predictions about what they will learn with partners. The group discusses the role of headings in an informational text. During reading, the students focus on looking for words to clarify and mark them with sticky notes. After reading, the students share their words. The teacher asks text-dependent questions and the students work in pairs to answer them. Then, the group works as a team to write a summary of the reading by returning to the headings to find main ideas and important details.

Reciprocal Teaching and Read-Aloud: During a read-aloud in a kindergarten and first-grade combination class, the teacher shares a big book on snakes and pauses every few pages to model one of the reciprocal teaching strategies. For example, after she models a prediction using evidence from the text, the students immediately turn to partners and use the same language to make predictions as well. The lesson continues as she alternates between modeling and inviting partners to share. The partners work to clarify confusing words, ask questions, and summarize the learning so far.

Scaffolding the Use of Informational Text

Using Think-Alouds and Gradual Release of Responsibility

Think-alouds show students what a good reader is thinking while reading and is an effective way to teach students how to comprehend informational text (Oczkus 2009). The gradual release of responsibility model (Pearson and Gallagher 1983) is a proven research-based process (Fisher and Frey 2007) that starts with teacher modeling and think aloud, followed by guided practice with the teacher and peers, and ending with independent practice coupled with teacher feedback. The goal is to provide practice and guidance so students become metacognitive and uses the strategies on their own.

Gradual release applies to any process one needs to learn. You can compare the gradual release model to learning to ride a bike with the adult modeling, holding onto the seat, running beside, and finally releasing the child to ride on his or her own (Oczkus 2010). In our household, we have one teen driver left to train, our youngest daughter, and the same gradual release process applies. We talk through what we are doing as we drive her around town. "Okay, now watch how I speed up to enter the freeway." Or "See how I am leaving a car's length and not tailgating?" When she practices driving with her driver's permit, we ride in the passenger seat guiding her with gentle suggestions and directions. Eventually, after the required months of guided practice with us, she'll be ready for the open road and driving on her own.

Another way to think about gradual release is to use the motto, "I do. We do. You do" made popular by master teacher Regie Routman, as part of her Optimal Learning Model (2008). Regie also added an extra step: "I do. We do. We do. You do." Notice the double "We do," which makes sense when students need more practice with you and each other before going it alone. Sometimes you might even add an extra "I do" for your modeling piece to provide more examples. For more challenging concepts or skills, we might provide several sessions of modeled and guided practice before students are ready to be released to work independently. The key to an effective think-aloud lesson is to engage students in each of the steps so that your think aloud does not become an ineffective "teacher talk only" that the students don't absorb or listen to (Think of the muffled trumpet sound Charles Schulz used for a teacher voice in his Charlie Brown videos!) You can easily make your think-aloud demonstrations more interactive by inviting students to talk to partners throughout the lesson, show their understanding with gestures, or by recording a response. English language learners and struggling readers will respond positively to the active engagement strategies that help make vocabulary and concepts easier to grasp. The lessons and samples in this resource provide many options for each of the steps in the think aloud using the gradual release of responsibility model so you can adjust for the needs of your students.

Classroom Connection

Primary Classroom Think Aloud

The first graders chime in as the lively discussion about earthquakes begins as the students study the cover of the text, *Earthquake!* by Cy Armour (2012).

"We stand in the doorway at our apartment," shares Jaime. "Terremoto," Petra whispers the Spanish word for earthquake. Mr. Robinson begins his think aloud by focusing the students' attention back onto the cover and table of contents. "Class, good readers use the table of contents to help think about their predictions for what they think they will learn. I see that the author uses question words *how*, *what*, and *where* for his chapters."

Mr. Robinson invites the students to take a quick text walk through the book and then he returns to the table of contents to model. "I think I will learn about what the Earth does to cause an earthquake in the chapter titled, 'How Earthquakes Happen,' because of the word *how* and also because I saw a picture of a crack in the Earth and arrows on page 8." He invites the students to show a thumbs up if they agree and to turn to partners to share by using the frame *In the chapter titled _____ I think I will learn about ____ because ____.* Students take turns sharing what they think they learn from each chapter with partners. They work independently to sketch what they think they will learn in each of the chapters.

Intermediate Classroom Think-Aloud

"Good readers consider the author's purpose and the way the author organized the text. Watch as I think aloud about the unusual organization of this exciting new book about volcanoes," says Mr. Ling. The fourth-graders settle comfortably in their desks after lunch as their teacher shares *Volcano Rising* by Elizabeth Rusch (2013) in a read-aloud. He also shows the text on a document camera so the students can see the text organization and illustrations. "I think the author chose an interesting way to organize her text. I noticed by the second page that she uses part of the page for her explanation, but does so in an entertaining, descriptive way. I know this because she incorporated cool sound, or onomatopoeia, words like *POW* and *Hisssss*. The author also includes a few paragraphs in smaller print on every page like this one about a volcano in Mexico."

Mr. Ling then asks the class to consider why the author organized the book this way with two running patterns. Partners discuss and the conclusion is that the author chose this organization to entertain and inform. He pages through the rest of the book asking students to skim the text and raise their hands when they see more "sound" words. *Whoosh, gurgle,* and *scrape* are among the words they find. Mr. Ling asks the students to work in pairs and become "experts" about one of the specific volcanoes mentioned in the book so they can retell for the class. He leads a discussion circling back to the author's choice of text structure and the class decides the duo of descriptive facts in smaller print plus the peppy narrative style make the book a hit. The class discusses the value of understanding text structure. "When you get the pattern of the book, it makes the book easier to understand," shares Jillian. Rebecca shares an insight, "And you can copy the pattern in your writing."

Steps to an Effective Think-Aloud Lesson

The think-aloud process includes teacher direction and explicit modeling using a text. Students view a purpose for each step of the lesson and exciting ways to engage students every step of the way with team- or partner-talk, gestures, or writing. The lesson may take place in one session or over multiple sessions. Steps may need repeating if students need more support before working independently.

Figure 3.3 Steps to an Effective Think Aloud

Scaffolded Step	Purpose	Ways to Engage Students
I Do (Teacher Modeling) • State the objective. *Today we will... Good readers...* • Ask what students know about the strategy. *What do you know about...* • Read and demonstrate. *Watch me while I ...on page _____.*	• To demonstrate for students *how* to employ a specific skill or strategy using a specific example from the text. • To share *why* the strategy or skill is important for future use.	• Invite students to use gestures such as thumbs up or down for nonexamples. • Share your examples from your own reading when appropriate. • Invite students to talk to partners about your example.
We Do (Guided Practice) • Pause throughout your lesson to invite partners/teams to try it with the same text. • Ask pairs or teams to try the strategy with a different text.	• To provide supported practice with the teacher commenting and assisting. • Students work in pairs or teams to practice. • Repeat guided practice as necessary.	• Students turn and talk to partners using your example, then other examples. • Students work in pairs or teams and record their examples in a notebook, graphic organizer, or on a sticky note.
You Do (Independent Practice) • Students respond on their own using notebooks, sticky notes, or an organizer.	• To independently practice the strategy or skill that was just modeled. • To give students specific targeted feedback.	• Students record responses in notebooks, sticky notes, or on graphic organizers.
Wrap Up • Discuss how the strategy helped the students read. *The strategy helped us _____ because _____. We will use it when _____.*	• To help students be metacognitive about the strategy. • To be ready to use the strategy in other situations as a "plan."	• Students turn to talk to partners or a team about how the strategy helped them.
Assessment Observe students in lessons and collect written responses to evaluate progress.	• To plan the next lesson based on how students do on practice.	• Students review your feedback and set goals. *Now I will...*

(Adapted from Oczkus 2009 and 2012)

Digging Deeper into Informational Texts

Informational text can be used for many instructional purposes and in many instructional settings. The rest of the chapter includes practical ways to incorporate your models for close reading, text sets, and ways to use informational text during guided as well as independent reading blocks in your classroom routines. Close reading offers students the strategies they need to work independently and together to tackle

© Shell Education

rigorous text. Text sets are a refreshing way to expose students to choices in their reading as well as experience with various text types, from books to primary sources and online articles. Students also learn how to synthesize information across texts when they read from multiple sources in a text set. When we meet with guided-reading groups to read informational text, we target student reading levels and specific needs. Teaching informational text structures, features, and comprehension

strategies is especially effective in small groups. By focusing on forming groups based on student reading level, interests, or needs we engage students with text. Students also need to be motivated to read informational texts during independent reading time.

First, let's look at powerful and practical ways to implement close reading to empower students with strategies for comprehending informational text.

Close Reading

What does it take for students to truly understand rigorous informational text laden with challenging content and vocabulary? Our students today desperately need to carry around an informational text tool kit to help them unlock comprehension in a wide variety of nonfiction texts. Close reading is one way for them to do this. The Common Core State Standards (2010) call for students to, "read closely to determine what the text says explicitly and to make logical inferences from it and cite specific textual evidence when writing or speaking to support conclusions drawn from the text." Instead of skipping reading or just skimming the surface of difficult texts, students need to develop the habits and strategies that good readers use to attack challenging texts on their own (Fisher and Frey 2012).

The Partnership for Assessment of Readiness for College and Careers (PARCC) says, "Close, analytic reading stresses engaging with a text of sufficient complexity directly and examining meaning thoroughly and methodically, encouraging students to read and reread deliberately. Directing student attention on the text itself empowers students to understand the central ideas and key supporting details. It also enables students to reflect on the meanings of individual words and sentences; the order in which sentences unfold and the development of ideas over the course of the text, which ultimately leads students to arrive at an understanding of the text as a whole" (2011, 7).

P. David Pearson (2013) suggests that there are many avenues to close reading. Close reading, when defined as an instructional routine, includes inviting students to critically examine a text especially though repeated readings for a variety of purposes (Fisher and Frey 2012). The key is to select text that is challenging and complex enough so students will need to reread it multiple times and with purpose. Literacy leader Pam Allyn (2012), recommends asking students to reread using various "lenses," looking for ideas such as:

- tone
- syntax
- word choice
- the gist
- author's purpose
- historical context
- evidence the author provides for his or her arguments
- how the text compares to other texts on the topic

In their book, *Falling in Love with Close Reading* (2013), Christopher Lehman and Kate Roberts expand the idea of close reading to include not just the messages found in written texts but the overt and sometimes subdued messages found in other areas of their lives. They invite students to consider themes in the texts they read and in other areas of their lives as well as to think deeply about messages in texts, the media, and even music or favorite books as they reread using lenses such as point of view or structure, patterns, and understandings including author's purpose. Close reading encompasses a rich variety of reasons for rereading and thinking about texts.

It is important that students learn good readers often need to reread informational texts when the text is confusing or challenging. Proficient readers underline, highlight, or use sticky notes to mark main ideas, questions, and points of confusion while reading. Students need to know that they might read closely for different purposes depending upon what they will do with the information. If they need to inform, persuade, or entertain an audience by writing a letter, making a presentation, writing a persuasive article, or teaching a younger student the information, close reading will come in handy.

Here are some questions educators ask about close reading:

- What exactly is close reading? Why should I do it?
- Is it really so different from what we've done before to teach reading?
- How do I conduct a close reading at a variety of grade levels?
- How do I select texts for close reading?

How Good Readers Use Close Reading Daily

In our adult reading, we read closely all the time. It is helpful to consider our own use of close reading as we examine practical ways to make it accessible to our students. Good readers exhibit certain habits when faced with difficult texts. They try not to give up easily. Instead they stick with it and persevere as they reread, highlight, underline, question, and even talk with others. Challenging informational texts force us to consider the author's point of view and the historical or social context and compare the text to other texts we've read.

Perhaps at some point in your college career you've purchased a used book with someone else's highlighted notes which provide the tracks or evidence of close reading. My own college-age children tell me they prefer purchasing used textbooks highlighted with notes to help them see the markings from another student's close reading experience. My high school daughter disagrees with her siblings and refuses to rely on a used text because she prefers drawing her own conclusions. Besides, she worries the former reader might be off base with his or her views!

Some examples of close reading in everyday life might include directions, professional reading, and informational reading on topics of interest to the reader. In each case some of the same close reading strategies apply with rereading portions of the text at the top of the list.

Figure 3.4 Examples of Close Reading in Everyday Life

Close Reading in the Real World	Why Close Reading Is Needed	Close Reading Strategies
Directions cookbooks, driving directions, technical manuals	Directions cause us to reread as we clarify challenging vocabulary, summarize the various steps, ask questions, and maybe even look up another set of directions for comparison. We ask who is the author and what is his or her viewpoint? Does this fit my needs?	• reread • highlight • underline • look up words • make annotations
Professional Reading articles, chapters in books, journals	We read professional articles for a variety of purposes including a graduate course, professional development presentations or sharing sessions, or lesson planning for our students.	• reread • highlight • underline • look up related texts
Informational Texts articles, magazines, newspapers, books	You might need to read a variety of sources on a medical condition or on a place you plan to visit. The daily news articles often require close reading to comprehend them. Or you might read to deeply learn something new.	• reread • sticky notes • look up words • highlight

What Close Reading Looks Like in the Classroom

You are already engaging students in some form of close reading when you reread texts to clarify and discuss confusing or interesting parts. Close reading begins with rereading a short, rigorous text that is worthy of being reread for different purposes. You may want to try a more formal model (Fisher and Frey 2012) where the teacher uses a document camera or other means of projecting a copy of the text during the lesson. Students also mark a copy of the text to show their thinking with a pencil, pen, highlighter, or colored pencil. To begin, students read the text silently to underline confusing words, sentences, or parts and write questions or comments in the margins. They may also use other symbols to leave tracks of their thinking. The teacher leads the charge as the class alternates between rereading the text for different purposes and discussing the reading with peers. The teacher also provides text-dependent questions to guide the discussions and to keep students focused on the text. Students may be encouraged to ask questions as well. A more informal close reading model may involve simply giving students sticky notes to use as they reread a page of text to mark, and then later discuss text evidence, questions, or clarifications.

The good news is that your classroom is already filled with many rich reading materials that you can grab to use for close reading lessons. Just choose a page or even paragraph from the news, magazines, content-area textbooks, leveled texts, big books, or read-alouds that go along with what you are already planning to teach. Choose a portion of text worthy of being reread numerous times for different purposes. You might also allow students to choose which portion of a text at which to pause and work through the close reading steps together.

Steps for Close Reading

1. Have students read the text silently on their own and mark confusing terms, questions, or connections.

2. Read the text aloud to students or ask a student to read the text aloud.

3. Have students reread the text in pairs and share ideas.

4. Have students reread the text to answer and discuss specific text-based questions.

Classroom Connection

Primary Close Reading During Guided Reading

Mr. Blore gathers the second-graders on the rug for a close reading lesson for page 10 of the text *Amazing Americans: Susan B. Anthony* by Stephanie Kuligowski (2013). Every student settles in with his or her close reading materials—a pencil, two sticky notes, and their copy of the text.

First, Mr. Blore asks the students to turn to a partner and quickly page through the book up to page 10 to review what they've learned so far about Susan B. Anthony. He encourages them to use text evidence by using the word *because* as they share their facts with examples from the text.

Next, Mr. Blore turns to page 10, displaying it on the document camera. "Read it silently first to yourself and mark with your sticky notes one word or sentence you think is tricky." The students whisper in first-grade "silent" reading mode.

When all appear to have finished the first pass, Mr. Blore compliments the group on finding tricky words. He then reads the entire text aloud to the students. Mr. Blore admits he thought the sentence "Her parents did not agree" was confusing. "I read it again looking for a *because* and found the part where it says her teacher did not think girls should learn the same things as boys. That is what her parents did not agree with. They *did* think girls could learn. I also looked at the heading for this page which was a few pages back. It was called 'Family Beliefs.' Her family believed girls could learn the same as boys because they taught her."

Then, he invites students to turn to their partners to share their tricky words on sticky notes. "I thought the word *taught* was tricky," says Ben. "This word is hard," shares Simon as he points to the word *agree*.

After the partners share, Mr. Blore directs the students to read the page again, only this time to answer the question, "What can you learn about Susan B. Anthony's parents from this page?" He asks students to reread and discuss with a partner using the verbal frame he writes on the board: " I learned that Susan B. Anthony's parents believed _____ because _____."

Classroom Connection

Intermediate Close Reading with a Primary Source

Fifth-graders participate in a close read of a primary source document, *Moral Precepts for Children*, from the colonies in 1805. Since the class is already engaged in studying what life was like in the colonies, Miss Janke only briefly sets the context for the reading by sharing, "This document is from 1805 and was actually used in the colonies. This appeared in their primer, or textbook."

Then, she passes out copies of the text for the students and projects a copy on the document camera. Students read silently first with pencils as they underline confusing words and ideas. Miss Janke circulates to prompt students who need more guidance. Several students haven't underlined anything yet, so she prompts students to find a challenging part to mark.

When Miss Janke calls "time," students focus on the text again from the beginning as she reads the entire text aloud.

After her reading, she circles back and shares a confusing word, *scorn*. "I didn't know what the author meant by 'scorn not the poor' so I underlined *scorn*. Now, I am reading on and I think that the author meant that when someone is in need, just help them because the next line says 'give them that want.' I think it means to not make fun of the poor."

She invites the partners to reread the text to share their underlined words with each other.

Miss Janke gives each table team a different text-based question to answer and then share with the class. Students reread again before answering their questions. The questions include the following:

- What do you think the author meant by "Live well that ye may die well?"
- What examples does the author include?
- What do the words "ill words breed strife" mean?
- What do you think the author meant by "learn to love your book?"
- Is this good advice or not? Why?
- What can you learn about education in Colonial America from this excerpt?

At the end of the lesson, students create a two-sentence summary and poster with drawings summarizing what they learned with their teams.

How Often to Teach Close Reading

In some form or another, you are teaching students to read closely as you guide them through challenging texts, clarifying confusions, discussing questions and answers, and rereading for different purposes. You might also try instituting five to ten minutes every day or a couple times per week that you call "close reading time" and follow the steps in Figure 3.5 with a page or paragraph from a text your class is reading. In an already busting-at-the-seams schedule, try weaving close reading moments into your lessons. During social studies, you might pause and share, "Class, these two paragraphs are worthy of a reread and a close read" and take a few minutes to follow the steps prescribed. During a read-aloud, pause and declare, "Oh this is a tricky page. Time for our close reading steps!" Once your class knows what it means to participate in a "close read," you can cue them in the middle of any text to stop and discuss using the steps.

Finding Good Text for Close Reading

Your classroom is filled with rich reading materials that can be used for close reading. Consider choosing a page or small section from a news article or magazine, content-area textbook, nonfiction children's book, big book, primary source, or Internet resource. The key is to find a text or portion of a text that is truly worthy of being reread numerous times for different purposes. You might also allow students to choose which portion of a text at which to pause and work through the close reading steps together.

Close Reading Helps Teachers Avoid Reading Lesson Pitfalls

Close reading helps teachers avoid some common problems that often occur during reading lessons. Many students easily become distracted by too many of their own connections and head off-topic. Close reading lessons provide opportunities for modeling and teaching students the discipline, concentration, and strategies for staying close to the topic at hand. The objective is to really focus on the author's message and purpose first before responding personally.

Another common lesson problem is the issue surrounding spoon-feeding, or providing too much teacher support. If we read everything aloud to students, we don't afford them the opportunity to develop the discipline and reading "chops" to dive into challenging texts independently. Close reading encourages students to take responsibility or to be accountable for attempting to read certain texts independently rather than depending on the teacher to read it aloud.

A Balance of Reading Experiences

It is important to balance reading experiences in the classroom. Close reading is just one of the techniques we use to help students become strong readers. Certainly, we will continue to provide rich background-building discussions and teacher read alouds throughout the day as our emerging and struggling readers and English learners benefit and need scaffolding. Close reading is helpful and useful in certain situations and helps students understand the text and the author's purpose (O'Connor and Snow 2013). However, close reading should not be used at the expense of other important comprehension building activities (O'Connor and Snow 2013). If we make close reading of challenging texts a tedious "drag," then kids won't be willing to draw on close reading skills when they read on their own (O'Connor and Snow 2013), and may be turned off to reading altogether. Close reading is an important tool that works well with our read-alouds, shared reading, guided reading and other classroom structures and techniques to promote independence and success for all of our students.

Figure 3.5 A Sample Close Reading Lesson Plan Format

Step	Details
1. Choose a text Choose a short, rigorous text.	• Select a short text that demands rereading from grade level content-area texts, primary sources, or articles. Text may contain challenging vocabulary, syntax, and complex content. • Display the text for students to see. • Provide copies of the text for students.
2. Students read silently Invite students to read the text silently first.	• Have students read with a pencil (or other writing utensil, highlighter, etc., or sticky notes) to mark difficult words, sentences, or ideas as they read. **Optional** • If absolutely necessary to help students with the background for the text, you may provide a one or two sentence brief lead-in to the silent reading.
3. Teacher reads aloud	• Read the text aloud once through. Have students follow along as you read aloud. • Read again to pause to think aloud to share words or ideas that you found confusing.
4. Students reread and discuss with peers	• Have students reread the text with partners or a small group. • Allow students to share words and ideas they found confusing with peers.
5. Teacher asks text-dependent questions.	• Pose text-dependent questions that require critical thinking and evidence from the text. • Instruct students to work cooperatively to reread the text again to find evidence to answer the questions. **Sample Text-Dependent Questions:** • What did the author mean by _____? • What examples does the author include? • What can you learn about _____ from this text? • Show evidence in the text that shows _____. **Optional** • Assign each pair or team of students a different text-dependent question to answer. Then have students share back with the whole class and show evidence from the text. • Allow students to ask their own text-dependent questions.

(adapted from Fisher and Frey 2012)

Text Sets

One of the best ways to understand the definition of a text set, or a collection of varied materials students use to explore content, is to visualize examples in the classroom. Picture students productively at work around the classroom using a variety of books, magazines, online sources, artifacts, or primary sources, with the common goal of studying a unifying concept, theme, or question. Mary-Ann Cappiello and Erika Thulin-Dawes (2012) from Lesley University have created many rich ideas for inspiring students with informational texts. For example, in third grade, students might participate in a unit

© Shell Education

on "Coming to America" by analyzing different reasons why people journeyed to the country. Texts could include trade books for the students to read in small groups, such as *Grandfather's Journey* by Allen Say (1993), *Molly's Pilgrim* by Barbara Cohen (1983), *The Dragon's Child* by Laurence Yep (2008), and Eve Bunting's classic *How Many Days to America* (1988). Students could also listen to a National Public Radio (NPR) series on immigration and read articles online. The text set model includes opportunities for students to listen to read-alouds, work in teams, read in small groups, fill in organizers to compare what they learn across texts, study online articles, view films and videos, and participate in writing or creating letters, journals, picture books, posters, presentations, and models. Cappiello and Thulin-Dawes (2012) call this type of unit a "multimodal, multigenre text set."

The concept of a text set is not brand new. Just like fashion, in education when something comes "back in style" it looks a little different than it did last time. The reentry of the text set on the scene could not be more timely or appropriate. With the content and rigor demands of the Common Core and the availability of technology, text sets now include a wider array of materials than the earlier models. In today's classroom, multimodal, multigenre text sets can be easier than ever to put together, with the world at our fingertips in just one Internet search. It doesn't take long to find a variety of texts, primary sources, films, clips, music, and articles to back any topic we want to research with our students (Cappiello and Thulin-Dawes 2012).

Classroom Connection

A Text Set in Action

Fifth-graders listen to Mr. Wright as he introduces the text set by reading aloud the Algonquin Indian version of Cinderella, *The Rough Faced Girl* by Rafe Martin (1992) to the class. Every time the students hear something that reminds them of Cinderella, they give a thumbs up. After reading, table teams fill in the Venn diagram with Cinderella on one circle and The Rough Faced Girl on the other, as they compare and contrast the two stories.

Then, Mr. Wright shares the central text set question, "How did conflict between white settlers and American Indian tribes in the 1800s change the lives of American Indians?" The students briefly discuss the central question and Mr. Wright gives an overview of the texts the students will read over the next few weeks including a close reading of a book filled with primary sources that discusses some famous American Indians and their experiences; a primary source from Sitting Bull; and a reader's theatre of "The Battle of Bear Paw Mountain." The students predict using the cause and effect graphic organizer. "I think we will learn what really happened to some of the American Indian tribes," shares Nadia. Fifth-graders, always ready to stand up for justice and fairness, can't wait to dig into the unit!

Here is a starter list of possible topics for text sets. Keep in mind any topic in your curriculum can become a text set.

Social Studies Ideas

- American Revolution
- Westward expansion
- Civil War
- Civil rights era
- Immigration
- African American history
- Latino heritage and history

Science Ideas

- Animals
- Endangered animals
- Weather
- Geology
- Marine life
- Dinosaurs
- Ecosystems
- Health topics

Reasons for Teaching with Text Sets

There are many reasons to use text sets as part of your high-quality literacy instruction. The list below highlights some of the most compelling reasons (Cappiello and Thulin Dawes 2012).

- **Common Core calls for challenging texts:** The Common Core calls for reading an array of "challenging informational texts in a range of subjects, students are expected to build knowledge, gain insights, explore possibilities, and broaden their perspective." (2010)

- **Captures the interest and engagement of students:** Students are involved with choices to explore on a range of topics with a variety of materials.

- **Prompts inquiry:** Students generate questions to guide their learning.

- **Reads for multiple perspectives:** Students analyze sources and compare and contrast information gained.

- **Builds prior knowledge:** Short texts provide background for longer, more complex ones. Students build knowledge through a variety of rich texts and sources including videos, maps, photos, and music.

- **Encourages writing:** Students can use any of the texts or sources in the text set as a model for writing (mentor text) and other projects.

- **Differentiates instruction:** Text sets with a variety of materials allows for flexible small group instruction for English language learners and struggling readers.

- **Supports vocabulary development:** The language-rich environment of a text set steeps students in vocabulary.

Some easy suggestions for starting a text set in your classroom include the following steps.

   © Shell Education

Steps for Creating Text Sets

1. **Identify the topic and content-area standards you want to address.** Choose a topic. Make a list of standards and skills you want (need) to teach. What do you want students to do, write, perform, draw, etc.?

2. **Search and gather materials for the topic.** Try to include a wide variety of reading levels and genres such as books, magazines, photos, artifacts, video clips, music, and primary sources. Make sure some materials are more complex for close reading and teacher-led lessons, while other materials may be used for student-led groups or independent reading. See Figure 3.6 for suggestions.

Figure 3.6 Material Suggestions for Text Sets

Materials	Sources for Materials
Books	• Internet searches • librarians • Internet searches for children's' book award lists such as Horn Book, Newbery, Notable Social Studies Trade Books, Outstanding Science Trade Books • Scholastic Book Wizard: http://www.scholastic.com/bookwizard/ • publishers' programs such as Teaching through Text Sets by Teacher Created Materials
Magazines	• Time for Kids: http://www.timeforkids.com • National Wild Life Federation (Ranger Rick, My Big Backyard): http://www.nwf.org/Kids.aspx • Kids Discover: http://www.kidsdiscover.com
Photos, Artifacts, Objects, Primary Sources	• search institutions, museums, libraries, zoos for video clips, photos and other unique sources for students to "read" and study

3. **Brainstorm questions with the students.** Present a central topic, question, or theme such as *How did the American colonies change during the two centuries following their founding?; Who came to America? When and why?* You can have students work in pairs or teams to generate their topic questions on sticky notes and then post the questions on a chart. Then, group the questions and label categories of like questions. It is important to allow students to add questions as they learn more and return to the topic or theme question throughout the unit of study.

4. **Have students read the materials in a variety of ways.** Depending upon reading level and the number of copies you have for each title, choose which materials are best suited for read alouds, whole-class lessons, small-group guided reading, and book clubs. When you have at least four copies of a book or article, students can work in groups in a book club. Students may read the text by taking on the reciprocal teaching roles of predictor, questioner, clarifier, and summarizer. The groups can then keep track of main ideas and details in their texts. You may also want to run some of the groups as teacher-led guided reading groups.

5. **All students respond to the reading.** Students should complete graphic organizers to track main ideas, details, and/or other important aspects of the reading. They may use sticky notes or write in a journal.

6. **Have students create projects related to the reading.** After reading a variety of sources in different settings, students can work in teams and/or alone to respond to the reading. Some possible projects include: book reviews, maps, brochures, picture books for younger students, presentations, art projects, debates, dramatizations, blogs, posters, and letters.

Small-Group Guided Reading

Whether, you are reading about the inside of a hornets nest with second-graders, the real story of Roanoke with fifth-graders, or cell division with middle-school students, small-group lessons with informational text are filled with wide-eyed wonder and amazement. Students naturally connect to informational text topics. In a small-group setting, students have more opportunities to engage, discuss, and question. When you combine small-group instruction with informational texts, the result is improved comprehension. All of our students, from our strongest readers to the students who struggle, benefit from small-group instruction (Allington 2011). Research tells us that struggling readers especially need frequent quality instruction in small teacher-led groups (Allington 2008). The more personalized environment allows for the teacher to target instruction to differentiate and meet students' needs. Informed by research, today's small group instruction is based on frequent assessments both formal and informal. I recall as a child the red, blue, and green reading groups that labeled us throughout our school careers. Always in the blue group, I envied the red group who read more challenging texts and chapter books. In our more fluid classrooms today, students move in and out of groups based on need, strategies, and interests. The small-group setting affords us the opportunity to teach a myriad of important skills and strategies for reading informational texts. All of the lessons

Helpful Online Resources

- **Teaching with Text Sets Website and Blog:** This is a great website with resources for your text sets from the authors of *Teaching with Text Sets.*
  http://teachingwithtextsets. blogspot.com/p/about-us.html

- **Booksource:** Includes book lists and ability to create custom bibliographies for trade books for units.
  http://www.booksource.com

- **Lit2Go:** This is an online collection of classic texts, including PDF and audio versions.
  http://etc.usf.edu/lit2go/

- **ReadWorks:** This online resource contains free passages with associated lessons, novel units, and reading skill units.
  http://www.readworks.org/

- **Columbia Reading and Writing Project:** The Columbia Reading and Writing Project supports text sets and suggests titles.
  http://readingandwritingproject. com

in this book (see Chapters 4 and 5) can be taught in a small-group setting. The small-group format is also ideal for intervention instruction with English language learners or struggling readers. Both of these groups of students gravitate to informational texts, especially many of the boys (Smith and Wilhelm 2002).

Classroom Connection

Primary Small-Group Example

The little band of readers hunch over their text *Animal Eyes* by Dona Herweck Rice (2012), anxious to open the book. Mr. Tatasio explains, "Good readers pay attention to the photos in an informational text. The photos help you understand the information." He invites the students to page through the text to study the photos. The students agree the book is about different kinds of animal eyes. Then he asks the students to turn to page 3 and read the page silently first. "I am going to show you what I am thinking about some of the photos," shares Mr. Tatasio. "On page three, I see a frog looking right at me! I think the author included this photo because it goes with the word 'watching'." Mr. Tatasio encourages the students to continue reading the text silently and to pay attention to how the photos help in understanding the text. Mr. Tatasio circulates around the outside of the table inviting each student to whisper-read to him. He asks each reader to explain why the author included the photo or why the photo was helpful. After the students finish reading, Mr. Tatasio continues by sharing in a think aloud from one of the two frames he writes on a chart:

I think the author included this photo because _____.

The photo was helpful (or not helpful) because _____.

He explains, "On page six the pictures were helpful because they show the frog peeking and the dog blinking. The author wanted to show us both actions." He invites the students to turn to page eight and share with a partner why they think the author included the photo. The group brainstorms words to describe what eyes do: view, see, cry, open, look, stare, peek, blink. Then, the students take out their dry-erase boards and Mr. Tatasio dictates words with the "ink" chunk as students say the words stretching the sounds to write each one: link, wink, sink, and mink. When the students leave the group, their "ticket out" is to tell which photo was the most helpful today and why.

Intermediate Small-Group Example

"Today, we are on page 22 of the book, *Animal Architects*, by Timothy Bradley," begins Mrs. Chan. The fourth-graders review briefly the pages they read yesterday in the text. Mrs. Chan asks the students to turn to a partner to share what they already know about beavers. "They look like they need braces," shares Sam. The students giggle as Mrs. Chan directs the students back to the text. "Glance at pages 22 to 25 to figure out what the author's purpose is today and how this information fits into the chapter." The students share with partners. Juan comments, "I see the steps to making a beaver lodge so that is one thing the author wants us to know." The students read pages 22 and 23 silently. Then, Mrs. Chan tells the students that good readers study the various text features found in informational texts. She invites the students to read along as she models how to read the first three steps in the sidebar for making a beaver lodge. She thinks aloud as she studies each illustration and reads the corresponding step. The students work in pairs and finish reading the steps. Then, she asks the students several questions about the order of the steps. Finally, the students turn to partners and share how rereading the text feature in an informational text helped them learn about beavers. "I remember the steps because I went slowly on that part," shares Destiny. The students reread the chapter, "Homes on Land," and then sketch drawings of the animals that live on land. Each student will then conduct research on approved websites to learn more about animals that build homes on land.

Selecting Texts

To select appropriate guided reading materials for your students, there are many factors to consider. Any informational text can be effective when used in small-group instruction. Types of texts can include leveled texts, magazines, articles from the newspaper or Internet, content-area textbooks, primary sources, and more. It is important to make sure that the selected text is an appropriate reading level for the group and that the topic is of high interest to the students. By getting to know what interests your students, you will be better able to select texts you know they will like. Typical high-interest topics include sports, extreme weather, animals, insects, gross things, scientific phenomena, pop culture, and technology. If your text topic can tie into the district science and social studies curriculum, that is even better.

Grouping Students

There are many effective ways to group students for guided reading including grouping by readiness level, reading strategies needed, or interest. Many educators teach in classrooms where the students are carefully placed in groups based on their needs determined by regular assessments including running records, retellings, and other comprehension checks. Students may move between groups if needed. The following are some grouping tips.

- Try providing several different books on the same or varied topics so students can sign up to read the text they are interested in. The students who select the same books become your reading groups.

- If you are providing opportunities for students to use to research and participate in project-based learning, have students sign up for the project they are interested in. The project groups become your guided-reading groups with each one reading texts to go with their project topic such as hurricanes or dolphins.

- Consider grouping students by reading strategies that they need support in developing, such as those students who need help inferring or finding evidence. When reading with students, keep a log to quickly note which strategies students need such as making logical predictions, using context to decode new words, or summarizing. Group students according to the strategies they need to work on.

- You can also group by reading level that may be determined by a formal measure such as Lexile® level (2014), Developmental Reading Association® (DRA) level (2003), or by your own observations and running records.

Planning for Instruction

Figure 3.7 shows some of the strategies, features, and structures unique and important to informational text that you may choose to teach during a small-group lesson. Choose one or two objectives to teach over the lesson.

Figure 3.7 Informational Text Topics for Small-Group Instruction

Text Structures	Text Features	Comprehension Strategies
• description	• table of contents	• setting a purpose for reading/predicting
• problem/solution	• headings	• determining author's purpose
• time-order sequence	• photos	• asking and answering questions
• compare/contrast	• maps	• monitoring for meaning
• cause/effect	• diagrams	• connecting to other ideas/texts
	• charts	• clarifying confusing words, parts, decoding
	• text organizers	• using mental images
	• graphs	• inferring
	• glossary	• summarizing
	• index	• synthesizing

This lesson structure can be used when planning for guided reading using informational text.

Figure 3.8 Informational Text Guided Reading Plan

Before Reading

Activate Prior Knowledge/Make Connections/Predict
Have students relate prior knowledge to the text through read alouds, discussions, or by paging through the text. Chart student responses, if desired. As appropriate, lead students on a "text walk" to introduce text structure, vocabulary, and make predictions.

Target Strategy/Skill
Choose a target strategy that is important for understanding informational text. Each target strategy lesson is designed as an engaging think aloud that is scaffolded so that after the teacher models and supports practice the students will learn to use the strategy on their own. See Figure 3.5 for a list of potential strategies and skills.

During Reading

        Reading Options
        ___ Individually
        ___ Silently
        ___ Paired
        ___ Aloud
        ___ Both

Have students read the text silently while you coach individuals. Or have students read in partners. You could also lead the group in a shared reading for a portion of the text followed by independent reading.

Target Skill/Strategy
Use the target skill or strategy instruction again, but the demonstration and scaffolding takes place further in the book during the reading process.

Assessment
Observe each student or just one or two reading and using the target strategy or any other strategy the student may need to work on. Record observations.

After Reading

Summarize/Respond
Have students share main points, important details, and favorite or interesting parts from the reading. Ask students critical thinking and text-dependent questions. Select vocabulary to discuss and act out.

Sample text-dependent questions:
What did the author mean by _____? What examples does the author include?
What can you learn about _____ from this text?
What evidence in the text shows _____.

Word Work
Conduct "word work" activities such as word sorting or writing on slates to target decoding and practice phonics patterns.

Target Skill/Strategy *(optional)*
Include one more teaching point or practice opportunity for the target strategy.

Reflect on Strategy Use
Have students think about how the target strategy helped them read.

Across Book Connections
Give students time to compare and contrast across texts.

Independent Reading Time

Whether you call it, Silent Sustained Reading (SSR); Wonderfully Entertaining Books (WEB); or Our Time to Enjoy Reading (OTTER), the independent reading block in your classroom is a key component to building students' literacy. Research suggests that the time students spend in independent reading is one of the best predictors of reading achievement (Anderson, Wilson, and Fielding 1988). The bottom line is that the students who read the most, read the best and score better on tests (Anderson, Wilson, and Fielding 1988). By providing time for students to practice reading in a book they have chosen, they grow in their vocabulary, fluency, comprehension, word-attack skills, and stamina. Most of all, they develop a lifelong love and appreciation of reading.

Independent reading is more important than ever with the Common Core requirement that students "will read and comprehend complex literary and informational texts independently and proficiently" (National Governors Association 2010, 10). Students are encouraged to read from a wide range of materials to deepen their knowledge base. This means our classroom libraries need to be stocked with lots of rich informational texts. Students need to read on a wide variety of topics such as people, places, history, and biographies from an interesting variety of informational text such as magazines, websites, and trade books. Try giving quick book commercials at the beginning of independent reading to spark interest in informational texts. Here are my "10 Best Ever Tips" for the classroom library and independent reading time (Oczkus 2012).

1. Set a consistent time every day for independent reading.

2. Set up a reading environment and classroom library.

3. Have students keep track of books read in a reading log.

4. Have students fill out interest inventories.

5. Establish procedures.

6. Teach students how to select books.

7. Make time for students to share books.

8. Give book talks and feature books.

9. Conference with students.

10. Teach mini-lessons on procedures and provide quick reading strategy lessons.

Model a Reading Log

When teachers share what they read, students are motivated and inspired to develop the habits of lifelong readers (Routman 2003; Miller 2009). I often cart piles of my own informational text reading titles into classrooms to show students. They love seeing my stacks of magazines, cookbooks, pet how-to volumes, and news magazines. The students really perk up when I show my collection of National Geographic magazines. The introduction of the Common Core Standards has made it increasingly important to read more informational text through all grades. Therefore, modeling the value and purposes for reading nonfiction must find its way into instruction.

If you want students to learn how to keep a reading log, then try keeping one of your own. Show students what you are reading and fill in the chart to share details. The sample reading log in Figure 3.9 invites discussion around the author's purpose for writing the text, and the reader even gets to be a mini-judge giving a score. The same book log format can be used with students.

Figure 3.9 Mrs. O's Informational Text Reading Log

Title and Author	Text Type	Author's Purpose Why did the author write this? *to inform* *to persuade* *to entertain*	My Purpose to learn about ___ to do something I am interested in	Score 1 Best 2 Good 3 Okay 4 Not great 5 Poor Tell why.
Lean In: Women, Work, and the Will to Lead by Sheryl Sandberg	__ magazine __ article __ online article __ book __ other	The author wrote this book to *inform* us about the stalled status of women in the workforce. She wants to *persuade* people to change it.	I read this because I am interested in equality for women in the workforce.	I rate it a 1 because it has so many wonderful stories and is easy to read. I really like the website and *Lean In's* online community with everyday women's stories.
Wild: From Lost to Found on the Pacific Trail by Cheryl Strayed	__ magazine __ article __ online article __ book __ other	The author shared this true story to entertain us.	I love going to Lake Tahoe and hike parts of this trail.	I rate it a 2 because it takes a while to get hooked.

Using Interest Inventories

Often students stall during reader's workshop or independent reading time. They run out of books to read or they can't decide what to read next. If you think about it, this may happen to you, too, sometimes! One helpful tool that keeps students reading is an interest inventory. Students fill one out several times per year as their interests change and they keep the inventory near their reading log in a folder or glued into a notebook. If you are conferencing with a student and he or she says, "I don't know what to read next," you can easily refer to the student's interest inventory to steer the student to new and varied informational text topics. This inventory can be found in Appendix B.

Figure 3.10 Interest Inventory for Informational Topics

Name: _____ Date: _____

My Interest Inventory

1. What topics do you know about? _____.

2. What do you enjoy doing? _____.

3. What are you good at? _____.

4. What do you want to learn about? _____.

Finish these sentences.

5. After school, I like to _____.

6. My hobbies are _____.

7. My favorite movie is _____.

8. My favorite television shows are _____.

9. I have a pet _____. I wish I had a pet _____.

10. I'd like to travel to _____.

Check all the topics you are interested in.

__ zoo animals	__ rainforest	__ heros	__ how-to books
__ farm animals	__ how things are made	__ travel	__ current news
__ ocean creatures	__ natural disasters	__ scientists	__ sports
__ dogs	__ volcanoes	__ inventions	__ football
__ cats	__ hurricanes	__ astronauts	__ baseball
__ horses	__ earthquakes	__ pilots	__ soccer
__ pigs	__ tornadoes	__ world records	__ basketball
__ snakes	__ rocks	__ firemen	__ wrestling
__ birds	__ weather	__ police men/women	__ other sport ____
__ frogs	__ health	__ immigration	
__ insects	__ solar system	__ wars	
__ butterflies	__ history	__ maps	
__ other _____	__ cars		

(Adapted from Harvey 1998; Moss and Terrell 2010)

© Shell Education

Figure 3.11 Informational Text Reading Log

Name: _____ Date: _____

Informational Text Reading Log

Title/Author	Text Type	Author's Purpose Why did the author write this? • to inform • to persuade • to entertain	My Purpose To learn about _____ to do something I am interested in	Score 1: Best 2: Good 3: Okay 4: Not great 5: Poor Tell why.
	__ magazine __ article __ online article __ book __ other			I gave it a ___ because...
	__ magazine __ article __ online article __ book __ other			I gave it a ___ because...
	__ magazine __ article __ online article __ book __ other			I gave it a ___ because...
	__ magazine __ article __ online article __ book __ other			I gave it a ___ because...
	__ magazine __ article __ online article __ book __ other			I gave it a ___ because...

 © Shell Education

Wrap-Up and Reflection

In order to arm our students with strategies for reading informational text, we need to inspire them to read such texts all day long! The routines and strategies shared in this chapter give you many options for bringing informational text alive in your classroom. By engaging students in reciprocal teaching routines, we arm them with the Fab Four power pack of strategies: predict, question, clarify, and summarize to help build comprehension of complex texts. When we involve students in think alouds with cooperative learning, physical movement such as gestures, and quick writes, students gain a deeper understanding of the reading. Close reading routines provide our students with many ways to reread challenging texts to uncover meaning. Hopefully, students will continue to hone and put to use the close reading model the rest of their lives. Support from the teacher makes guided reading in small groups the perfect setting for teaching informational text structures, features, and comprehension strategies like summarizing and inferring. Text sets make learning fun by offering students choice, variety in texts and the opportunity to work in small groups with others. By simply encouraging that students read more informational text of their choice during independent reading, their fluency, vocabulary, and comprehension grows.

Here are some key ideas to think about from this chapter:

- Reciprocal teaching (Palincsar and Brown 1986) is a powerful method that yields results in as little as 15 days with bolstered confidence and in just a few months, gains of one to two years (Cooper et al 2000; Rosenshine and Meister 1994; Hattie 2008). Reciprocal teaching strategies, or the Fab Four (Oczkus 2010) predict, question, clarify, and summarize work together to help students improve comprehension.

- The gradual release of responsibility model (Pearson and Gallagher 1983) is a proven research-based process (Fisher and Frey 2007) that starts with teacher modeling and think aloud, followed by guided practice with the teacher and peers, and ending with independent practice coupled with teacher feedback. Used in think alouds and coupled with interactive strategies such as gestures and writing comprehension, lessons become more engaging (Oczkus 2009).

- In close reading, students learn that instead of skipping reading or just skimming the surface of difficult texts, they develop the habits and strategies that good readers use to attack challenging texts on their own (Fisher and Frey 2012).

- Text sets are a creative way of offering students multiple texts on the same topic and may include books, magazines, online sources, artifacts, and primary sources, with the common goal of studying a unifying concept, theme, or question.

- Meeting with small guided-reading groups is an effective way to target student needs and interests using informational texts.

- Research suggests that the time students spend in independent reading is one of the best predictors of reading achievement (Anderson, Wilson, and Fielding 1988).

Reflect and Discuss

1. What are some ways you can increase the amount of informational text students are reading in your classroom?

2. Why is reciprocal teaching a powerful strategy to use with informational texts?

3. What is close reading and why is it so critical in helping students read informational texts? How can it be implemented in the classroom and across the curriculum?

4. How can text sets be used to teach content and reading strategies with informational text?

5. What are some ways that you can group for and use informational texts during guided reading lessons?

© Shell Education

Chapter 4

Promoting Comprehension with Engaging Text Feature Lessons

This chapter contains lessons to help you teach students about text features, the unique "glue" that holds informational texts together. Text features are one of the aspects that distinguish informational text from fiction and are designed to support the reader. Yet, if students do not understand how text features may help them, they miss valuable information that the author intended for the reader to enjoy and understand. Informational text looks distinctly different from fiction or narrative text because of its often features including the table of contents, headings, visuals (maps, diagrams, photos, charts), the glossary, and the index. Not all informational texts include each of these text features. It is up to the reader to utilize the text features to benefit his or her reading experience.

These lessons provide many creative and engaging ways to support students with instructional practices such as modeling, cooperative guided practice, and independent practice. Special considerations for English language learners and struggling readers are provided. The lessons are designed to be used over and over again to teach as needed all year long using a variety of informational texts.

Text Feature Lessons Chart

Page	Table of Contents Lessons
95	Guess My Prediction: Using the Table of Contents to Predict
98	Table of Contents Wonderings: Using the Table of Contents to Question
101	Symbol Summaries: Using the Table of Contents to Summarize
	Headings Lessons
104	Pause to Predict: Using Headings to Predict
107	Presto-Change-o: Using Headings to Question
110	All Aboard the Heading Train! Using Headings to Clarify Text
112	What's My Heading? Using Headings to Summarize
	Other Text Features Lessons: **Photos, Maps, Diagrams, Charts, Graphs**
115	Say Cheese: Using Photos to Understand the Text
118	Photo Awards! Evaluating Photos

Guess My Prediction: Using the Table of Contents to Predict

Objective/Standards

Use the table of contents to make logical predictions about the text; read closely to determine what the text says explicitly and to make logical inferences from it (CCSS); cite specific textual evidence when writing or speaking to support conclusions drawn from the text (CCSS); know and use various text features to locate key facts or information in a text efficiently (CCSS)

Materials

- table of contents from a book

- *Predicting with the Table of Contents* (See Appendix B)

- sticky notes

Tip

The nickname, or acronym, for Table of Contents in the publishing world is the "TOC." The table of contents is a rich source of information that your students can dive into prior to reading to help them set purposes for reading and to predict what they will learn from the text. Try giving students the same text and even different texts to study the TOC's.

Set Purpose/Preview the Text

1. Invite students to study the cover, skim the table of contents, and quickly flip through the text to get a feel for the content. Ask what they know about the topic and provide a few minutes for partners to discuss.

2. Turn to the table of contents together and ask students to tell their partners what they know about the purpose of a table of contents. Tell students, "A table of contents is called a TOC for short. Good readers use it in a variety of ways like a roadmap to guide their reading. We use the TOC to see how the author has organized the book, predict what it will be about, and to set our purpose for reading."

Teacher Model

3. Ask students to turn to the table of contents and read it over silently while paying attention to the topics and how the author organized the content. Tell students, "Start to think about what the author wants to teach us in each chapter as you study the TOC."

4. Read the chapter titles chorally with the students. Demonstrate predicting with the table of contents. Say, "As I look over each of these chapter titles, I see there are chapters called (read the titles of all or a few of the chapters). I think I will learn_____ in chapter_____ because _____." (I saw information in the preview above or the title helps me predict the possible content.)

5. Read aloud the chapter titles again. Discuss as a group whether the chapters should or even could be read in order or out of order.

6. Select a chapter to model a prediction. "I think I will learn____ from chapter ____." Have students show a thumbs up if they agree. Provide one or two examples of information you think you will NOT find in a chapter using the frame, "I don't think this chapter on ____ will tell me about____ because____." Check student understanding with a thumbs up or down.

7. *Option:* Use the *Predicting with the Table of Contents* organizer (Figure 4.1) to model how to select a chapter from the table of contents and then fill in the information including what you think you will learn and a sketch. After reading, return to the sheet to check off whether your prediction was met by reading the text or not.

Guided Practice

8. Play a quick guessing game with the table of contents. To begin, share some of your predictions and ask students to point to the chapter title that goes with it. For example, "I think I will learn about how to ____. Which chapter might give me that information?" Have students point to the chapter and discuss with a partner why they think that chapter fits the prediction. Share one or two more examples of predictions and invite students to indicate which chapter might fit the prediction.

9. Ask students to each think of a prediction using the frame, "Guess which chapter might teach us about ____ (what, how, why, when, where… examples of… causes of… etc.)." Have students work in pairs to point to the chapter or chapters they think goes with their partner's prediction. *Option:* write the predictions on sticky notes. Post them on a chart to check after reading. Or post them directly on the table of contents.

10. *Option:* Students work in pairs to fill in the *Predicting with the Table of Contents* organizer with partners or teams. After reading, students return to their predictions to check whether they were met or not by reading the text.

Independent Practice

11. Ask students to make one prediction per chapter on a sticky note and put it on the table of contents page of the book. After reading each chapter, have the students return to the table of contents to put a check mark on their sticky note for that chapter. Assist students who are having difficulties making logical predictions and provide additional models when necessary.

12. Students fill in the *Predicting with the Table of Contents* organizer independently, or with a partner at their desks, or in a workstation. After reading, students return to their predictions to discuss whether they were met or not by reading the text.

Assessment

Circulate and note student predictions for the chapters. Guide students in making logical predictions based on text clues. Direct students to share with a partner after reading whether each of their predictions were met or changed as they read. Were students surprised by the content included or not included in a given chapter? Do they agree with how the author presented the material in each chapter? Which chapters were strongest, weakest? Why?

Figure 4.1 Predicting with the Table of Contents

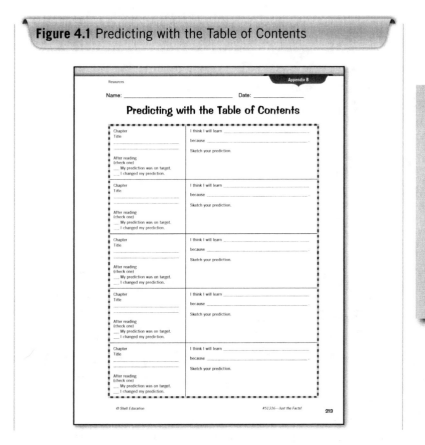

Struggling Readers Support

Encourage students to use the language, "In the chapter titled _____ I think I will learn _____ because _____." Turn to the pages in a given chapter to assist students in using headings and illustrations to create logical predictions that go with the TOC.

Table of Contents Wonderings: Using the Table of Contents to Question

Students enjoy "wondering" about informational text topics. The trick is to keep their wonders close to the text rather than off topic. One way to do that is to focus their attention on the organization of the text topics and the table of contents.

Objective/Standards

Use the table of contents to help students formulate and answer text-based questions before and during reading; read closely to determine what the text says explicitly and to make logical inferences from it (CCSS); cite specific textual evidence when writing or speaking to support conclusions drawn from the text (CCSS); ask and answer questions about key details in a text (CCSS)

Materials

- book with table of contents
- *Table of Contents Wonderings* (See Appendix B)
- sticky notes
- chart paper

Set Purpose/Preview the Text

1. Show students the cover of the selected book. Ask them to discuss what they think the book will be about. Allow a few minutes for students to page through their copies, or if you are conducting a read-aloud, flip through the pages of the book to show some of the illustrations.

2. Tell students to turn to the table of contents and skim the chapter titles. Ask students to share what they know about the purpose of a table of contents. How does it appear this author has organized the information? Why? Read the table of contents together aloud. Ask students to point to the chapter they think looks the most interesting and that they have the most questions about.

Teacher Model

3. Select one of the chapter titles to ask questions about. Share your reason for picking that particular chapter. Explain, "Good readers look over the book and use the table of contents to begin thinking about questions they have about the topics in the book."

4. Read aloud your selected chapter title. Tell students, "I picked this chapter because _____ and I am wondering _____." Be specific about your wonders and base them on what you saw in the text preview in step 1 and on what you know about the topic. Write your wonders on a sticky note and post on a sheet of chart paper titled *Wonder Wall* (Murphy 2009). Tell students that the table of contents helps the reader to wonder and ask questions about the topic.

5. *Option:* Use the *Table of Contents Wonderings* organizer (Figure 4.3) to model by guiding the students in a discussion about the author's organization and by filling in one specific chapter from the text and sharing what you are wondering about in that chapter.

Guided Practice

6. Ask students to work in pairs and take turns pointing to the chapters they are most interested in reading. Have students share one wonder about their chosen chapter with each other and write it on a sticky note to post on the Wonder Wall.

7. *Option:* Students may use the *Table of Contents Wonderings* organizer with partners or teams as they write what they are wondering about in each chapter.

Independent Practice

8. During reading, have students sketch or write other wonders on sticky notes to add to the Wonder Wall.

9. Have students complete the *Table of Contents Wonderings* organizer as they think about what they wonder about in each chapter.

Wrap-Up

10. After reading, ask students to return to the Wonder Wall and the original questions about the table of contents. Were their questions answered in the text?

11. Create a chart as shown in Figure 4.2. As a class, sort questions according to the three categories shown in the figure.

English Language Support

Provide wonder starters for students to use for their wonders. Post these on a chart or on sticky notes. Encourage students to share their thinking.

- I wonder why ____ because ____.
- I wonder how ____ because ____.
- I wonder what ____ because ____.
- I wonder who ____ because ____.
- I wonder when ____ because ____.

Figure 4.2 Question Sorting Chart

Questions Answered in the Text	Questions Answered with the Text Plus My Head or Inferred	Unanswered Questions

Assessment

Ask individual students to show you the table of contents and share what they are wondering about one of the headings. Are the wonders related to the text topic or is the student asking tangentially related questions? Does the student need prompting? Assist the student in asking related wonders using the table of contents.

Figure 4.3 Table of Contents Wonderings

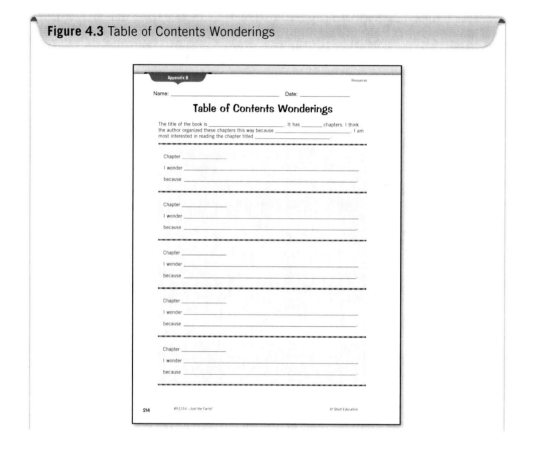

Symbol Summaries: Using the Table of Contents to Summarize

Students enjoy sketching during lessons. Try using sticky notes in different colors for each chapter to create symbol summaries. Assign different chapters to each student to summarize.

Objective/Standards

Use the table of contents to help summarize; determine central ideas or themes of a text and analyze their development (CCSS); summarize the key supporting details and ideas; know and use various text features to locate key facts or information in a text efficiently (CCSS)

Materials

- book with table of contents
- *Symbol Summaries Organizer* (See Appendix B)
- sticky notes in different colors

Warm Up/Review the Content

1. After reading the selected text, ask students to turn back to the table of contents. Tell students, "Good readers use the table of contents throughout the reading process to help them understand how the author organizes the information. After reading, we can return to the table of contents and use it to help us summarize what we have learned about the book."

2. Ask students to turn to the table of contents and reread silently each of the chapter titles. Then, read the chapter titles chorally. Ask students to tell a partner which was their favorite chapter and why.

Teacher Model

3. Demonstrate how to fold a sheet of paper to create a flip chart. Write each of the chapter titles in a box. Have students create one to use to record their own summary symbols.

4. Select a chapter to model a symbol summary. Explain: "I liked the chapter titled ____ so I am going to summarize it now, and I will choose a symbol to represent what I learned."

5. Model how to turn back to the chapter and review using headings and visuals from the text. In the box with the chapter title you've selected, tell students what symbol (or drawing) you've chosen to sketch to represent a summary of the content and why. Invite students to sketch it, too. Invite partners to turn and repeat your summary as they discuss their sketches.

6. *Option:* Fill in the *Symbol Summaries Organizer* (Figure 4.4) with an example or two using chapter titles from the text to model for students how to wonder using the table of contents.

Guided Practice

7. Ask students to begin with their favorite chapter and review it briefly and then sketch a symbol summary to go with it. Use either a flip chart or the *Symbol Summaries Organizer* (See Figure 4.4). Invite students to share their work with partners. Circulate around the room to support students as they summarize. Encourage a discussion with the whole class and invite students to show their symbols.

Independent Practice

8. Have students finish filling in their symbol summaries for each chapter of the text using either a flip chart or the *Symbol Summaries Organizer*. Assist and coach students in determining which symbols to use. Interrupt work to share inventive symbols students sketch that other students may wish to use as well.

Wrap-Up

9. Ask students to identify and share with a partner which chapter they think is…

   • the easiest chapter to summarize and tell why.

   • the most difficult chapter to summarize and tell why.

   • the favorite chapter to summarize and tell why.

10. After partners have discussed their ideas about the chapters, tally and vote as a class on the chapters that are easiest, most difficult, and favorite. Ask students to share their reasons for their choices.

Assessment

Circulate and note student summary symbols for the chapters. Guide students in selecting main ideas from each chapter.

Figure 4.4 Symbol Summaries Organizer

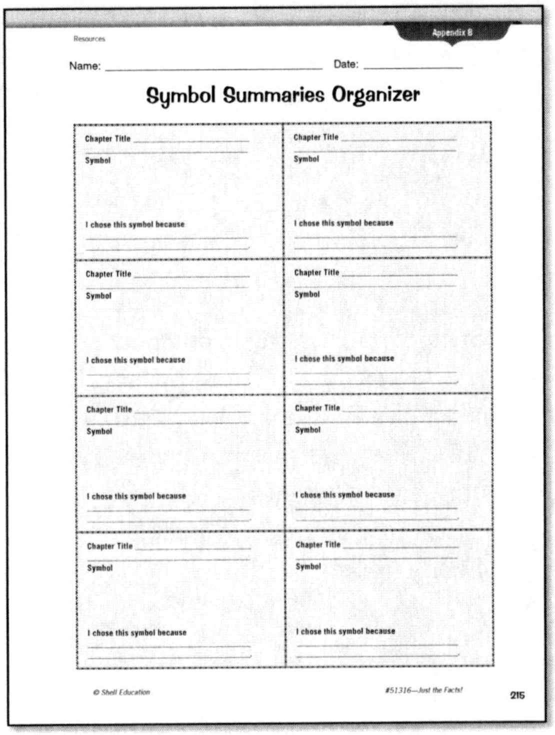
Resources

Appendix B

Name: ______________________ Date: __________

Symbol Summaries Organizer

Chapter Title ______ Symbol I chose this symbol because ______	Chapter Title ______ Symbol I chose this symbol because ______
Chapter Title ______ Symbol I chose this symbol because ______	Chapter Title ______ Symbol I chose this symbol because ______
Chapter Title ______ Symbol I chose this symbol because ______	Chapter Title ______ Symbol I chose this symbol because ______
Chapter Title ______ Symbol I chose this symbol because ______	Chapter Title ______ Symbol I chose this symbol because ______

© Shell Education #51316—Just the Facts! 215

Struggling Readers Support

Assist students in summarizing chapters by encouraging them to use visuals and headings to come up with a symbol for each chapter. You may wish to invite students who are experiencing difficulty to work with you at a separate table. Model how to reread and select a symbol to represent the material.

Pause to Predict: Using Headings to Predict

Using headings to predict is a great way to keep students on target throughout the reading of a text. Predicting helps them to stay interested in the text and focused on the purpose the author intended. Encourage students to think of the headings as stop signs where they stop and think about what is next.

Objective/Standards

Use each heading in a text to make logical predictions about the text and confirm or change predictions based on reading; read closely to determine what the text says explicitly and to make logical inferences from it; cite specific textual evidence when writing or speaking to support conclusions drawn from the text (CCSS); know and use various text features to locate key facts or information in a text efficiently (CCSS)

Materials

- text
- *Pause to Predict: Partner Bookmark* (See Appendix B)
- sticky notes

Teacher Model

1. Guide the class to look at the headings in the selected text. Read each heading together.

2. Explain to students, "Headings are like road signs that the author uses to signal what each little part of the text is about. You can use them when you read to help you predict what you are going to learn." Discuss the headings in the text and what they have in common. "These headings all have to do with (topic) because (the author used… it says… I can tell…, etc.)."

3. Select one of the headings and say, "Watch me as I demonstrate how to use a heading to think about what the author is going to teach us in this part of the text." Read aloud the heading. Share your prediction using the frame, "I think the part under the heading _____ is going to be about _____ because _____." Share any other clues that helped you make your prediction (e.g., visuals, photos, graphs, text, bold words).

4. Read aloud the text under the heading. After reading, ask students whether your prediction was confirmed by having them show a thumbs up or a thumbs sideways if you changed your prediction.

Guided Practice

5. Write on the board or display each of the headings from a portion of text. Guide students in making an overall prediction as they discuss what all of the headings have in common. "All of these headings are teaching us something about _____."

6. Have students work in pairs to select another heading from the same section of text you just modeled. Have them take turns skimming the text under the

heading to make predictions. "I think the part under the heading _____ is going to be about _____ because _____."

Independent Practice

7. Instruct students to read alone or in partners and each time they come to a heading have them pause to make a prediction about the next portion of text. *Optional:* Allow students to use sticky notes to write their predictions. Have them put a + sign on their note if the prediction was met and an editor's swervy line (𝓛) if they had to change their prediction.

Wrap-Up

8. Ask students to reflect on how headings help them predict what a text is about. Which headings were most helpful today and why?

Assessment

Put a positive emphasis on predicting rather than making it a "right or wrong" exercise. Coach individual students by asking them to make a prediction and either tell whether it was met or if they changed it after reading. Ask, "Was the text what you expected?" Watch for wild or off-target predictions and ask, "What in the text made you think that?" Model for students how to keep predictions "text based" using clues from skimming the text rather than based entirely on prior knowledge.

English Language Learner Support

Write prediction starters on the board so students can use them as a conversation guide with partners. Include the following: "All of these headings are about _____ because _____." "I think the part under the heading _____ is going to be about _____ because _____." Help students who struggle use the starters to make predictions by selecting a heading and making a prediction together. Show students how to use other clues on the page such as photos, maps, or visuals to help make predictions along with the headings.

Figure 4.5 Pause to Predict Bookmark

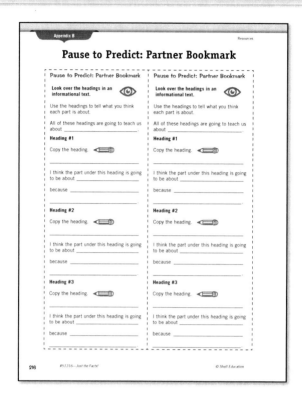

Presto Change-o: Using Headings to Questions

The name Presto Change-o will remind students to turn headings into questions as they read to stay on target as they make their way through a text.

Objective/Standards

Learn how to effectively use question words and turn headings into logical questions to then answer after reading

Materials

- informational text
- *Presto Change-o Headings to Questions* (See Appendix B)
- chart paper
- sticky notes
- notebook

Teacher Model

1. Tell students that good readers often turn headings in an informational text into questions. Say, "Turning headings into questions helps the reader stay interested in the reading and helps the reader pay attention, too. Plus it can be fun to quiz yourself after reading to see if you understood what you just read." Explain that you are going to model using several headings from the reading.

2. Write the following question words on the board: who, what, when, where, why, and how. Read aloud one of the headings from a text. Turn it into a question. For example, if the heading says **Types of Ants**, show how to look at the pictures and briefly skim the text to figure out which question word you might use. You say, "I see three paragraphs in this section that each starts with the name of an ant. I think I will ask, 'What types of ants are there?'" Record your question on a chart.

3. Read aloud the text under the selected heading. Return to your question to answer it. Invite students to turn to a partner and answer the question as well. Select another heading and model how to skim for clues, and then turn the heading into a question.

Guided Practice

4. Select a different heading and skim the text with the class. Invite students to each turn the heading into a question. Have partners share and then read to answer their questions.

5. Invite pairs of students to continue the process of reading headings, skimming, turning headings into questions, and then answering questions verbally. Rotate between pairs to listen in and provide guidance when necessary.

Struggling Reader Support

Struggling readers experience difficulty asking and answering questions using headings. Read headings and provide just two question words to choose from to focus their thinking. Emphasize rereading of both the question and the section of text to answer the question.

Extension

Try modeling different kinds of questions using headings.

Question Word Questions	Post question words, who, what, when, where, why, and how. Students use clues from the text and the heading to ask and answer text-based questions.
I wonder...	These questions start with, I wonder what, why, when, who, or where and promote critical thinking.
Question the Author	The students may ask questions of the author and the content. Why did the author organize the text this way? Why did the author include these points? What was the author attempting to teach us? What reasons did the author have for including this information?

Independent Practice

6. Have students practice independently in a variety of ways.

   - **Sticky notes**: Students turn headings into questions and place next to the heading on the page in the text.

   - *Presto Change-o Headings to Questions:* Have students use the graphic organizer shown in Figure 4.6 to turn each heading into a question and then answer the question after reading. (See also Appendix B)

   - **Notebook:** Have students write their headings to questions directly in a notebook.

Wrap-Up

7. Ask students to turn to a partner and review the steps for how to turn a heading into a question (reread, think of a question word, ask, and answer).

Assessment

Instruct students to evaluate not only how well they did asking and answering questions using headings, but also to evaluate the author's choice of headings. Were these headings helpful or on target for the text? Why or why not? What would students change? Observe students and ask individuals to turn headings into questions. Model again for students in small groups to provide more assistance.

Ask students to quiz one another on the reading material by asking and answering their heading questions.

Figure 4.6 Presto Change-o Headings to Questions

Sample Lessons

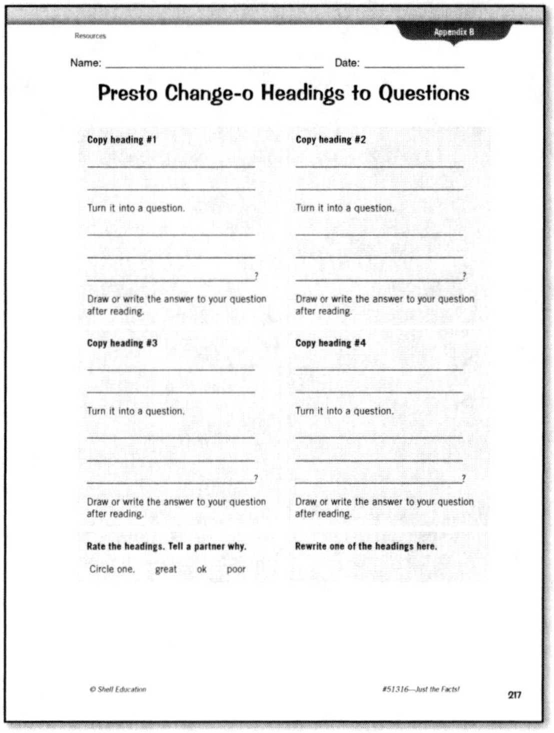

Resources
Appendix B

Name: _____ Date: _____

Presto Change-o Headings to Questions

Copy heading #1

_____

_____

Turn it into a question.

_____

_____

_____?

Draw or write the answer to your question after reading.

Copy heading #2

_____

_____

Turn it into a question.

_____

_____

_____?

Draw or write the answer to your question after reading.

Copy heading #3

_____

_____

Turn it into a question.

_____

_____

_____?

Draw or write the answer to your question after reading.

Copy heading #4

_____

_____

Turn it into a question.

_____

_____

_____?

Draw or write the answer to your question after reading.

Rate the headings. Tell a partner why.

Circle one.   great   ok   poor

Rewrite one of the headings here.

© Shell Education   #51316—Just the Facts!   217

All Aboard the Heading Train!
Using Headings to Clarify Text

Headings are helpful to readers as they make their way through a text. Students need to use headings to determine main ideas, generate questions, and help them think about confusing words and points. The heading train is a helpful metaphor for staying on track when reading.

Objective/Standards

Use headings to help monitor and keep track of their comprehension; analyze the structure of texts, including how specific sentences, paragraphs, and larger portions of the text relate to each other and the whole (CCSS); determine the meaning of general academic and domain-specific words and phrases in a text (CCSS); know and use various text features to locate key facts or information in a text efficiently (CCSS)

Materials

- text
- *All Aboard the Heading Train* (See Appendix B)
- chart paper

Teacher Model

1. Guide the class to look at the headings in a text. Read over each heading together. Ask students to share what they know about headings. Tell them that headings are like road signs that the author uses to signal what each little part of the text is about. You can use headings when you read to help you keep track of what you are reading if you are confused while reading.

2. Say, "Watch me as I demonstrate how to use a heading to help me keep track of what I am reading." Read aloud one of the headings. Pause at some point to share something confusing (sentence, word, or idea). Share your clarifying strategies using the frame, "I am confused about _____ , so I am going to reread the heading. It says _____. So this part is about _____. The next heading is about _____. Now I understand this part!"

Guided Practice

3. Select another heading. Read aloud with the class and pause to clarify a confusing idea or sentence. Guide students to reread with a partner the heading as well as the next heading to help them figure out where the author is headed with the information in the text.

4. Using chart paper, keep a class running list of strategies besides headings to use to clarify confusing words and ideas. Include such strategies as: rereading, reading on, substituting words of similar meaning, breaking words into parts, sounding out, looking up words, and cross-checking illustrations and visuals.

Independent Practice

5. Have students practice with a partner identifying confusing words and parts and using headings to help them clarify the meaning of the text. Students may fill in the *All Aboard the Heading Train* activity sheet, if desired. (See Figure 4.7 and Appendix B)

Wrap-Up

6. Ask students to reflect on how headings can be used like a train to stay on track during reading. How does it help sometimes to reread the headings or to read ahead to the next heading? Are all headings helpful? Why or why not?

Assessment

Observe how students identify confusing points and ideas. Do they only identify confusing vocabulary and not ideas? What strategies do students use besides rereading headings? Do they use a variety of strategies such as looking up words and checking the visuals? Coach individual students by modeling and guiding them as they find examples of confusing ideas in the text to clarify and then using the headings as one way to figure out meaning.

Struggling Readers Support

Provide a language frame to help students use headings to clarify. Select examples from the text and fill in the first blank for students. Distribute these examples to partners or individual students who then read the confusing parts you've identified and the headings to help clarify. **Sample frames:** This part about _____ is confusing so I am rereading the heading _____ and reading ahead the heading _____ to see if that helps.

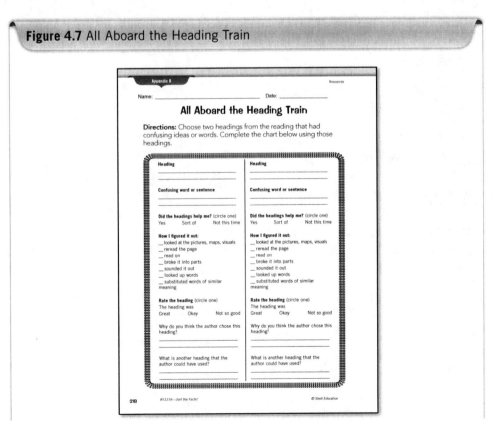

Figure 4.7 All Aboard the Heading Train

What's My Heading? Using Headings to Summarize

Using headings to summarize after reading is a useful text that students can take in their reading tool kit all the way through college! Making games out of headings helps elementary students to slow down and pay attention to the road signs of informational text headings!

Objective/Standards

Practice summarizing portions of text while classmates guess which heading goes with their summary; determine central ideas or themes of a text and analyze their development (CCSS); summarize the key supporting details and ideas; know and use various text features to locate key facts or information in a text efficiently (CCSS)

Materials

- informational text
- *What's My Heading? Concentration Game* (See Appendix B)
- cards

Teacher Model

1. Tell students that today you are going to play a game using the headings in the text. Tell students that they will take turns selecting the text that goes with a heading, summarizing it, and then the class guesses which heading the student is summarizing.

2. Share that you will go first. Say, "Watch me while I summarize from one of the headings in the book. First, I will reread." Don't allow students to see which heading you are going to summarize. Give a two to three sentence summary including the main ideas and details of one section of text. Encourage them to flip through the text as they guess your heading. Have partners share their guesses, then discuss as a class.

3. Select another portion of text to model from by summarizing and asking students to guess the heading, or model using the concentration game, *What's My Heading?* and demonstrate for students how to select a chapter, make one card with the title of a heading and a symbol, and another card with a two sentence summary. (After students make more pairs of concentration cards during guided practice, demonstrate how to play the game.)

Guided Practice

4. The following includes two options for guided practice.
Team Practice: Have students work in teams to select a heading and the text that accompanies it to summarize. Or you can write the headings on strips and have the groups each draw one. Have teams prepare and present their summaries to the class in one of two ways with a two sentence summary: 1) acting out the main ideas and details, or 2) drawing the main ideas and details. Allow the class to guess which heading goes with each summary. Circulate to assist students as they reread and select main ideas and details to summarize for the group.
Partner practice: Have students take turns summarizing sections of text and having the partner read the corresponding heading. Provide small group practice for students experiencing difficulty.

English Language Learner Support

Encourage students to use either drama or drawing to summarize the text headings. Serve as a scribe to record short summaries of each heading in the reading material. Underline words that students can draw or dramatize in the summaries.

Independent Practice

5. Have students work independently or with partners to summarize each portion of text. Allow them to record summaries using art or writing.

6. Have students work independently to create cards for the concentration game. In pairs, have students use their cards to play the game. (See Figure 4.8 and Appendix B)

Wrap-Up

7. Ask students to share how summarizing with headings is helpful to learning the material. Discuss the following: What is easy about it? What is difficult?

Assessment

Observe how students are summarizing each portion of the text. Are they including main ideas and important details? Give a quick +, ✓, or – to each student in your records to indicate whether they need more support for summarizing. Call up small groups to practice summarizing chunks of text. Ask students to lay out the summary and headings cards that they made for the What's My Heading? game and ask them to match for you. Note how they do it. Can they recall main ideas and details?

Figure 4.8 What's My Heading? Concentration Game

What's My Heading? Concentration Game

1. Write each heading. Then, sketch a drawing and write one or two sentences to go with the heading. Be sure to reread to include main ideas and details. If you want, you can write in very small lettering at the bottom of the summary card the heading your summary goes with.

2. Cut apart your headings and summaries.

3. Mix them up, turn them over, and play concentration matching with a partner. You may want to use both your and your partner's deck of headings and summaries. Make sure you've both read the texts.

4. Take turns turning over two of the cards. If you have a matching heading and summary, it is a match. If you turn over two cards and they don't match, put the cards back and it is your partner's turn.

5. To make the game more challenging, use headings and summaries from several different chapters or texts.

6. Save your cards in an envelope. Label the envelope with the title of the book.

7. You can glue the envelope into your notebook to save.

Say Cheese: Using Photos to Understand the Text

Students naturally gravitate to the photos in informational texts. This lesson forces them to get the most out of photos. As they look away to try to remember the photo and then sketch it, they not only have fun, but they practice the skill of close observation while reading visuals.

Objective/Standards

Study photo(s) from informational texts to analyze their content and effectiveness; integrate and evaluate content presented in diverse media and formats, including visually and quantitatively, as well as in words; use information gained from illustrations (e.g., maps, photographs) and the words in a text to demonstrate understanding of the text (CCSS)

Materials

- photos from a selected informational text
- *Say Cheese!* (See Appendix B)
- interactive board or a document camera

Teacher Model

1. Tell students that authors often use photographs as a text feature to convey information in their informational texts.

2. Display the selected text using a document camera or interactive whiteboard and provide students with a hard copy. Ask students what they know already about how photos are used in texts.

3. Display a specific photo from the selected text. Ask students to take a moment and silently study the photo and the caption or label that accompanies it.

4. Use a think-aloud to describe what students are seeing in the photo as well as the author's purpose for including this photo. For example, say, " Watch how I study the photo to get the most out of it to help me understand the text more. First, I am going to look at the page around the photo. I see that this page is mostly about _____ because I see the _____ (headings, etc.). As I study the photo I see _____ and _____. The caption says _____ (if there is one)."

5. Share what you find confusing or interesting about the photo. Also, share questions you have: "I wonder (why, how, what, when, where) _____." Then, tell why you think the author included this photo. "I think the author included this photo because _____." Also, share whether you found the photo helpful in understanding the text. "This photo was helpful (not helpful) because _____." Finally, tell what you found most memorable about the photo.

6. Stare at the photo. Pretend to take a photo of it and say "cheese" as you take a mental picture of it. Cover the photo and try to sketch what you remember about it. Then, look back at the photo.

7. Tell students that this is a fun game because good readers really do remember the photos in their minds after they read. Remembering the photo helps us understand the content of the text. Share your thoughts on the photo, such as "The author included this photo to show (explain, etc.) _____. The photo was or was not helpful because _____. The hard part (confusing part, etc.) was _____."

Guided Practice

8. Select a photo to play "Say Cheese" from either the same text you just modeled from or another text of which the students have a copy.

9. Ask students to study the photo you selected quietly. Then, have them "Say Cheese" and photograph it in their minds. Ask them to look away from the photo and turn to a partner and describe what they remember. The pair can either work together to draw a quick sketch of the photo or each draw their own and compare. They may add items they forgot as they share.

10. Invite students to work in pairs and page through the text and select a photo to study, cover, sketch, and evaluate. *Option:* Use the *Say Cheese* reproducible.

Independent Practice

11. Have students select two or three photos and with each one study, cover, sketch, and evaluate the photo. Circulate to assist students and observe whether they need guidance as they study photos and evaluate their usefulness.

Wrap-Up

12. Ask students to share which photos were most helpful, least helpful, and tell why. Also ask, "Which photos were the easiest to remember? Which were the most difficult? Why did the author include these? How did the photos help you learn more about (topic)?"

Alternative Wrap-Up Option: Have students place their "Say Cheese" sketches on their desks for others to see. Then, have them leave a paper out next to their sketches for others to write comments. All students rotate around the room in a "gallery tour" and try to guess which photo each student sketched. Students write their guesses including page numbers on the papers next to each sketch.

Assessment

Observe students as they study the photos. Are they able to discuss the author's purpose for the photo and evaluate whether it was useful? Can they sketch the "gist" of important information from the photo?

Figure 4.9 Say Cheese!

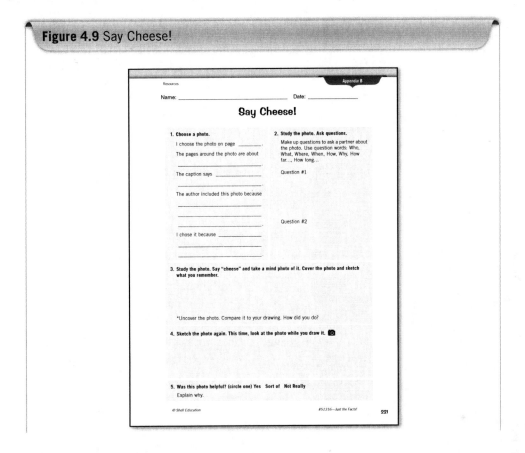

Photo Awards! Evaluating Photos

This is a fun lesson that will motivate students to pay further attention to photos as they read. Students may enjoy holding a mini awards show for the photos. They might even pretend to be the different photographers and make speeches or explain their photos.

Objective/Standards

Evaluate the author's use of photographs in an informational text; integrate and evaluate content presented in diverse media and formats, including visually and quantitatively, as well as in words (CCSS); use information gained from illustrations (maps, photographs) and the words in a text to demonstrate understanding of the text (CCSS)

Materials

- informational text with photographs
- *Photo Awards* (See Appendix B)
- construction paper

Teacher Model

1. Explain to students that informational text authors often choose to include photos to help make their point in the text. Today, they will give photo awards or prizes to the photos they think are the most helpful in the text.

2. Choose an informational text that has lots of photographs. Provide copies for students, and display the text so students can see your modeling.

3. Allow students to flip through the text and select a favorite photo to share with a partner. They may comment using a sentence frame such as, "This looks interesting because _____."

4. Allow students to read the text silently. Then, read the text aloud to the class.

5. Select a photo that you think illustrates a key point from the text. Tell the class, "I picked this photo of the _____ because it helps us learn more about the topic of _____." Share your thoughts on why the photo is helpful for illustrating key points the author is making in the text. Ask questions such as, "Why is a photo more helpful than a diagram here?"

6. Select at least two more photos and tell why they are helpful in explaining the text content. Then, tell the students that you are going to rank them by giving them a first, second, or third place for their helpfulness. Allow students to talk to partners to guess which photo you will choose for the first, second, and third place winners.

Guided Practice

7. Use the next section of the text you modeled from or another informational text with photos. Ask students to work in partners to select their top three (or just top

two for a text with fewer photos) photographs. They must tell why they thought the photo was helpful in understanding the main ideas of the text.

8. Assign a different photo from the text to each corner of the room. Invite students to walk to the corner of the most important photo and discuss it. When they arrive at the corner, have students partner with another student and make a list of three reasons why they like that photo.

9. Select a volunteer to represent each photo and to stand in front of the room to "defend" their choice and tell the following:

   • *two reasons why the photo is the most important one in the text*

   • *how the photo helped them understand the text better*

   • *why they think the author included it*

10. If students are experiencing difficulty giving reasons for selecting their photos, provide some examples, such as:

   • *This photo helped me understand how _____.*

   • *This photo helped me understand why _____.*

   • *The photo added some very important information including _____ that was not in the text.*

   • *The photo explained the information in the text about _____.*

   • *The author included this photo to _____.*

English Language Learner Support

Invite students to work with you to act out some of their favorite photos. Have each student act out a photo and the others in the group tell which one he or she is depicting by turning to the page. Make construction paper award ribbons to represent first place (blue) second place (red), and third place (yellow) photos. Students vote on and award the ribbons to their top three photos. Encourage them to share their reasons for their selections.

Figure 4.10 Photo Awards

Independent Practice

11. Have students read informational texts with photos and use the *Photo Awards* activity sheet (See Figure 4.10 and Appendix B) to select and rate photos for ranking.

Wrap-Up

12. Discuss how photographs can help the reader understand the text better. Ask, "Were there any places in the text where a photo was **not** included but a photo would have enhanced the concepts in the text?"

Assessment

Observe as students rate the photos. Can they use the text to articulate information presented in the text? Do they give varied reasons for their rankings of photos? Can they tell how the photos helped them gain an understanding of the text?

Sketch it! Diagram it! Reading Diagrams, Charts, and Graphs

Objective/Standards

Learn to use diagrams as useful text features (e.g., diagrams, charts, or graphs) that support deep comprehension of informational texts; integrate and evaluate content presented in diverse media and formats, including visually and quantitatively, as well as in words (CCSS); use information gained from illustrations (maps, photographs) and the words in a text to demonstrate understanding of the text (CCSS); know and use various text features to locate key facts or information in a text efficiently (CCSS)

Materials

- informational text with one or more diagrams
- *Sketch It! Diagram It!* (See Appendix B)
- sentence strips

Teacher Model

1. Select an informational text that has one or more diagrams. Display the text and provide copies for students.

2. Explain to students that diagrams are visuals authors use to convey important information. Diagrams usually include labels and come in a variety of forms including drawings or photographs. Good readers pause on diagrams to further their understanding of the text.

3. Ask students to turn to a partner and share what they know about diagrams (drawing, cross section, labels, etc.). Also, have students discuss the purpose of diagrams when reading. Support this discussion by asking questions such as, "Why do authors include diagrams? How are diagrams helpful when reading about science topics, history topics, or other informational texts?"

4. Select a diagram from the text. Make observations about the surrounding text by reading it aloud up to the diagram. Share your thoughts by saying, "These pages are about _____."

5. Pause to study the diagram. Demonstrate how to read the diagram by reading the labels, etc. Then, think aloud about the reasons the author included the diagram and whether you found it useful. Use language such as, "I think this diagram is _____ (helpful, sort of helpful, not helpful) because _____. I think the diagram is included because the author wants us to learn about _____."

6. Invite students to study the diagram on their own first to try to figure out the author's purpose and some of the details about the diagram. Tell students, "You have one minute to try to figure out this map on your own. Ready, go!" After a minute, ask students to turn to partners to quickly share what they think is confusing or interesting about the diagram.

Sketch it! Diagram it!

7. Model how to take a mind photo by saying, "When I want to remember what I read I will also want to remember the diagram in my head. To practice this, I am going to look at it now for a minute. Then, I will try to recreate it."

8. Look at the diagram for a moment and pretend to take a mind photo. Cover or hide the diagram and without looking, quickly sketch what you remember from it on paper. Take one "sneak peek" to recall some of the details. Compare the diagram you drew to the original. How did you do?

9. Give students the opportunity to take a mind photo of the diagram and then without looking, sketch it and compare it to the original.

Guided Practice

10. Using the same diagram from the teacher model, have students work in pairs and take turns asking questions of one another about the information found in the diagram. Circulate and guide students in their question formulation.

11. Students work in pairs to cover the same diagram you sketched and try sketching it. Or both may sketch at the same time. Try timing them and allow only a few minutes before looking back at the original to compare. Emphasize having fun with this and just going for the basic outline, etc., not getting it perfectly! Students may sketch the diagram a second time while looking.

12. Invite students to choose different diagrams from the text and to work in teams or pairs to practice covering and sketching. Circulate around the room to assist.

English Language Learner Support

Use question stems to help students study a particular diagram. Write questions about the features, such as the key, legend, distances, etc. and put them on strips. Have students draw questions to ask the group and to answer.

Independent Practice

13. Assign or allow students to choose a diagram from the text to study and create questions to go with it, using the *Sketch It! Diagram It!* activity sheet (See Figure 4.11). Students should consider the author's purpose for the diagram and whether it was a useful tool in understanding the content. Then, have students sketch the diagram without looking and then while looking.

Wrap-Up

14. Instruct students to evaluate a series of diagrams from a text. "Which diagrams were most useful in the text? Why? Or How? What was easy to understand? What was hardest to understand?"

Assessment

Observe students as they study the diagrams. Are they able to ask and answer questions about the content? Can they sketch the basics of the diagram and do they have the "gist" of its purpose?

Figure 4.11 Sketch It! Diagram It!

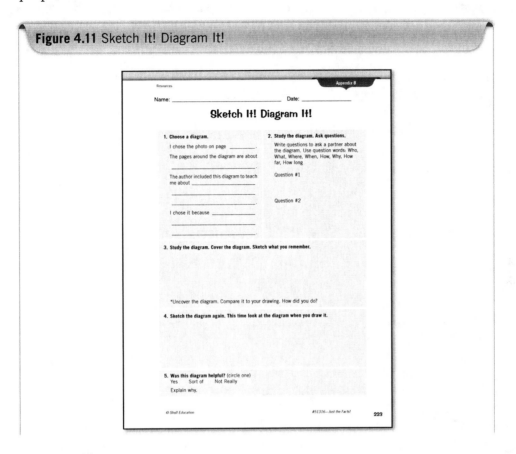

Thumbs Up, Thumbs On: Using the Glossary to Understand Words

Some students feel uncomfortable admitting that they do not know a word. In this lesson, instead of asking students to show which words they don't know, they are asked to put their thumbs on words they would like to learn. **Note:** This lesson can be completed as written or by using a text the class has already read.

Objective/Standards

Skim the glossary and indicate familiarity with words using gestures; interpret words and phrases as they are used in a text, including determining technical, connotative, and figurative meanings, and analyze how specific word choices shape meaning or tone (CCSS); determine the meaning of general academic and domain-specific words and phrases (CCSS); know and use various text features to locate key facts or information in a text efficiently (CCSS)

Materials

- informational text with glossary
- *Thumbs Up, Thumbs On Glossary* (See Appendix B)
- display board

Teacher Model

1. Ask students what they know about the glossary in an informational text. Tell them that good readers use the glossary throughout the reading process to help figure out difficult words and concepts.

2. Tell students about how a glossary can be used to activate knowledge prior to reading a text. Say, "Sometimes I use the glossary before I read to skim and see what words and concepts I already know something about and to get a quick idea of what is in the text. I usually do this after I also flip around in the pages of the text a bit as well."

3. Select a text that includes a glossary and that you and the students have not read yet, and page through it. Share your thoughts, such as what you already know or want to know about the text topics.

4. Turn to the glossary and read some of the words aloud. As you read, put a thumbs up for a word you already know, sideways for one you sort of know, and touch the word with your thumb for one you are not familiar with but would like to learn. Think aloud when touching a word by saying, "Here is a word I do not know. I am going to touch it with my thumb because I want to 'get it' or remember it as I read."

5. After modeling with a few words, share with students your evaluation of the glossary entry. Say, "I found the glossary entry helpful for the word _____ because _____."

Guided Practice

6. Review the rest of the glossary and select several more words to read aloud and show your thumb response (up, sideways, or down). As you read each word, invite the class to also indicate familiarity with the words with their thumbs.

7. Have students turn to a partner and share reasons for their "thumb" response and their thoughts about the words.

8. Invite students to select glossary words to share with a partner and discuss their "thumb" responses.

Independent Practice

9. Have students skim the glossary and record interesting words they know, sort of know, and want to know. If desired, students can use the *Thumbs Up, Thumbs On Glossary* organizer (See Figure 4.12) to support with independent practice.

10. During reading, instruct students to stay on the lookout for their selected words and sketch drawings to go with the text. Also, have students rate the glossary entries and the author's use of the word in the text.

11. After reading, have students share their responses in partners or small groups. Circulate to assist students as they select words, read, and look up the words in the glossary.

Struggling Reader Support

Work with struggling readers in a small group. Review the text and glossary as a group. Ask students to turn to the same page. On the count of three, each student points to a key word of their choice. Each member of the group shares their word and their "thumb" response and invites the other students to do the same. Write several of the key words on the board and make up actions to go with each one. When the students encounter the words in the text, ask them to remember the actions.

Wrap-Up

12. Ask students to reflect on how the glossary is useful before and during reading to help spark interest in vocabulary. Did they enjoy and find helpful using their thumbs in the lesson? Why? Which words were hardest and which were the easiest to understand? Was the glossary helpful? Why or why not?

Assessment

Observe students as they show their thumbs in the lesson. Are they varying their responses? Can they identify difficult words and concepts? Do they use the glossary to help them figure out the word? Do they remember the words?

Figure 4.12 Thumbs Up, Thumbs On Glossary

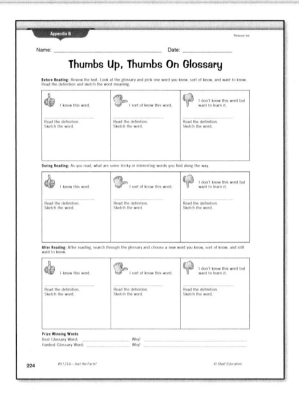

Glossary Sense Walk: Visualizing and More with the Glossary

Informational texts are loaded with visual and sensory images that are critical to comprehension. This lesson helps students to develop the skill of using sensory images when reading informational texts.

Objective/Standards

Use the glossary to find words that elicit the senses and find specific examples of the glossary words in the text; interpret words and phrases as they are used in a text, including determining technical, connotative, and figurative meanings, and analyze how specific word choices shape meaning or tone (CCSS); determine the meaning of general academic and domain-specific words and phrases (CCSS); know and use various text features to locate key facts or information in a text efficiently (CCSS)

Materials

- informational text with glossary
- *Glossary Sensory Bookmark* (See Appendix B)

Teacher Model

1. Ask students what they know about the glossary in an informational text. Tell them that good readers use the glossary throughout the reading process to help figure out difficult words and concepts.

2. Select a text that students have already read. Introduce the lesson by saying, "I am going to flip through the glossary and pick some words that help me to use my senses to understand the concepts we've learned. I am looking for words that help me see, hear, touch, taste, or smell the topic. That way, I will remember what I've learned."

3. Skim the glossary and read some of the words aloud. For each one, pause and tell which sense comes to mind. Also, flip back through the text for examples of the word on specific pages. Instruct students to follow along in their texts. You might invite them to also sketch each word and a symbol for the sense that you suggest using the following frames.

   - The word _____ helps me to see _____. An example is on page _____.

   - The word _____ helps me to hear _____. An example is on page _____.

   - When I read the word _____ , I can smell _____. An example is on page _____.

- When I read the word _____ , I can almost taste _____. An example is on page _____.
- The word _____ helps me to think about what it would feel like to touch _____ and it would feel _____. An example is on page _____.

Guided Practice

4. Write a glossary word on the board and the page number where it is found in the text. Have students read the text with partners and look up the word in the glossary. In pairs, have students decide which sense they think goes with the word and discuss this as a class.

5. Post symbols around the room to represent the senses: eye, ear, mouth, hand, and nose.

6. Read glossary words and passages aloud from the text. Ask students to choose which sense they associate with the word, and walk to it with their text in hand so they can discuss with others, who made the same choice, their reasons for selecting that sense and use evidence from the text to support their response.

Independent Practice

7. Have students work in teams or alone to complete the *Glossary Sensory Bookmark*. (See Figure 4.13 and Appendix B.) To do this, students read the text and use the glossary to help them remember the words. Then, they return to the text to provide evidence of the sense from words in the glossary definition or the text itself.

8. Circulate around the room while students are working and provide help when necessary to find the words in the text, look them up in the glossary, and reflect upon which sense best "fits" the word.

Wrap-Up

9. Ask students to reflect on how the glossary is useful in thinking about sensory images while reading. How does rereading the text and glossary definition help understanding?

Assessment

Observe students as they work back and forth from the text to the glossary. Is there more than one way to think about the senses and the words? Do students use the glossary when reading to help them understand words?

Figure 4.13 Glossary Sensory Bookmark

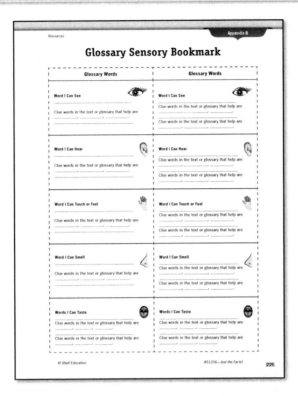

English Language Learner Support

Assign a sense to each student in a small group. Give them a card with an ear, eye, mouth, hand, or nose on it. Select glossary words. As the group reviews the text and glossary entry, ask students to tell how or if their sense goes with the word.

Favorite Word Summaries: Choosing, Ranking, Sorting Words

Many students do not bother looking up words in the glossary during reading. This lesson helps build motivation for using the glossary to get the most out of reading an informational text. When students self-select vocabulary, they are more interested in the text and retain what they read.

Objective/Standards

Use the glossary to find words that represent important ideas or details in the text, write them on sticky notes, and then sort them; interpret words and phrases as they are used in a text, including determining technical, connotative, and figurative meanings, and analyze how specific word choices shape meaning or tone (CCSS); determine the meaning of general academic and domain-specific words and phrases (CCSS); determine central ideas or themes of a text and analyze their development (CCSS); summarize the key supporting details and ideas (CCSS)

Materials

- informational text with glossary
- *Favorite Words Bookmark* (See Appendix B)
- sticky notes
- chart paper
- scratch paper

Teacher Model

1. Ask students what they know about the glossary in an informational text. Tell them that good readers use the glossary throughout the reading process to help figure out difficult words and concepts.

2. Select a text your students have already read and model the process that students will follow by saying, "As I flip through the glossary I am going to choose five words that are some of my favorites and that I think are important to the text." Read aloud from the glossary as you skim for your favorite words that you think are important to the text. Tell why you chose each one. "I am choosing the word _____ because _____. I think this word is a main idea because _____." Or, "I think this word is an important detail because _____."

3. Write each word on a sticky note. With two of the selected words, flip back in the text to the page or pages where the word can be found. Read aloud the heading (if there is one) that goes with the word. Place the sticky note on the page where the author first uses the word. Read the portion of text around the word. Discuss why you think the author decided to include the word in the glossary.

Guided Practice

4. With your remaining three words, invite students to join in by also writing the words on sticky notes with a partner. Have students look up your words in the text and discuss their importance with their partners.

Independent Practice

5. Instruct students to work in teams or pairs to find their own five favorite glossary words to write on sticky notes. Instruct students to also complete the *Favorite Words Bookmark* using the five words they selected. (See Figure 4.14 and Appendix B.) Circulate to assist students as they hunt for favorite and important words.

6. Once the bookmark is complete, have students join with another team or pair and combine all ten words. Have the teams analyze which words go together and remove any duplicate choices.

7. Instruct teams to use their sticky notes to post their words on a class chart in an order that makes sense to them. Then, have teams either sketch a drawing to go with each word or create a skit to teach the class the words. Teams may also choose to write a summary using their words.

8. Allow each group time to share their sketches or skits and explain why they selected their words.

English Language Learner Support

Put each student in charge of several pages of the glossary (or letters of the alphabet) and have students choose at least three important words to share with the group.

Wrap-Up

9. Ask students to reflect on how the glossary is useful in reviewing material they have already read. What is easy or hard about selecting just a few favorite words? Did the author do a good job illustrating and explaining the words? Why or why not?

Assessment

Observe students as they work back and forth from the text to the glossary. Students may need more practice in selecting important words and in evaluating the author's use of the key words. Can students verbalize and/or write a summary using the selected words?

Figure 4.14 Favorite Words Bookmark

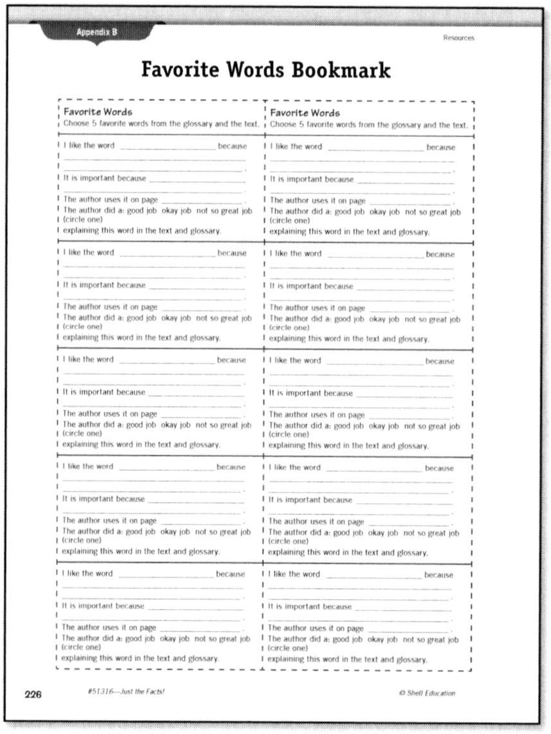

Appendix B

Resources

Favorite Words Bookmark

Favorite Words Choose 5 favorite words from the glossary and the text.	**Favorite Words** Choose 5 favorite words from the glossary and the text.
I like the word ____ because ____. It is important because ____. The author uses it on page ____. The author did a: good job okay job not so great job (circle one) explaining this word in the text and glossary.	I like the word ____ because ____. It is important because ____. The author uses it on page ____. The author did a: good job okay job not so great job (circle one) explaining this word in the text and glossary.
I like the word ____ because ____. It is important because ____. The author uses it on page ____. The author did a: good job okay job not so great job (circle one) explaining this word in the text and glossary.	I like the word ____ because ____. It is important because ____. The author uses it on page ____. The author did a: good job okay job not so great job (circle one) explaining this word in the text and glossary.
I like the word ____ because ____. It is important because ____. The author uses it on page ____. The author did a: good job okay job not so great job (circle one) explaining this word in the text and glossary.	I like the word ____ because ____. It is important because ____. The author uses it on page ____. The author did a: good job okay job not so great job (circle one) explaining this word in the text and glossary.
I like the word ____ because ____. It is important because ____. The author uses it on page ____. The author did a: good job okay job not so great job (circle one) explaining this word in the text and glossary.	I like the word ____ because ____. It is important because ____. The author uses it on page ____. The author did a: good job okay job not so great job (circle one) explaining this word in the text and glossary.
I like the word ____ because ____. It is important because ____. The author uses it on page ____. The author did a: good job okay job not so great job (circle one) explaining this word in the text and glossary.	I like the word ____ because ____. It is important because ____. The author uses it on page ____. The author did a: good job okay job not so great job (circle one) explaining this word in the text and glossary.

226 #51316—Just the Facts! © Shell Education

© Shell Education

The GGG: Glossary Guessing Game: Looking Up Words

By playing games and acting out words, students make the meanings memorable and their own. Try playing the games in a station or during independent work time.

Objective/Standards

Use glossary skills to play a guessing game as they act out words from the glossary and then look up the words; interpret words and phrases as they are used in a text, including determining technical, connotative, and figurative meanings, and analyze how specific word choices shape meaning or tone (CCSS); determine the meaning of general academic and domain-specific words and phrases (CCSS); know and use various text features to locate key facts or information in a text efficiently (CCSS)

Materials

- informational text with glossary
- *Glossary Guessing Game* (See Appendix B)
- dry-erase board (optional)

Teacher Model

1. Ask students what they know about the glossary in an informational text. Invite them to share their thoughts and to flip through a glossary in a text to spark their responses.

2. Explain that a glossary is a tool for understanding the difficult words and concepts in the book. Tell students, "Today we will play a fun glossary guessing game called the GGG to help us learn how to use the glossary to figure out hard words and concepts."

3. Select an informational text with a glossary to model the game. Model from a text you have already read or are in the middle of reading so students will be somewhat familiar with the words. Display the glossary and provide copies for the students to follow along.

4. Select a word for the students to guess. Act it out several times and ask, "What is my word? Guess and hunt for it in the glossary. When you find it, point to it and put your thumb up." You may also ask students to write their guesses on a small dry-erase board. Circulate to see responses. Wait for all students to respond, and if necessary, act out the word again or even give a clue such as:

   - The word begins with _____.
   - The word means the same as _____.

- The word is found on page _____.

5. While students wait for others to find the word, they may sketch the word. Try not to make this a "race," but rather praise students for finding the word.

6. Turn to the page in the glossary and read aloud the word and definition. Also, show students where the word is in the text. Or ask students to hunt for the word in the text.

7. Using the glossary word you just acted out, invite students to work with a partner to repeat the actions you chose to demonstrate the word and to put the definition into their own words.

Guided Practice

8. Select another glossary word, act it out, and encourage students to find it in the glossary and the text. Then, have partners act it out as they recite the meaning and pronunciation.

9. Have partners take turns selecting a word and acting it out while the other partner guesses the word and finds it in the glossary and the text. Circulate and coach students as they act out words, look them up, and provide clues for partners.

Independent Practice

10. Instruct students to sketch four words on the *Glossary Guessing Game* organizer and write definitions to match. (See Figure 4.15 and Appendix B.)

11. Have students share their words with a partner by mixing up all the cards faceup. To do this, students match drawings, definitions, and page numbers. After the matches are made, students also take turns acting out the words for one another and guessing the words. As an alternative to play, students can turn the cards facedown and play concentration.

Wrap-Up

12. Ask students to reflect and discuss the questions that follow. Be sure to encourage students to tell why.

- Which word was the most difficult to demonstrate using an action?

- Which word was the easiest to make up an action for?

- Which word was the most fun to demonstrate?

- Which words were the easiest/hardest to find in the text?

- How is understanding the use of a glossary helpful when reading?

English Language Learner Support

Turn to a page in the text and tell students you will select a glossary word to act out and for them to guess. Give clues as needed. Support students in a small group activity rather than in pairs.

Assessment

Circulate as students work in pairs and see if they can:

- Select glossary words
- Act out the words with an appropriate action
- Find words in the text
- Pronounce the words
- Tell the meaning of the words

Figure 4.15 Glossary Guessing Game

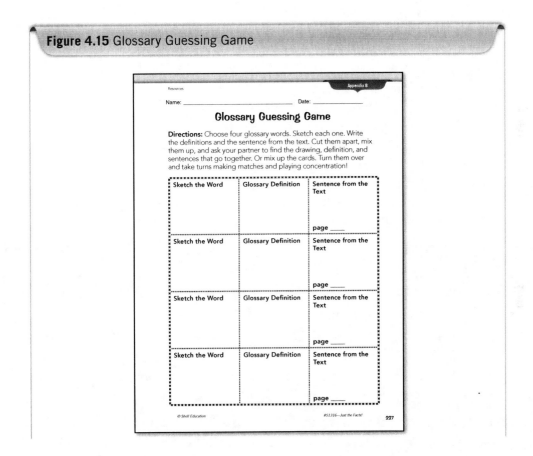

Index Hunt: Using the Index to Locate Information

This lesson gives students the opportunity to learn the purpose of an index in an informational text. If you also teach the lessons on the glossary, students will gain a working knowledge of the purposes and differences of both tools.

Objectives/Standards

Participate in an index hunt to quickly locate words in an index and the corresponding pages in the text; discuss the usefulness of an index in researching topics for a variety of purposes; interpret words and phrases as they are used in a text, including determining technical, connotative, and figurative meanings, and analyze how specific word choices shape meaning or tone (CCSS); determine the meaning of general academic and domain-specific words and phrases (CCSS); know and use various text features to locate key facts or information in a text efficiently (CCSS)

Materials

- informational text
- *Index Hunt* (See Appendix B)
- dry-erase board or scratch paper

Teacher Model

1. Ask students to turn to the index in an informational text. Ask students what they know about using an index. How is it organized? What do they notice?

2. Explain that the index is used to help the reader skip around in the book to find out on which page topics of interest are found. Tell students today they will participate in a fun index hunt and that looking things up quickly in an index is a good skill to develop.

3. Prior to the start of the lesson, select one topic to use to model. Tell students, "Good readers use the index before, during, and after reading to find out what page a topic is on. For example, if I want to look up _____ (topic), I need to first think about what letter it starts with, then look under the letter _____ words. I may need to go to the second or third letter to find the word. Then, I look at the page number and flip to that page. Here I see the topic _____ that I wanted is on page _____."

4. Flip to the specific page to look over the topic covered. If there is more than one page on the topic in the book, go back to the index and tell students you are seeing what other pages to flip to for more information.

Guided Practice

5. Several types of hunts can be done with an index.

Individual Hunt: Provide a topic from the index and have students hunt to find the topic in the index. Have students put their finger on the topic and quietly raise a hand. Instead of racing each other, set a time such as 10–20 seconds and see how many students can find the topic in the time frame. Then, try it again and see if they can beat their own times.

Team Hunt: Call out an index word and have student teams hunt to find it. They point to the word and raise their hands to show they have found it. Every student in the team must find the word in the index before other teams for a point. Teams must be absolutely silent and "flip, don't rip" with the page turning. After looking up the word, have teams find one page that the word is featured on as well and raise their hands when they do. Then, have them turn to teammates to talk about what the word means. **Student-Lead Variation:** Ask a student to provide words for all of the teams in the class to find or at each table designate a leader who dictates words to look up. Words may be selected by the leader or put on cards in a container and drawn by the leader.

Partner Hunt: Call out a word and write or display it for all to see. Have students work in pairs. One partner looks up the word in the index and raises a hand. Then, the other partner flips to the page in the book. Partners talk about the meaning of the word after reading the page. Provide small dry-erase boards or paper for students to use to sketch a drawing that goes with the word.

Struggling Reader Support

Work with small groups of students and allow them to take turns selecting the index words to race to find. Put the emphasis on beating the clock, not each other.

Independent Practice

6. Have students work in pairs and complete the *Index Hunt* organizer to select and race to index words. (See Figure 4.16 and Appendix B.)

Wrap-Up

7. Ask students why knowing how to use an index is a useful skill. Why are finding topics in an index quickly important? What is hard or easy about looking up topics in an index?

8. Ask partners to review the steps in looking up words in an index, and then finding the pages where the words are featured.

Assessment

Observe students to see if they can easily find topics in the index and then find the page numbers in the text. If needed, teach this skill to small groups of students and try providing practice during independent or center time with partners.

Figure 4.16 Index Hunt

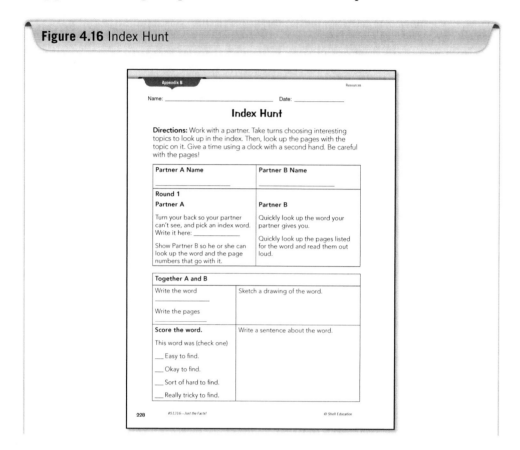

Index It! Using the Index to Locate Words

Try using self-stick notes to teach this lesson. Students often experience difficulty going back and forth from the text to the index. This lesson gives them practice doing just that with the added task of thinking critically about the words as they go. Use this activity with self-selected informational text reading as well as content-area required reading.

Objectives/Standards

Select index words to write and label as main ideas (+), supporting details (√), or interesting facts that are not considered main ideas or details (*); create an oral or written summary; interpret words and phrases as they are used in a text, including determining technical, connotative, and figurative meanings, and analyze how specific word choices shape meaning or tone (CCSS); determine the meaning of general academic and domain-specific words and phrases (CCSS)

Materials

- informational text
- *Index It!* (See Appendix B)
- sticky notes (3 different colors or sizes)
- scratch paper

Teacher Model

1. Explain to students that the index is useful throughout reading a text. After reading, you can refer to the index to review the concepts in the book.

2. Turn to the index in a selected text and model for students how to skim and then choose a word that is likely related to the main idea in the text. For example, "I am going to skim the index to see if I remember some of the important things we learned from this book. I see the word _____ and am going to turn to the pages it is found on to review it. This was one of the main ideas in the book, so I am going to write it on my sticky note and label it with a +." Then, do the same for another word that is a supporting detail in the text using the symbol √. (You may wish to use different colored pens/markers for each of the symbols as well.)

3. Select one interesting word that is not a main idea or supporting detail and write it on a sticky note. Write a * next to it. Tell students, "Authors often include extra information to make a book interesting. This fact about _____ is an example of something that is not one of the main ideas or details. But we may enjoy knowing about it."

4. Continue skimming the index looking for words that are either main ideas, details, or interesting fun facts.

5. When you have collected four to five sticky notes, stop and continue thinking aloud. Tell students you are going to group the ideas that go together. Group any related words and give a summary using the words.

Guided Practice

6. Have students work in pairs or teams at their tables. Provide sticky notes for them to find and write words from their text that are:

+ main ideas

√ details

* interesting facts

7. Encourage students to go back to the page numbers of each word to reread the actual text where the word is found to help them figure out how to classify the word.

8. Circulate to assist students as they label their words. Model for individuals and teams as necessary.

Variations

- Provide a sheet of paper with three columns for the students to sort their facts. The columns should be labeled main ideas (+), details (√), and interesting facts (*).

- Assign letters of the alphabet so tables can study and label all the words that go with certain letters. (e.g., a table may be assigned the A–D words to go over)

- Provide a limited number of sticky notes in three different sizes or three different colors and let students skim the entire index hunting for main ideas, details, and interesting facts.

Independent Practice

9. Have students work alone or in pairs to collect words that are part of main ideas, supporting details, or fun facts. Have students record their words and complete the *Index It!* activity sheet. (See Figure 4.17 and Appendix B.)

English Language Learner Support

Distribute sticky notes in different sizes. Use the larger notes for main ideas and smaller ones for supporting details. Use even smaller ones for interesting facts. As students take turns and share one of their selected index words, have them use the frames, *"This word is _____. I learned _____ about it on page _____."*

Wrap-Up

10. Ask students why the index is useful before, during, and after reading. For some of the words selected in the lesson, guide students to explain why they think those words are the main idea, supporting details, or just interesting facts. Use frames such as:

- "I think the word _____ is a main idea word because _____." (Possible responses include: The author gave us many pages on it. The word appears in the major headings, chapters, illustrations.)

- "I think the word _____ is a supporting detail word because _____." (Possible responses include: The word is found on pages with the main ideas. It is not featured as much as the main idea. It is a part of the main idea.)

- "I think the word _____ is an interesting fact because _____." (Possible responses include: The author only mentioned it once. It was put it in a sidebar. It is just found in an illustration. It is not a main idea or supporting detail.)

Assessment

Observe the words students are collecting for the three categories. Are students experiencing difficulties identifying which words are related to main ideas? Do you need to meet with some students in small groups to model and practice finding main ideas and important details?

Figure 4.17 Index It!

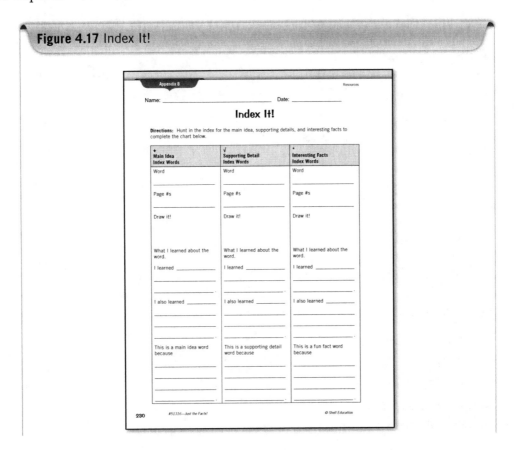

Favorite Words of the Day: Using the Index to Review Content

Objectives/Standards

Use the index to review concepts learned from the text; make inferences about which words might be the author's favorites and tell why; interpret words and phrases as they are used in a text, including determining technical, connotative, and figurative meanings, and analyze how specific word choices shape meaning or tone (CCSS); determine the meaning of general academic and domain-specific words and phrases (CCSS); know and use various text features to locate key facts or information in a text efficiently (CCSS)

Materials

- informational text
- *Favorite Index Word Awards* (See Appendix B)
- scratch paper

Teacher Model

1. Tell students that the index is important to use for finding the pages of favorite topics or topics of interest in the reading. Using an index from a familiar text, select a word to use to model for students by saying, "I am going to flip through the index to see if there are any words I enjoyed learning about. Here is the word _____ that is one of my favorites from this text. I am going to turn to the page(s) that it is on and reread to remember what I learned about it."

2. Turn to the page(s), skim the text, and encourage students to do the same with you, using their copies of the text. Then, tell one or two things you will remember about the word.

3. Select another word and repeat step 2. ***Optional:*** Write the word and either sketch or write a sentence about what you learned about the word.

Guided Practice

4. Ask students to review the index and when you signal, have them point to a favorite word from the text. Invite students to turn to a partner and share why they selected this word. "_____ *is one of my favorite words in the text because* _____."

5. Tell students to look up the pages that correspond with their words and sketch or write a sentence about the word and what it means.

   Variation 1: Have students work in teams, taking turns sharing their words with team members by acting out the word and then asking the other students to guess which word they are enacting. Students may give clues such as, "My word begins with the letter _____."

© Shell Education

Variation 2: Hold a word of the day contest. Have students work with others at their tables or in teams and select one word to be their group nominee for class favorite word of the day. The team must also come up with at least two reasons why their word should be number one and present their argument to the class. After each team presents their word choice, have the class vote on just one word as the winner.

Independent Practice

6. Have students find four words they find interesting and write or sketch about them. Students may use the *Favorite Index Word Awards* organizer to complete this part of the lesson. (See Figure 4.18 and Appendix B.)

Wrap-Up

7. Have students turn and talk with partners about why it is important to be able to pick topics from the index and share about them. Ask students questions such as, "What is hard about summarizing your topic? How does rereading and looking up the pages help? What words do you think the author would say are his or her favorite and why do you think that?"

English Language Learner Support

Encourage students to use the following frame to help them talk about their favorite words: *"I thought learning about the word ____ was interesting because ____."*

Assessment

Observe whether students can select words they liked learning about and then give reasons why they thought those words were interesting. Coach and give examples, if necessary. Allow students to share so they can learn from one another as well.

Figure 4.18 Favorite Index Word Awards

Resources   Appendix B

Name: _____   Date: _____

Favorite Index Word Awards

Directions: Choose your four favorite words from the index to complete the chart below. Put the words in order with #1 as your very favorite.

#1 Word	#3 Word
The Favorite Word Award goes to	The Favorite Word Award goes to
because	because
Draw the word.	Draw the word.
#2 Word	#4 Word
The Favorite Word Award goes to	The Favorite Word Award goes to
because	because
Draw the word.	Draw the word.

© Shell Education   #51316—Just the Facts!   231

Wrap-Up and Reflection

Text features are the hallmarks of informational text. Text features such as visuals, graphics, headings, tables of contents, glossaries, and indices are uniquely designed to support the reader's comprehension throughout the reading process. Unfortunately, many of our students gloss over text features, or skip them completely! When we teach students to pause and pay attention to text features, their comprehension improves (Lubliner 2001; Recht and Leslie 1988). Engaging students in explicit instruction and lessons on the various text features helps them to see the value of these features and to use them more effectively in their reading.

Here are some key ideas to think about from this chapter:

- The table of contents holds many opportunities for meaningful lessons that can be taught throughout the reading process including before reading, to anticipate content and organization as well as set a purpose for reading, during reading to ask questions and wonder, and after reading to summarize.

- Headings provide a rich source for lessons that teach students by showing students how to pause throughout the reading to consider the author's purpose for each section of the text, ask relevant text-based questions, clarify words and unclear phrases, and summarize content for each section of material.

- Text features including visuals such as photos, maps, charts, diagrams, and graphs present endless opportunities for lessons where students judge and evaluate visuals. Students should be able to discuss the following: what each visual in the text does for the content, why the author included the visual, and how helpful the visual was or was not to the reader.

- Diving into the glossary and index before, during, and after reading offers students ways to explore rich and interesting vocabulary. From admitting that one doesn't know a given word to choosing a favorite glossary word to dramatize or sketch, the glossary and index provide endless opportunities for instruction.

Reflect and Discuss

1. Discuss how text features impact student comprehension of informational text.

2. How does studying the table of contents aid students in their comprehension?

3. Name five important text features that are found in informational texts and tell how each one helps the reader. What are some ways to teach students about each of these?

Chapter 5

Interactive Strategy Lessons For Informational Text

Comprehension Strategies for the Common Core Standards

Students need a toolbox of flexible strategies to employ as they make their way through a variety of challenging informational texts. The research-based list of comprehension strategies (Dole, Duffy, Roehler and Pearson 1991; Pressley 1997; Keene and Zimmerman 1997) that educators rely on includes inferring/predicting, asking questions, clarifying, summarizing, synthesizing, and evaluating. Classrooms in the age of Common Core State Standards still incorporate this proven set of strategies to unlock deeper meanings in a variety of increasingly complex texts. Organizing strategies around the updated thinking in the Common Core provides a new framework for the familiar proven strategies. By modeling using strong mentor texts and interactive think alouds, teachers scaffold the reading experience and then provide support for use of comprehension strategies in cooperative guided practice. The many options for engagement and independent practice along with solid suggestions for working with second-language students and struggling readers make these lessons practical and fun! Student comprehension will improve as they work in teams to *Text Walk This Way*, play text structure bingo in *Building Inspection*! or judge informational texts for their content in *Compare it! Contrast it!* Filled with many rich options, these lessons are designed to use over and over again all year long with complex informational texts.

Page	Setting a Purpose for Reading Informational Text Lessons
147	Purpose, Purpose, What's the Author's Purpose?
151	Purpose, Purpose, What's My Purpose?
155	Text Walk This Way!
	Key Ideas and Details Lessons
159	Wonder Walk, Wonder Wall
162	Interview Show
165	(QBTTT) Question Back to the Text

Purpose, Purpose, What's the Author's Purpose?

Students need to understand that when they predict with informational text, they need to consider why the author wrote the book. Consider looking up author information on book jackets or online to see what authors share about their reasons for writing their books, articles, and other texts.

Objectives

Students will preview an informational text and consider the author's purpose and also identify whether the author set out to either inform, persuade, or entertain the reader; assess how point of view or purpose shapes the content and style of a text (CCSS); read closely to determine what the text says explicitly and to make logical inferences from it (CCSS); cite specific textual evidence when writing or speaking to support conclusions drawn from the text; identify the main purpose of a text, including what the author wants to answer, explain, or describe (CCSS); determine an author's point of view or purpose in a text and explain how it is conveyed in the text (CCSS)

Materials

- informational text
- *Purpose, Purpose, What's the Author's Purpose?* (See Appendix B)
- real or pretend microphone (optional)

Teacher Model

1. Explain to students that authors of informational texts write for a reason. Give examples by holding up texts students have read recently or that are appropriate for your grade level. You can do this over the course of a few days or in a "blitz" of examples in one lesson for older students. Or ask students to hunt through their grade level and independent reading materials for examples of all three types of texts. Use the information in Figure 5.1 for support.

Figure 5.1 Informational Texts and Author's Purpose

Explain	Examples	Sample Mentor Text
describe explain answer tell how explain steps	how a seed grows into a tree, or how a bill becomes a law	**Primary** *A Rainforest Habitat* by Molly Aloian and Bobbie Kalman *The Boy Who Drew Birds: A Story of John James Audubon* by Jacqueline David **Intermediate** *Great White Sharks* by Josh Gregory *Volcano Rising* by Elizabeth Rusch
Persuade	**Examples**	**Mentor Text**
convince point of view share sides to an issue give evidence argue	a persuasive essay or article on recycling or composting that shares reasons for trying the practice	**Primary** *The Great Kapok Tree* by Lynne Cherry *Should We Have Pets?* by Sylvia Lollis **Intermediate** *The Librarian of Basra: A True Story from Iraq* by J. Winter *Everglades* by Jean George
Entertain	**Examples**	**Mentor text**
more narrative story like	a true account of what happened to a dolphin or turtle, or a biography about someone famous such as Helen Keller	**Primary** *Ice Bear* by Nicola Davies *Out on the Prairie* by Donna Bateman **Intermediate** *The Star-Spangled Banner* by Peter Spier *Insectopedia* by Douglas Florian

2. Tell students that you want to share an informational text with them so that together you can figure out what the author's purpose was and answer these questions. ***Optional:*** Share the hand gestures to go with each question. Invite students to join in with them as they repeat the questions.

   • Why did the author write the text? (Gesture: Pretend to write with a pen in the air.)

   • What does the author want us to learn? (Gesture: Put hands together with palms up to make a "book," and gesture to pass the information by moving hands away from the body as if to give something away.)

   • What does the author think about the topic? How do you know? (Gesture: Point to head or tap head gently while looking pensive.)

3. Display the text you are modeling from (students may have a copy) and conduct a think-aloud to predict the author's purpose as you read aloud. Skim through the text first discussing what you see in the headings, illustrations, etc. Predict the author's purpose using any or all of the following prompts.

   • **Why did the author write the text?** Say, "I see _____ and _____ so I think the author wrote this to (pick one: inform, persuade, entertain) the reader." Share evidence for your response.

   • **What does the author want us to learn?** Say, "The author wants us to learn _____. I can tell that because I see _____ and _____." Give examples of how text is organized and what the author is conveying.

   • **What does the author think about the topic? How do we know?** Say, "I can tell the author believes _____ about the topic of _____ because he or she includes _____ on page _____."

4. Encourage older students to read the text silently first before you read it aloud. Read a portion or all of the text aloud if it is brief. Pause along the way and think aloud about your predictions regarding the author's purposes. When you are done reading the selection, return to the three questions and share evidence from the text.

- Why did the author write the text?

- What does the author want us to learn?

- What does the author think about the topic _____ and how do we know?

Guided Practice

5. Have students play a role play game where one is the interviewer and the other acts as the author of a text. Invite a student to help you model before having students do this on their own. The student may role-play as the author. Ask the questions below as the student answers from the perspective of the author. *Optional:* Rather than put the student on the spot, you may ask students to talk to partners first to answer each question and then have the student "author" respond. If he or she is stuck they may call on another student to help. You may wish to use a real or pretend microphone in the interview, or have students use their fists or pencils as pretend microphones.

- Why did you write this text?

- What did you want us to learn?

- Why is this important?

- How did you accomplish this goal in the text?

- Give examples of what you think you did well in this text.

- What is your opinion of the topic _____?

Check for Understanding

6. Read aloud either from texts or examples like those provided in Figure 5.1 (or make up your own fictitious ones to fit your grade level!) and ask students what the author's purpose is: to inform, persuade, or entertain. Have students hold up one finger for inform, two for persuade, and three for entertain. Or you might post three signs in different parts of the room that say *inform, persuade, entertain* and have students walk to the signs to indicate their understanding of the author's purpose.

Struggling Reader Support

Select a text to read with a group of students who need extra support. Together, use the hand gestures to signal the categories of author's purposes including inform, entertain, and persuade.

Independent Practice

7. As students read informational texts have them reflect on the author's purpose before, during, and after reading. They may work independently or with partners to complete the *Purpose, Purpose, What's the Author's Purpose?* organizer (See Figure 5.2 and Appendix B). Then, have students work in pairs to role play as the author to share their responses.

Wrap-Up

8. Review the three main questions about the author. Discuss which question was the easiest or hardest to answer. Which was most helpful? Why?

Assessment

Observe students as they analyze the author's purpose in the various options suggested in this lesson. If students express difficulty with one part of the lesson such as the independent organizer, try teaching students in a small group using the gestures and discussion only. Do they need extra support in understanding how to categorize the author's purposes to inform, entertain, and persuade? Bring in more examples to share.

Figure 5.2 Purpose, Purpose What's the Author's Purpose?

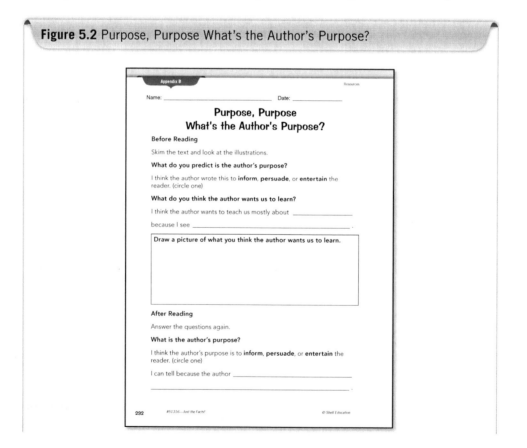

Purpose, Purpose, What's My Purpose?

Students love it when you bring in your reading material from home to demonstrate and model reading strategies. This lesson's teacher modeling will be a hit if you do just that. Look around your home (and car!) grabbing informational text. Maybe even have a family member videotape you as you share where the texts were found and why you need each one.

Objective/Standards

Identify possible reasons and purposes for reading informational texts; assess how point of view or purpose shapes the content and style of a text (CCSS); read closely to determine what the text says explicitly and to make logical inferences from it (CCSS); cite specific textual evidence when writing or speaking to support conclusions drawn from the text (CCSS)

Materials

- informational text
- *What's My Purpose?* (See Appendix B)
- *What's My Purpose? Bookmark* (See Appendix B)
- sticky notes

Teacher Model

1. Explain that good readers often read informational text for a purpose or reason. Give quick examples from your own life using informational texts such as maps, recipe books, computer manuals, newspapers, internet searches, etc. If possible, bring texts to hold up or show on your computer.

2. Tell students, "We read informational texts for different purposes such as to answer questions, learn how to do something, learn more about a particular topic so we can present it or write a report, or to learn general information then narrow down what we want to learn about a topic or to study a viewpoint on a topic. Once I figure out my purpose, then I decide how closely I need to read the text."

3. Share the frames below as possible comments on purposes for reading:

- Why am I reading this book? What is my overall purpose?
- I had a question about _____, so I read _____.
- I wanted to know more about the entire topic of _____, so I read _____. That helped me to choose the smaller topic of _____ to focus on.
- I needed to _____ so I read _____.
- I wanted to find out what _____ said about _____.
- I just wanted to read about _____ for enjoyment because _____.

4. Select one text at a time to model setting a purpose for reading. This lesson can be conducted over a few days and you can model from several different types of texts. The guided practice section of the lesson includes ways for students to practice

setting purposes that go with each type of text. Select a text from your adult reading or from the grade level and use the following prompts to model each one.

- **To learn how to do something:** *I am going to read a manual that explains how to _____. I want to know this because I have to (or want to) _____.* Read part or all of the text aloud to students. After reading, tell whether the text met your purpose for reading it.

- **To answer a question:** *I want to read* (book, article, etc.) *_____ because I have to (or want to) find out _____.* Read part or all of the text aloud to students. After reading, tell whether the text met your purpose for reading it.

- **To "do" something with the information:** *I am giving a report* (taking a test, or writing a letter, writing a report, giving a presentation or making a video, or writing a blog, putting on a play, etc.) *on the topic _____ so I am reading to find out information to use in my presentation.*

- **To choose a topic:** *I want to try to learn about the topic _____ but it is too broad and too much information to learn all at once. I need to choose just part of the topic to study so I will read this _____ to figure out what part of the topic is most interesting to me so I can read more about that in other texts.* Read part or all of the text aloud to students. After reading, tell whether the text met your purpose for reading it.

- **To study a point of view:** *I wanted to know what _____ thought or found out about the topic _____. How does this point of view fit into what other sources say about _____?* Read part or all of the text aloud to students. After reading, tell whether the text met your purpose for reading it.

- **To read just for pleasure:** *I think it would be fun to read about _____. It looks like something I'd enjoy reading. It caught my eye because _____.* Read part or all of the text aloud to students. After reading, tell whether the text met your purpose for reading it.

Guided Practice

5. Hold up sample texts and share your purpose for reading each one. *Note:* The texts may be from your own reading (articles, books, manuals, etc.) or reading from the grade level texts including content-area textbooks and high interest informational articles or magazines. Simply use what you have to model a variety of purposes.

6. Display and number each of the sample purposes (from step 4) and ask students to discuss with a partner what purpose goes with your response. They each hold up a finger to indicate the purpose.

7. Hold up or show, or just mention a book or article about dogs or another topic you are interested in. Say, *"I am interested in reading this to learn about my hobby, training a dog to do tricks. What is my purpose?"*

8. Continue using one or all of the prompts below to go with texts/purposes. Mention articles from newspapers, online sources, and other texts.

- I am wondering about _____. What's my purpose?

© Shell Education

- I am reading this general article or book on _____ so I can figure out what aspect or part I want to read more about. What's my purpose?

- I am reading this to find out what _____ thinks about the topic of _____. What's my purpose?

- I am reading _____ to learn about the topic of _____, which I have always loved! What's my purpose?

- I am reading this _____ about _____ so when I am done I can (make, write, share, report, blog, etc.) _____. What is my purpose?

9. Distribute a variety of informational texts onto desks or the student's tables. Ask students to work with a partner and select a text that looks interesting to them. As they text walk through the pictures, ask pairs to think about which purpose fits the text best (see step 4).

Independent Practice

10. Have students work in pairs or alone to complete the *What's My Purpose?* organizer (See Figure 5.3). They may use the content-area textbook, basal reader, leveled texts, or other books from the school or classroom library. You may also want to provide magazine articles and other high-interest materials for students to use to practice setting purposes for reading. Also, give students the *What's My Purpose?* bookmark to use during lessons as you discuss informational texts (See Figure 5.4). Students use the prompts to discuss their book choices with partners and their teams. They may write in their book logs which purpose they have for reading their independent-choice books.

Struggling Reader Support

Meet with students and model how to read for one of the purposes, such as answering questions. As a group, skim over the pages and visuals and come up with something the group is wondering. Give pairs of students sticky notes and ask them to read to find out the answer. You may assign different pages to each pair or they can all read the same pages. Discuss. Read either another text or another portion of the text you used for questions and select a new purpose for reading to model and practice.

Wrap-Up

11. Discuss with students any or all of the following reflective questions:

- Why it is important to know what purpose one has for reading informational texts?

- Is there a particular purpose they use more than others?

- What is the relationship between one's purpose and how closely one reads the text?

- Do we sometimes have more than one purpose for reading informational text? When? Why?

- Can one enjoy reading for all the purposes? Why? How?

- How can we make reading informational texts we are required to read in school for more interesting purposes than just learning for a test?

Assessment

Observe students as they participate in the partner discussions during the guided practice. Are they able to identify the purpose for reading with each text or example shared? Also, observe students as they use the *What's My Purpose?* organizer and the *What's My Purpose? Bookmark* to reflect on their purposes for reading informational texts. Continue providing examples of your own in whole class and small group settings.

Figure 5.3 What's My Purpose?

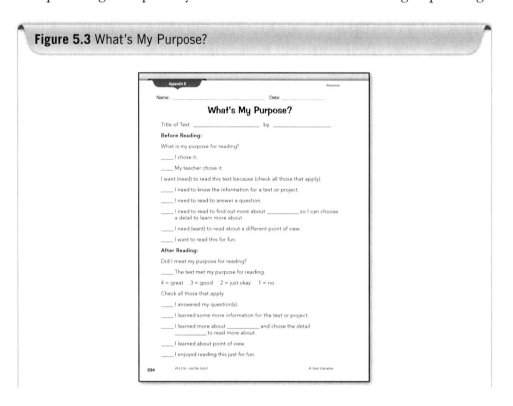

Figure 5.4 What's My Purpose? Bookmark

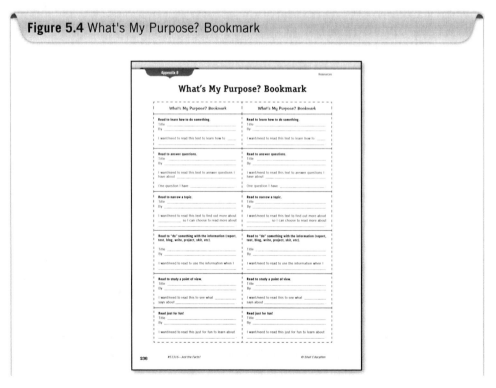

Text Walk This Way!

The saying, "Walk this way," a line from Mel Brook's 1974 classic hit comedy movie *Young Frankenstein*, was adapted for the title of this lesson. Lead a quick walk around the classroom or playground walking in different ways: skipping, lumbering, dancing, hopping, etc. Then, share that there are different ways to "walk" through a text as well that include a "quick flip" or a "slow look" depending upon your purpose for reading the text.

Objective/Standards

Preview a text by "walking" through the pages and skimming the visuals, headings, and text for a variety of purposes; read closely to determine what the text says explicitly and to make logical inferences (CCSS); ask and answer questions to demonstrate understanding of a text (CCSS); integrate and evaluate content presented in diverse media and formats, including visually and quantitatively, as well as in words (CCSS); know and use various text features to locate key facts or information in a text efficiently (CCSS)

Materials

- informational text
- *Text Walk This Way Group Discussion Bookmark* (See Appendix B)
- *Text Walk This Way: My Own Bookmark* (See Appendix B)

Teacher Model

1. Explain that when good readers read informational texts, they often flip through the text (or online they scroll through a text) before actually reading it word for word. This is called taking a "text walk" before reading and resembles a "picture walk" except when reading an informational text, the reader also studies the text features such as headings and bold words.

2. Tell students that text walking before reading helps us understand and better remember what we read in an informational text. A good reader may text walk multiple times for different reasons before settling in to read the text all the way through.

3. Choose an informational text to model from and provide copies for students. Display the text so everyone can see as you demonstrate. Text walk three times using the following language frames as guides.

   - **First Text Walk—What I Think I Know Already…** Say, "Watch me as I page through the text. My first text walk is going to be quick as I flip through the text to see what I already know about the topic." As you page through say, "I think I already know…" and share some facts you already know. Ask students to work with partners and use the frame *I think I know…* as they quickly page through and skim the text looking for what they may already know about the topic.

- **Second Text Walk—Text Features: I Think I Will Learn...** Say, "As I go through the text this time I am going to go slower and identify each text feature and tell what I think I will learn from it." As you text walk, pause on each feature to study and make predictions/infer using the frame, "I think I will learn _____ in/from this _____ because...." Have students work in pairs and take turns pausing on each text feature (heading, visual, etc.) to identify the feature and tell what they think they will learn about in that portion of text. "The text feature _____ shows (says) _____ so I think we will learn _____."

- **Third Text Walk—What I Want to Know: I wonder...** Share, "As I flip through the pages this time my text walk will focus on what I want to know about the topic of _____ and what I am wondering." Page through again and share a few of your wonderings and questions. Then, have students work in pairs with the same text and walk through the text a second time to share what they want to know about the text. They may use the frame "I wonder _____." Or "My question about _____ is (what, when, where, why, how,) _____."

Guided Practice

4. Guide the class to go on three text walks using a text all students have a copy of. Students may work in pairs or teams of four, taking turns as they text walk using the jobs below:

- **Text Walker #1** walks by skimming for what the group knows already.

- **Text Walker #2** walks, pausing through the text identifying text features to determine/predict what the group will learn by reading the text.

- **Text Walker #3** walks to preview the text a final time before reading to determine what questions the group has about the text.

- **Final Text Checker #4** walks through the text after reading to help evaluate the learning and the text features that helped the readers the most.

English Language Learner Support

Work with students in a small group. Practice as a group just one of the text walking jobs (1, 2, 3, or 4) together. Focus on modeling for students and on asking students to use the various sentence frames in this lesson to guide their oral responses. **Option:** You may ask students to text walk several different ways while assisting a younger student in another class to practice text walking with an easier text and to role play as a "teacher" or tutor. Debrief the experience as a group. What was easy, hard, or the most fun? How did text walking help the younger student understand the material better?

Independent Practice

5. Have students use the *Text Walk This Way: Group Discussion Bookmark* to read with a partner (See Figure 5.5 and Appendix B). Students may practice using the *Text Walk This Way: My Own Bookmark* on their own with a text you assign or text of their choice (See Figure 5.6 and Appendix B). Conference with students and ask them to choose one or more of the text walks to demonstrate for you.

Wrap-Up

6. Poll students and ask them which of the text walks—1, 2, 3 or 4—is their favorite to participate in, and share why. Which text walk is most helpful or least helpful? Why?

Assessment

Observe students as they work in their teams and pairs to see if they are text walking and using the text clues to stick to what the text says. Also, collect student responses on the *Text Walk This Way: My Own Bookmark* and form small groups based on which of the text walks (1, 2, 3, or 4) students need help with. Model for groups and ask students to work in pairs to practice each type of text walk.

Figure 5.5 Text Walk This Way: Group Discussion Bookmark

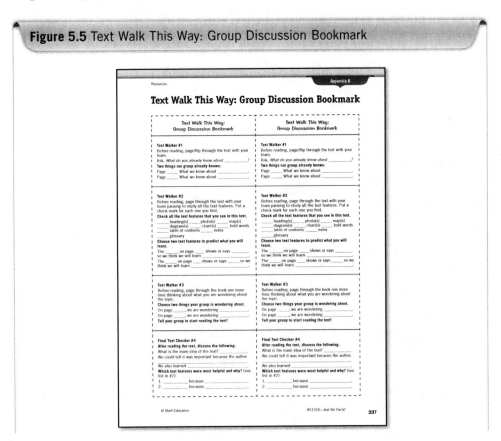

Figure 5.6 Text Walk This Way: My Own Bookmark

Text Walk This Way: My Own Bookmark

Text Walk This Way: My Own Bookmark	Text Walk This Way: My Own Bookmark
Text Walk #1 Before reading, quickly flip through the text. What do I already know? Page _____ I know about _____ Page _____ I know about _____	**Text Walk #1** Before reading, quickly flip through the text. What do I already know? Page _____ I know about _____ Page _____ I know about _____
Text Walk #2 Before reading, page through the text pausing to study all the text features. Check all the text features that you see in this text. _____ heading(s) _____ photo(s) _____ map(s) _____ diagram(s) _____ chart(s) _____ bold words _____ table of contents _____ index _____ glossary **Choose two text features to predict what you will learn.** The _____ on page _____ shows or says _____ so I think I will learn _____ The _____ on page _____ shows or says _____ so I think I will learn _____	**Text Walk #2** Before reading, page through the text pausing to study all the text features. Check all the text features that you see in this text. _____ heading(s) _____ photo(s) _____ map(s) _____ diagram(s) _____ chart(s) _____ bold words _____ table of contents _____ index _____ glossary **Choose two text features to predict what you will learn.** The _____ on page _____ shows or says _____ so I think I will learn _____ The _____ on page _____ shows or says _____ so I think I will learn _____
Text Walk #3 Before reading, page through the book one more time thinking about what you are wondering about the topic. **Choose two things you are wondering about.** On page _____, I am wondering _____ On page _____, I am wondering _____ **Start reading the text!**	**Text Walk #3** Before reading, page through the book one more time thinking about what you are wondering about the topic. **Choose two things you are wondering about.** On page _____, I am wondering _____ On page _____, I am wondering _____ **Start reading the text!**
Final Text Check #4 After reading the text, answer the following: The main idea was _____ I could tell it was important because the author _____ I also learned _____ **Which text features were most helpful and why?** (see list in #2) 1. The _____ on page _____ was helpful because _____ 2. The _____ on page _____ was helpful because _____	**Final Text Check #4** After reading the text, answer the following: The main idea was _____ I could tell it was important because the author _____ I also learned _____ **Which text features were most helpful and why?** (see list in #2) 1. The _____ on page _____ was helpful because _____ 2. The _____ on page _____ was helpful because _____

Wonder Walk, Wonder Wall

If you ask students to share questions they have about a topic, they often shut down because when they hear the word "question" they think we are looking for a right answer. When you ask students what they are wondering about a particular topic, the thinking opens up and they share more openly. (Adapted from Murphy 2009; Oczkus 2004.)

Objective/Standards

Ask questions and add to a wonder wall throughout the reading process; read closely to determine what the text says explicitly and to make logical inferences (CCSS); ask and answer questions to demonstrate understanding of a text (CCSS); integrate and evaluate content presented in diverse media and formats, including visually and quantitatively, as well as in words (CCSS); know and use various text features to locate key facts or information in a text efficiently (CCSS)

Materials

- informational text
- *My Wonders* (See Appendix B)
- chart paper
- sticky notes

Teacher Model

1. Tell students that asking questions is the hallmark or sign of a good reader. Good readers often ask questions that start with, *"I wonder…."* Wondering helps keep the reader interested and focused on the text.

2. Post a chart with the words I WONDER at the top. This will become the Wonder Wall.

3. Using an informational text that students also have a copy of, ask them to look at the title and spend just a few minutes flipping through the book. Have students return to the beginning of the text and watch as you model how to "wonder walk" through a text. Glance at photos, headings, etc. on each page and say things like, "Hmm, I wonder how the…, I wonder why…, or I wonder if…."

4. Record several of your "wonders" on sticky notes and place them on the Wonder Wall.

5. Read a small portion of the text and share what you are wondering now. Add to the Wonder Wall. Tell students that good readers wonder the entire time they are reading. Not all of their wonders will be answered in the text and that is acceptable.

Guided Practice

6. Invite students to turn to a partner to try a "wonder walk" and as they skim the headings and visuals, they repeat the phrase, "I wonder…" on each page.

7. Ask pairs of students to put one of their wonders and the page number on a sticky note and to bring it to the Wonder Wall or collect them for the Wonder Wall.

8. As a group, sort the wonders into categories for the topic. Guide students to find larger main ideas verses smaller supporting ideas. Refer back to the text to show how one can tell which ideas are more important by using headings and other text features.

9. Read more text with students. Then, ask them to share wonders with their partners and invite some students to add their questions to the Wonder Wall.

Struggling Reader Support

Distribute sticky notes, one per student. Assign one page or one visual or heading on a page and ask the student to write a wonder to go with it. Guide students by helping them decide if an I wonder who, what, when, where, or why fits the page best. Or try reading a small portion of text and pausing for students to share wonders with the group or in partners. Select some of the wonders to answer after reading.

Independent Practice

10. Have students write wonders before reading and throughout reading at various natural stopping points. Encourage students to add to the wonders they already came up with or to think of new ones. Students can use the *My Wonders* organizer to record their wonders through the reading process (See Figure 5.7 and Appendix B).

11. Instruct students to share their wonders with partners or in teams.

Wrap-Up

12. Ask students to reflect upon how wondering helps them to better understand the texts they read. What is easy and hard about wondering? How does talking to others about your wonders aide in understanding the text?

Assessment

Observe students in pairs and working independently as they pause to wonder. Do their wonders make sense? Are they text-based on big ideas, only trivia, or based on their background knowledge? What do you need to model next to ensure students are thinking deeply and asking good questions?

Figure 5.7 My Wonders

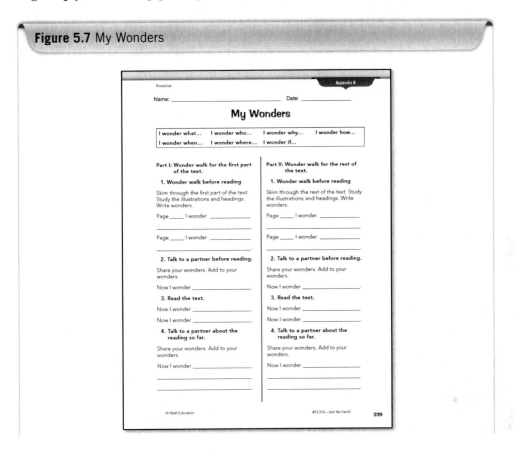

Interview Show

Students see microphones and interviews on television on a regular basis and are motivated when we run mock interviews using either real or fake microphones. When you want them to dig deeper, think critically, and infer meaning, try role-playing interviews about nonfiction topics. Be sure to conduct this lesson on a regular basis so students become more proficient in questioning the text. (Adapted from *Pop the Question*, Oczkus 2010)

Objective/Standards

Create questions about the text after reading in order to role play characters and objects from an informational text; read closely to determine what the text says explicitly and to make logical inferences (CCSS); ask and answer questions to demonstrate understanding of a text (CCSS)

Materials

- informational text
- *Interview Show* (See Appendix B)
- toy or real microphone (optional)
- camera (optional)

Teacher Model

1. Tell students that good readers ask questions when they read and that today the students will role-play to ask and answer questions. *Optional:* Use a toy or real microphone. You may also want to use a camera and record students as they participate.

2. Select an informational text that students have copies of. Ask them to silently read the first portion of text. Tell students that you will reread the text aloud to them and that you will pause when you see a place where you might ask an interview question of someone or something in the text.

3. Begin reading. Read a few paragraphs and pause. Tell the student, "Lets ask the _____ (object, or person) a question. I am rereading to figure out what I want to ask."

4. Reread the text in front of the students as you create your question. Ask students in the class to turn to a partner to answer the question you just posed. Then model the answer. You may want to role-play as the object or person as you answer.

5. Invite a student up to the front of the room. Tell students, "You are the _____ (character or object) in the text." You may wish to put a label for the student to hold. Use a real or pretend microphone (or your fist as a pretend microphone) and ask the student some questions such as, "Why did you _____?" or "What does _____?"

6. Ask the class to turn and answer the question with a partner, going back to the text as they formulate their answers. Then, guide the volunteer as he or she answers the question in front of the group.

Guided Practice

7. Have students work in pairs as they read another portion of text and take turns being the interviewer or the person in the text or object. You can choose to indicate how far the students should read (e.g., page, paragraph, section).

8. Circulate as students role play and guide them back to the text to formulate answers. Help students create strong questions that do not have a yes or no answer as well as reasonable answers.

9. Invite volunteers to perform their interviews for the class. **Optional Stroll Line:** Place students in two lines facing one another. Have students bring their text with them in line. Tell one of the rows of students that they are the character or object. The other row of students is the interviewers. Have students take turns asking and answering questions. When you cue them (ring a bell, play music, clap hands) one of the lines takes a step to the left and the student at the front of the line goes to the back (on the outside of the row) so that they now have new partners to interview. You can choose to provide the questions or students can create their own.

Independent Practice

10. Have students work independently to create questions to go with the text. Allow them to use the *Interview Show* organizer to record their questions as well as sketch their answers and provide page numbers from the text where the answers are found (See Figure 5.8 and Appendix B).

Wrap-Up

11. Have students share which portions of text were most difficult to create questions for and which questions were most difficult to answer. How does rereading and discussion help when asking and answering questions?

Assessment

Observe the types of questions students are asking each other. Do you need to model for small groups how to ask or answer questions?

Struggling Reader Support

Model how to read a portion of text and create a strong question to ask. To scaffold the language of questioning, provide students with two to three word question starters such as Why did you _____? or How does the _____?

Figure 5.8 Interview Show

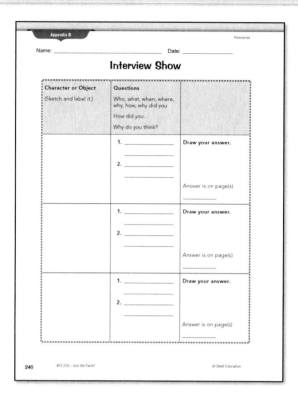

QBTTT (Question Back to the Text)

Asking text-dependent and evidence-based questions land on our top list of "must teach" lessons. Why not make it fun so that the learning will stick? Students will stay engaged as they use the optional hand gestures to point to the text, try out the question starters, or toss questions in the paper wad activity.

Objective/Standards

Study the text and answer and discuss text-dependent questions that require returning to the text for answers; read closely to determine what the text says explicitly and to make logical inferences (CCSS); ask and answer questions to demonstrate understanding of a text (CCSS); integrate and evaluate content presented in diverse media and formats, including visually and quantitatively, as well as in words (CCSS)

Materials

- informational text
- *QBTTT (Question Back To The Text) Bookmark* (See Appendix B)
- sentence strips
- index cards

Teacher Model

1. Explain to students that good readers ask questions throughout the reading process. Tell students that today they will practice the art of reading for the purpose of asking and answering questions by returning to the book for evidence. **Optional hand gesture:** Draw a question mark in the air (say Q—QUESTION), and then point to the book three to four times (chant BTTT—Back to the text!).

2. Display an informational text and provide students with copies. Choose just one paragraph or a few select sentences to use to model how to ask and answer text-dependent questions. Ask students to read the paragraph or sentences silently, first. Then, read the selected portion of the text aloud to the students as they follow along.

3. Say, "Watch me while I use the text to help me as I ask and answer questions by going back to the book. (Use the hand gesture from step 1.) I am going to choose just a few sentences to read and then make up a question to go with what I just read."

4. Read aloud a few sentences. Use the following list of question starters and give reasons for which one you think fits best.

Turn a heading into a question using who, what, when, where, or why?

- Read a sentence. Ask a question using a word that fits—who, what, when, where, why, how?

- Ask a question about a paragraph, page, map, or photograph.

- What do you think the author means by (word, sentence, passage) _____? What are some examples?

- Why did the author use the word _____?

- What can you learn about _____ by reading this? Give examples.

- What part of the text was confusing? (choose a word, sentence, or paragraph)

- Why did the author include the (caption, map, other text feature) _____?

- What did the author want us to understand or know about the topic _____? Give evidence.

- What was the author's purpose for writing this text? (inform, persuade, entertain) Give evidence.

Guided Practice

5. Select the next portion of the text (a sentence or two) and encourage students to read silently first. Then, choose one of the QBTTT Starters for students to work in partners to create a question using that starter. For example, all students work in pairs to create a question using the starter *Why did the author use the word _____?* for a word they select from the text.

English Language Learner Support

Select one or two sentences from the text and one of the QBTTT Starters. Use the hand gesture from step one as students take turns asking and answering questions using the text. Consider putting several of the QBTTT Starters on sentence strips and allow students to choose one to use. Or write them on index cards and put them in your hand for students to "draw" one. Ask students to point to exact sentences in the text for their evidence and answers. Every time a student asks a question as a group, point to the text and whisper chant, "Back to the Text!"

6. Have students work in pairs to read the text and select their own sentences as they create text-based questions. You can assign one of the QBTTT Starters for all students to use or you can allow them to choose. Students may also use the *QBTTT Bookmark* (See Figure 5.9) to guide them through creating their own questions.

7. Circulate and assist students as they ask their questions of one another and return to the text for the answers. Be sure students are cueing one another to return to the text to figure out answers.

Independent Practice

8. Have students work independently to read and then ask text-dependent questions. Allow students to share their questions with classmates in fun formats including:
Stroll Line: place students in two lines facing

one another. Have students bring their best question and the text with them in line. Have students take turns asking and answering questions. When you cue them (ring a bell, play music, clap hands), one of the lines takes a step to the left and the student at the front of the line goes to the back. Then, students ask their question of their new partner.

Paper Wad and Toss: Divide students into groups of four and have them read and share their questions and answers from their independent work. They select just one question and write it on a paper, wad it up, and when you signal, they toss (not throw) it at another table. You can also choose to indicate which table each team will toss to. The receiving team opens the text-based question and answers it using evidence from the text.

Wrap-Up

9. Ask students to think about why it is important to ask and answer questions when they read informational text. How does going back to the text help you understand the text better? What is hard or easy about asking and answering text-dependent questions?

Assessment

Observe students' text-based questions and answers. Which question starters are easiest or most difficult to prompt their thinking? Work with small groups to help students come up with better text-based questions, if needed.

Figure 5.9 QBTTT Bookmark

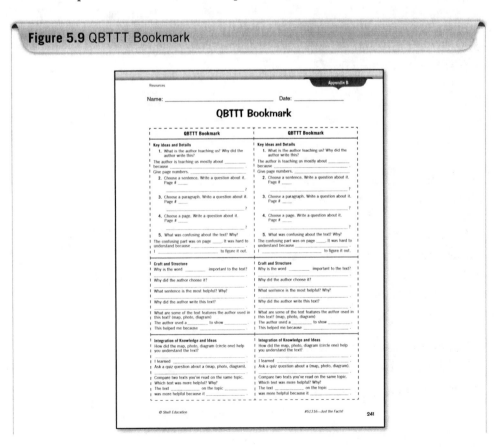

Building Inspection! Identifying Informational Text Structures

Understanding text structures unlocks nonfiction texts for our students. This lesson is designed to teach over and over using a variety of text examples all year long. Collect examples of the different text structures all year long and create a chart listing them or displaying them in your room. *Note:* This lesson includes some brief texts to use to get you started. However, it will be most meaningful if you use your own classroom materials in subsequent lessons.

Objective/Standard

Read informational text and identify which text structures are included in the text; analyze the structure of texts, including how specific sentences, paragraphs, and larger portions of the text relate to each other and the whole (CCSS)

Materials

- informational texts with different text structures
- *Bingo Card* (See Appendix B)
- sticky notes
- dry-erase board

Teacher Model

1. Explain to students that buildings have different shapes and structures both inside and out. With your finger in the air sketch the shape of the school or home where you live. Or, sketch the shape of a building on the board. Ask students to turn to a partner and, in the air, sketch a building they know such as the school, their home or apartment building, or a store.

2. Tell students that just like buildings, texts also have a structure or are built around a frame. The author of an informational text uses sometimes just one structure to build with, or sometimes uses more than one on different pages/sections of the text.

3. Use a variety of texts (see step 4 for examples) to give students an overview of informational text structures. You may choose to take several days to give students examples of each of the types of text structures. For older students, point out and find examples of multiple organizers in the same book. For example, a social studies chapter may contain a few pages explaining an event in chronological order, then another page with the causes and effects of one event. Each heading or topic may signal a new organization.

4. Read each text aloud while students follow along.

   - **Content-area texts**—Use your content-area textbooks, such as science, social studies, health, or mathematics.

   - **Weekly newspapers**—If you subscribe to a weekly newspaper or monthly magazine for your class, the short articles make great examples of short informational texts that you can use to study text structures. (examples:

Time for Kids Nonfiction, Weekly Reader®, Scholastic News®, National Geographic)

- **Basal anthology**—If your school district has adopted a reading basal anthology, it may contain texts from which you can use the informational text selections for this lesson.

- **Leveled texts**—Leveled texts make great sources for studying text structures.

- **Mentor Texts**—See the list of informational mentor texts in Chapter 2.

Option: Build a chart for text structures. Use the sample texts provided plus ones you and your students find in your classroom texts. Use the *Building Inspection* organizer to support the understanding of the types of text (See Figure 5.10 and Appendix B). This can be made into a class chart.

Figure 5.10 Building Inspection! Examples of Informational Text Structures

Text Structure	Example Circle the clue words in each example.
Description The author explains a topic and lists examples. **Clue Words:** for example, in addition to, most important, another, such as, has, have, in fact	
Time Order Sequence The author lists events or the topic in order. **Clue Words:** first, next, then, finally, before, after that, not long after	
Problem/Solution the author explains a problem and solutions. **Clue Words:** The problem is, solve, a question is…, one answer is, one reason is, the puzzle is	
Compare/Contrast The author explains how two or more topics are alike/different. **Clue Words:** **Compare Words** same as, alike, not only but also, either or, similar to, compared with, as well as, likewise **Contrast Words** different from, in contrast to, less than, instead of, however, while	
Cause /Effect The author explains why or how something happens. **Clue Words:** because, since, if, then, so that, for this reason, because of, consequently, in order to	

Guided Practice

Here are several suggestions for guided practice:

- **Building Inspection:** After you show students one of the informational text graphic organizers, types of words, and clue words, have students use their own version of the *Building Inspection!* organizer to underline the clue words in each example.

- **Text Organizer Hunt:** Have students work in pairs or teams to hunt in the classroom for informational texts to add to their versions of the *Building Inspection!* organizer.

- **Informational Text Desk Dump!** Once all of the text types and organizers have been shared using the examples given or mentor texts, you may wish to participate in an informational text "dump" by giving a pile of informational books to groups of four to six students. Students use sticky notes to label examples they find of the various types of informational text.

- **Guessing Game:** Check for understanding by playing a guessing game where you read aloud from an informational text. Have students sketch on a dry-erase board the graphic organizer that goes with the text structure. Then, have students turn to partners to discuss and share the "answer."

- **Informational Text Bingo:** Have students play BINGO with text organizers. The teacher or another student reads aloud from an informational text. The students must figure out which type of text it is and place a game chip on the correct graphic organizer. Play continues until someone has three in a row or the complete card filled in and raises their hand to say "Info Bingo!" See Appendix B for a blank BINGO board. Create boards for this game by drawing graphic organizers that represent the various text structures.

English Language Learner Support

In a small-group setting, review the organizers for informational text. Teach students to sketch the organizers in the air with their fingers.

Independent Practice

5. Have students identify text types as they read by participating in an additional guided practice activity. Or students can read just one text and complete the corresponding graphic organizer that goes with that text structure.

Wrap-Up

6. Discuss with students the importance of identifying informational text structures. Do students prefer a certain type of organizer? Which is the easiest to identify? Hardest? Which are the easiest/hardest to understand? Which text structure seems to be the most common in the texts they read?

Assessment

Observe students in a variety of settings as they identify informational text organizers. Can they read a text and tell you which one it is? If not, further model and show students more examples.

Looking In and Around Tricky Words!

Many students only use one strategy at a time to figure out words. In this lesson, students benefit from looking both in and around words to figure them out. For younger students, bring in different pairs of funky glasses to make the point about "seeing" and "clarifying" words.

Objective/Standard

Experience different strategies for figuring out words by looking within the words for word parts and at the context around the words; interpret words and phrases as they are used in a text, including determining technical, connotative, and figurative meanings, and analyze how specific word choices shape meaning or tone (CCSS)

Materials

- informational text
- *Tricky Words* (See Appendix B) or a piece of paper
- chart paper
- sticky notes

Teacher Model

1. Explain to students that informational texts often contain many tricky words. It is helpful to know strategies for looking within the words as well as around the words to figure them out. **Optional hand signal:** Have students hold up an index finger and point for "in the word" and have them make a circle with their index fingers for "around the word."

2. Choose an informational text. Provide copies for students and display the text so students can see your modeling. Ask students to read silently a portion of the text and to be on the lookout for tricky words. If students tell you there are no tricky words and that they know them all, ask them to find words that a younger student (name a grade level below yours) would not know.

3. Model looking "in" the word. Pause your reading when you come to a challenging word in the text. Tell students, "This word is tricky. I will try looking within the word first." Demonstrate how to:

   - look for the largest chunk you know (prefix, suffix, base word, or word family)

   - look from left to right at sounds you know (what does the word begin and end with?)

   - try to figure out the word using syllables

   - look at the visuals

   - put the word together and say it

4. Model looking "around" the word. Tell students, "I am going to look around the word for clues to figuring it out." Demonstrate how to:

   - reread

   - look at the words before the tricky word

   - look at the words after the tricky word

   - read the sentences before and after the word

   - substitute a word of similar meaning (optional)

   - look the word up in the glossary

5. Select one or two more words from the text and model how to look in and around the word to figure out what it means.

Guided Practice

6. Read more of the text and pause on a tricky word for students to work in pairs to figure out.

7. Discuss whether they used more of the looking "in" the word strategies or "around" the word strategies.

8. Read more of the text aloud and invite students to raise their hands when they hear a tricky word they'd like to pause to figure out. Invite students to work in pairs to either all figure out the same word, or choose different words to figure out. Then, have students share which "in" and "around" strategies they used to figure out the word.

9. Have students work in pairs or teams to find at least two more tricky words and prepare to share with the class what strategies they used to figure them out. Encourage students to use at least two strategies per word.

10. Use chart paper to make a class tally (See Figure 5.11) of strategies used for in and around words. Which strategies are students relying on most? Which do they need to try?

Figure 5.11 Class Tally Chart

Look for chunks you know.	Look at the beginning sound.	Say the word.	Look it up in the glossary.
Look at syllables.	Look at the ending sound.	Ask a friend.	Put in a word that means the same thing.

Reread the sentence from the start.	Read on a few sentences after the word.	What is another word that makes sense here?	Use the glossary.
Look at the words around the tricky word.	Look at the picture, map, diagram, etc.	Reread a few sentences that are before the word.	Ask a friend.

Independent Practice

11. Have students read informational texts and keep track of tricky words and ways to figure them out. Students can use the bookmark as a reference tool.

12. Ask students to fold a paper into four boxes (or divide with pencil) and record tricky words or you could choose to use the *Tricky Words* activity sheet (See Figure 5.12). Have students tell which of the bookmark strategies helped the most with each word.

Struggling Reader Support

Invite students who need extra support to work with you to find words that are tricky, and to find two strategies for figuring out each one.

Wrap-Up

13. Discuss with students their favorite strategies for figuring out tricky words. What strategies are ones they need to try next? Ask students to set a goal and share it with a partner. "I want to try to use one new 'inside' the word strategy and one 'around' the word strategy. Those strategies are _____ and _____."

Assessment

Observe students as they figure out tricky words and encourage them to use a variety of both inside the word and around the word strategies. Keep a record of which strategies students are using and coach them on ones they need to try. Model for small groups and individuals, when necessary.

Figure 5.12 Tricky Words

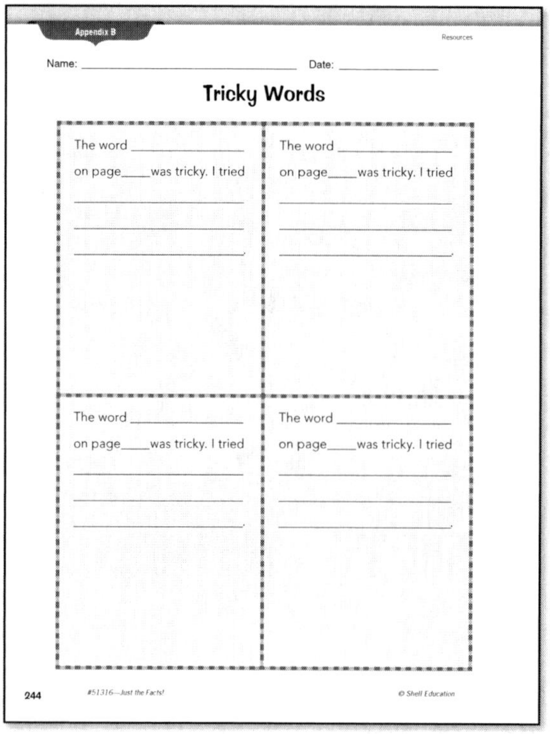
Appendix B Resources

Name: ______________________________ Date: ______________

Tricky Words

The word ______________ on page____was tricky. I tried ______________ ______________ ______________.	The word ______________ on page____was tricky. I tried ______________ ______________ ______________.
The word ______________ on page____was tricky. I tried ______________ ______________ ______________.	The word ______________ on page____was tricky. I tried ______________ ______________ ______________.

244 #51316—Just the Facts! © Shell Education

Picture This!

Visualizing while reading informational texts requires concentration, rereading, and paying close attention to key words and details. Invite students to be on the lookout all day long for strong sensory images in their reading (adapted from Mind Movie, Murphy 2009).

Objective/Standards

Identify words, sentences, and passages that evoke mental images while reading informational text; read closely to determine what the text says explicitly and to make logical inferences from it (CCSS); cite specific textual evidence when writing or speaking to support conclusions drawn from the text (CCSS); interpret words and phrases as they are used in a text, including determining technical, connotative, and figurative meanings, and analyze how specific word choices shape meaning or tone (CCSS)

Materials

- informational text
- *Picture This!* (See Appendix B)
- chart paper
- sticky notes or index cards
- sentence strips

Teacher Model   1.   Explain to students that informational texts use photos and other visuals to help us picture the topic. Authors also help us see a "mind movie " in our heads using words, sentences, and passages that help us to experience the reading using our senses.

2. Choose an informational text. Provide copies for students and display the text so students can see your modeling.

3. Tell students you will show them how to use their "mind cameras" to read informational text and build pictures in their heads. Share a passage from the selected text by reading it aloud. Pause when you encounter a descriptive sentence such as 'Leafcutter ants use their sharp mandibles to chew plant leaves into small pieces and carry them to the nest.' (from TCM Time for Kids Nonfiction) Reread the sentence and use a think-aloud to describe what you see in your "mind camera."

4. Copy the descriptive sentence onto chart paper. Underline or highlight two or three words that helped you "see" a picture of the topic in your head. (In the example from step three, the descriptive words are chew, carry, and next.) Say, "I am underlining the word _____ because I can see the _____." (Repeat for each word selected.)

Guided Practice

5. Ask students to close their eyes to try to see the topic in their heads as you read the next portion of text. Invite students to turn to a partner and tell one word that helped them "see" a mind picture or movie.

6. Distribute index cards or sticky notes for students to sketch what they just heard from the text. Encourage them to reread the text. Older students may copy the sentence or passage and underline the words that helped them visualize.

7. Invite students to find one more example of a descriptive sentence in the text and copy it on a card or sticky note. Then, have them underline at least two to three key words that helped them visualize the most, and then share them with a partner.

8. Ask individual volunteers to share one of the words they thought evoked visual images. Invite other students who also chose that word to stand up. Call on other volunteers to share their words and again invite the class to stand up if they too choose that word.

Independent Practice

English Language Learner Support

Select a sentence for students to study. Ask them to visualize each key word. Make up gestures for some of the words. Invite students to sketch pictures and share which of the words are their favorites and which they think are the strongest. Write some of the sentences on strips or the board and ask students to underline or highlight the strongest words for mental images. Pass out the key words on cards and have students act them out. Play "which word am I acting out" and have other students guess.

9. Have students read informational texts and collect sentences that evoke visual images. Then, have them identify which words are the strongest for making mental images and give reasons for their selections. Students may also rank their choices.

Wrap-Up

10. Discuss how visualizing or making mind pictures is helpful when reading informational texts. Ask students to rank the first, second, and third most helpful words for mental images and tell why.

Assessment

Circulate and observe as students select sentences and underline passages or words. Are they able to select important ideas? Can they tell which words matter most and why? As students read to you, can they identify words and sentences that evoke images?

Figure 5.13 Picture This!

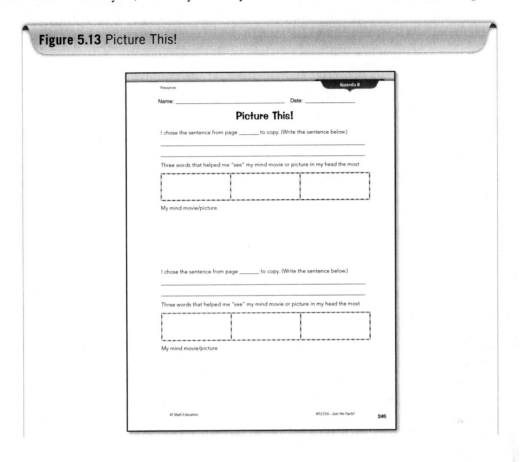

Sample Lessons

Presto Change-o: Say It in Your Own Words

Paraphrasing is challenging for students. Try taking small chunks of text to paraphrase and summarize. The "Presto Change-o" term helps students remember what to do as they hunt for ways to repeat the message of the text "in other words." Provide students with lots of examples and be sure to make some examples "good" and others "not so good" so that students can give you a thumbs up or thumbs down for paraphrasing and summarizing.

Objective/Standard

Learn and practice summarizing portions of text by paraphrasing what the text says and putting their summary into their own words while maintaining the meaning of the text; determine central ideas or themes of a text and analyze their development; summarize the key supporting details and ideas (CCSS)

Materials

- informational text
- *Presto Change-o* (See Appendix B)
- *Presto Combine-o* (See Appendix B)
- index cards or sticky notes
- drawing paper

Teacher Model

1. Explain to students that paraphrasing is rewording a part or all of a text while stating its meaning in another way. When we paraphrase, we often reread a few times, think about the meaning of the text as we look away, and then summarize in our own words. Say, "Putting the author's ideas in my own words or substituting different words can help me better understand and remember what I read."

2. Ask a volunteer to come up and tell what he or she did over the weekend, or about a favorite sport or activity. Retell the student's account in just a sentence or two. Ask students if what you said was the same or not. What did you do? (possible responses: used different words, made it shorter) Tell students, "When we paraphrase or summarize, we change the words the author said and keep the meaning, but we do not copy exactly what the author said."

3. Select a sentence or passage from an informational text that you can display and provide students copies as well. Read the selection aloud. Then say, "I am going to read it again to get the idea of what the author is saying. Now, I am going to cover it with my hand and not look at the text while I try to say the same thing in my own words." Give your example. You may wish to write down your paraphrased version.

4. Repeat step 3 with another example. This time give a "not so great" example where you barely change the text or you leave out main ideas or copy the original text exactly.

5. In subsequent lessons, you may choose to model paraphrasing using these ideas:

Focus on changing key words—Copy a sentence from a text or a short passage. Underline the key words. Cross out the key words and put synonyms in their place. Cover the passage with your hand and write a new version using your words. Be careful not to just change one or two words but to make it sound different. For younger students, use the phrase, *presto, change-o!* as you underline key words, cross them out, and come up with new words that mean the same thing. You might want to use a pointer or a wand to point to the words as you go through this process.

Make it shorter—Read a paragraph or two and write a one-sentence summary to recap the main ideas. Show how to combine sentences and ideas by using one's own words.

Guided Practice

6. Invite students to work in pairs to try summarizing and paraphrasing small portions of the text. Provide index cards or sticky notes for students to write their sentences on. Or provide index cards with sentences copied from the text on them.

7. Have students underline key words in the sentence and replace those words with synonyms. Then, have them sketch a drawing to go with the sentence. Finally, have students turn the cards over to rewrite the sentence. Then, turn the card back to check their work. Students can use the *Presto Change-o* activity sheet for support.

8. As an alternative, have students copy one or two more sentences from the text while crossing out words and writing synonyms above the words. Then, have students reread their "new " sentences and cover up the entire text to recite their new paraphrased version. Students can use the *Presto Combine-o* activity sheet for support (See Figure 5.14 and Appendix B).

Independent Practice

9. Observe students as they change words in sentences to synonyms and as they combine sentences to summarize. Meet with students in small groups to model and construct verbal and written examples.

10. As an extension, have students play Sketch It and Guess, where they read a page (without revealing which page it is) and sketch a picture with symbols to summarize the text. A partner has to guess which page is represented and give a verbal summary or paraphrase the text. The artist confirms and shows the correct page that goes with his or her sketch.

Struggling Reader Support

Try this activity in a small group with students who are struggling with summarizing and paraphrasing. Be sure to also participate and model for the group. Focus on using synonyms, rereading, and making the summary shorter than the actual text by combining ideas.

Wrap-Up

11. Ask students to summarize the steps to paraphrasing—read, reread, cover the text, remember what you read, and say it in your own words. Ask students to tell what is hard/easy about doing this. What activities in the lesson did they enjoy most?

Assessment

Observe students as they first substitute words with synonyms and then as they combine sentences. Are they experiencing trouble with remembering key ideas and words? If needed, try using the various suggestions in the lesson with small groups to promote more practice. Use the *Presto Change-o* organizer repeatedly for a few weeks until students begin to paraphrase more naturally.

Figure 5.14 Presto Change-o

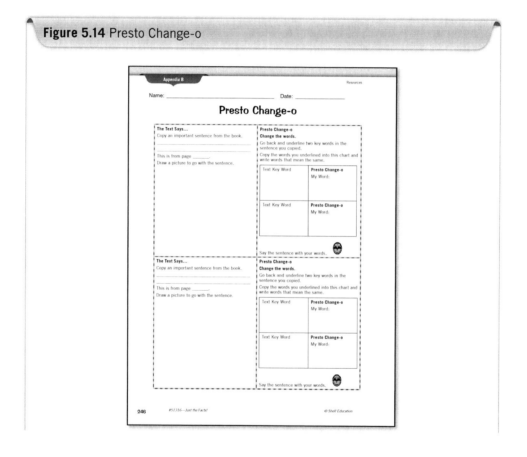

Figure 5.15 Presto Combine-o

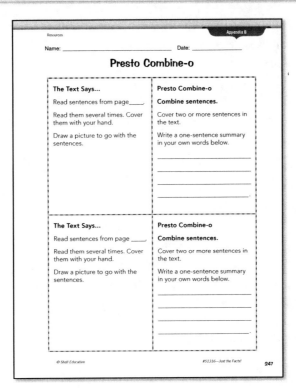

Show the Evidence!

Students already know how to argue and defend claims with reasons or evidence. They lobby to eat a snack *because* they didn't have one yet today, or to stay up late *because* they finished homework early, or to pawn their turn to empty the trash onto a sibling *because* he or she hasn't done his share. Kids today are "mini-attorneys" at work all day long, presenting evidence for their cases. My youngest daughter wrote "Why I Need a Dog" for her fifth-grade persuasive essay, and after years of hounding (excuse the pun!) us, her father and I caved. Your students will enjoy studying authors' claims, arguments, and statements, and defending them with solid evidence from the text.

Objective/Standard

Study an author's claim, idea, opinion, or argument and defend it with evidence from the text; delineate and evaluate the argument and specific claims in a text, including the validity of the reasoning as well as the relevance and sufficiency of the evidence (CCSS)

Materials

- informational text
- *Show the Evidence Bookmark* (See Appendix B)
- chart or board

Teacher Model

1. Tell students that in this lesson they will learn how to do something they are already pretty good at. Ask students if they know what it means to argue. Share the following scenario: You want to go to your friend's house. Your mom says, "No, you have to do your homework!" What reasons or evidence can you give that might convince her to let you go?

2. Ask students to respond in complete sentences to a partner "I think you should let me go to my friend's house because…" Possible student responses might include: I finished my homework; The homework is not due until the next day; We will do homework at the friend's house. **Optional "because" hand gesture:** Students may make a fist and pound it in their other hand to stand for the word *"because"* as they share evidence throughout the lesson.

3. Tell students that while they try to convince their parents at home by sharing reasons for something they want, authors in their informational texts also attempt to convince readers using evidence.

4. Model reading aloud a page from a high interest text such as *Animals Nobody Loves* by Seymour Simon (2001) or an interesting article. Select a page to read to the students and project the text so the students can see it. Focus on a claim that the author makes such as "The rat is the animal that many people dislike the most." (Simon 2001, 28). The author includes evidence that people dislike rats by allowing the reader to make some inferences about the abundance and persistence of rats, their sharp teeth, their presence in rich and poor neighborhoods alike, and their dirtiness that spreads disease, including the Bubonic plague.

5. Write the following sentence frame on a chart or the board: *The author says that _____ because _____*. Tell students that the author shares this claim or statement and then provides evidence in the text to prove it. Then, record several reasons found in the text and point to where the reasons or evidence is located in the text.

6. As an option, share how to infer a claim in this lesson or in a subsequent lesson. Explain to students that sometimes the author does not come out and explicitly make a claim—the reader has to infer it. Say, "Watch me infer with the statement, 'I can tell that the author believes (thinks, feels, etc.) because _____.'"

Guided Practice

Use any of the following suggestions for guided practice:

- **Partners Find Evidence**: Read aloud a main idea statement or claim from an informational text. Ask students to work with partners to find the evidence in the text to back the claim. Students may repeat the frame, "The author says that _____ because _____." (List several reasons found in the text.)

- **Page Teams:** Invite students to work in teams to find other examples in the text of statements, arguments, or claims and evidence to back them. Assign different pages to each team and have them prepare to show text evidence either by rewriting it, underlining and highlighting, or by showing the text on a projector.

- **Stroll Line:** Place students in two lines facing one another. Have students bring their copies of the text with them. Tell one of the rows of students that they are to read a statement from the text. The other row of students gives the *"because"* or the evidence from the text. When you cue students (ring a bell, play music, clap hands), one of the lines takes a step to the left and the student at the front of the line goes to the back. The lines switch roles and the process repeats. You can provide the questions for the partners or they can create their own.

Independent Practice

7. Ask students to use their *Show the Evidence Bookmark* as they find evidence in the text (See Figure 5.16 and Appendix B). They may write their responses directly on the bookmark or in a notebook. Meet with small groups or circulate to tables to practice and guide.

English Language Learner Support

Use the "because" hand gesture as a concrete symbol for the word *because* as students give evidence from the text. Ask students, "How do you know?" as you guide their explanations. Provide extra language support with additional textual evidence starters such as: The author says _____ because _____; On page _____, it said _____; The map, diagram, chart showed _____; An example is _____.

Wrap-Up

8. Discuss with the class what they learned about finding authors' claims and giving evidence from the text. Does it help to know who the author is and his or her background when considering the text? What was their favorite piece of evidence? How do the starters help? How does the hand gesture help?

Assessment

Are students able to find the author's claims or infer them? Can students provide evidence to go with the author's claims? If needed, meet with small groups to demonstrate using additional texts. Provide copies of pages from texts so students can underline main ideas and claims in one color and evidence in another.

Figure 5.16 Show the Evidence Bookmark

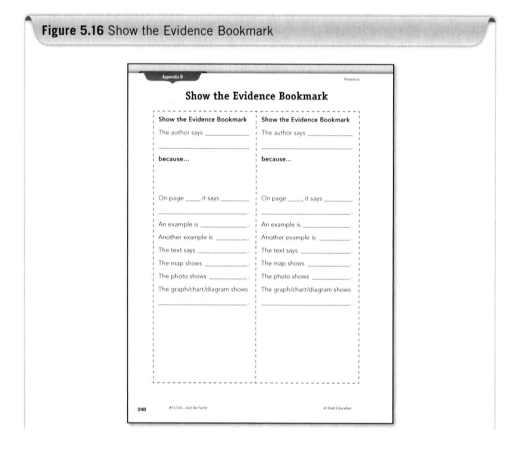

Where'd You Get It—T or V? (Text or Visuals?)

Some students only glance at the visuals in a text, and they do not think about what the visuals contribute to the author's entire message. Try making a classroom chart with two categories, visuals and text, at the top and allow students to list examples and page numbers.

Objective/Standards

Reflect on the text and summarize the information learned and concluded from reading the text and the visuals; analyze the structure of texts, including how specific sentences, paragraphs, and larger portions of the text relate to each other and the whole (CCSS); integrate and evaluate content presented in diverse media and formats, including visually and quantitatively, as well as in words (CCSS); use information gained from illustrations (maps, photographs) and the words in a text to demonstrate understanding of the text (CCSS)

Materials

- informational text that includes several visuals

- *Where'd You Get It—Text or Visuals?* (See Appendix B)

- chart

Teacher Model

1. Select an informational text that includes several visuals (photos, diagrams, charts, maps, etc.). Display the text on a screen and provide copies for students.

2. Share with students that when authors write informational text they include visuals to help convey some of the information they want the reader to learn. Ask students to tell a partner what some of these visuals might include (e.g., photos, diagrams, charts, maps). Discuss briefly with the class. You may wish to list the student responses on a chart.

3. Preview or text walk a few pages from the informational text you've selected. Share your predictions using comments that will encourage students to use text evidence such as the following examples:

   - I think I will learn _____ from this part of the text _____ because the heading says _____ and the chapter is about _____.

   - I think I will learn _____ from this visual (photo, diagram, chart, map, etc.) because the title/caption says _____ and I see _____.

4. Encourage students to read the text silently first. Then, read aloud from a page or two of the text. After reading, summarize what you learned from the T-text and V-visuals. Also, share what both had in common. Use the following sentence structure for your summary: The most important points I learned from the text are _____, _____, and _____ (show where in the text). I also learned _____ from the visual _____ (show where in the text). Together, from both I learned _____.

Guided Practice

5. Select another page of the text or another text. Ask students to work in pairs to figure out what they can learn from the T (text) and the V (visuals). Circulate to assist students as they do so. Be sure to have them point to the evidence in the text.

Struggling Reader Support

Invite students to work with you in a small group. Select a page of text and assign a sentence, paragraph, or visual to each student in the group. Using the following starters, ask students to tell what they learned and to show the evidence.

- I learned _____ from the text because it says _____.

- I learned _____ from the visual because it shows _____.

- On page _____ it says _____ so I know that _____.

- The author says _____.

- The graphic (photo, map, etc.) shows _____ so this means _____.

Optional: Put the starters on the board and number them 1–5 with 6 for free choice. Using a number cube, allow students to roll the cube and then use that starter to find an example on the page.

6. Allow students to work in pairs or teams to select pages from the text. Ask them to share their "evidence" for what they learned or concluded from both the visuals as well as the text. Invite teams to share.

Independent Practice

7. Have students use the *Where'd You Get It –Text or Visuals?* organizer to select pages from a text and tell what they learned, backed by evidence.

Wrap-Up

8. Discuss whether the visuals or the text was most helpful and why. Which visuals were most helpful? Did the visuals add to the information in the text, by illustrating it? Or did the visuals add more detail or new information that is important to the topic?

Assessment

Observe students as they make claims, infer, and summarize using evidence from the text and visuals. Are they stating the obvious or using critical thinking to infer deeper themes and ideas from the text and visual evidence?

Figure 5.17 Where'd You Get It—Text or Visuals?

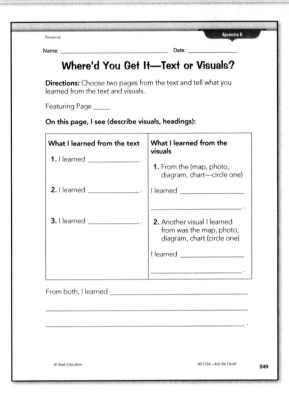

Compare It! Contrast It! Rating Informational Texts

Good readers synthesize across texts and evaluate the information they learn from each of them every day. With the wealth of online information available today, it is essential that students learn how to evaluate and compare texts.

Objective/Standards

Read text and compare and contrast the information as well as the effectiveness of texts on the same topic; analyze how two or more texts address similar themes or topics in order to build knowledge or to compare the approaches the authors take (CCSS); compare and contrast the most important points and key details presented in two texts on the same topic (CCSS)

Materials

- informational text
- *Compare It! Contrast It!* (See Appendix B)
- chart paper
- sticky notes or index cards

Teacher Model

1. Tell students that when good readers research topics, they often need to read information from more than one source. Give an example of a time where you needed information and read two sources either online or in books. Tell how you used both sources to help you gain the information you needed. Ask students if they have ever done the same—used more than one source for information.

2. Explain to students that when we use two or more sources we compare and contrast the two books or articles as we think about which one was more useful. We might use information from both or from one—however, the text is most helpful.

3. Select two texts on the same topic to model from. You may want to use a high-interest topic such as animal training or a sport. Read a portion of one of the texts aloud. Or, if the texts are brief, read both of them. Create a chart that will help evaluate what you learned from each text (use *Compare It, Contrast It!* as a guide).

4. Show both texts and briefly skim through them. Share one question you have about your topic or something you want to know. Involve students by asking them to turn and tell a partner what questions they have about your topic after you model yours. Write your question at the top of the chart.

   Text #1—Read the portion of text that may answer your question. Write your answer.

   Text #2—Read the portion of text that may answer your question. Write your answer.

Share what else you learned by reading each text. What did you learn from each one that was NOT in the other? How would you rate each text? Which was the best? *Optional:* Model again using another question.

Guided Practice

5. Using the two texts you just modeled from, guide students to ask a question that they can research in both texts. Have students work with a partner or table teams to fill in a simple chart, such as what is shown below (or use an index card.)

Text #1	Answer to our question
	_____
	_____
Text #2	Answer to our question
	_____
	_____

Which text was most helpful in answering your question?

Why?

_____

_____

_____

_____

Options:

Table or Partner Book Switch: The class discusses one thing they want to know about or a question they want answered about the topic. Give each team just one of the two texts that the class is reading. The entire class researches the answer to the same question but teams use different books. Teams share what they learned. Tables switch books and hunt for the same question in a different book.

Partner Switch: Two students each read a different book to find the answer to the same question or a "what we want to know" issue. When the teacher signals "record," the pair stops reading and records their answers on a sticky note or on an index card. When the teacher signals "switch," the students swap books and read for the same question or issue in the different text. When the teacher signals "record," the students flip their index card and write their responses for the second text on the other side. Have students discuss which text they found most helpful for answering their question.

Independent Practice

6. Provide students with two texts on the same topic to compare/contrast. If you have limited copies, give half the students one title and half the other, and swap at some point.

7. Students may think of a topic they are interested in and use two texts for research. They should use the *Compare It! Contrast It!* organizer to record their questions, answers, and evaluation of the texts (See Figure 5.18 and Appendix B).

Wrap-Up

8. Discuss what students enjoy about evaluating and using two texts to research a topic. What did they learn? How can they use this information when they research other topics?

Assessment

Observe students as they work together and alone to research topic questions and find answers in two or more texts. Do they experience difficulty finding a topic question or finding the answers? Can they compare the usefulness of a text in answering their questions?

Struggling Reader Tips:

Work with struggling readers in a small group. Guide the students to come up with something they are wondering about a topic after picture walking through a text so that their wonders will stick closer to the text. Use the frames "I wonder" (why, how, when, where, who, what), and ask students what they see in the text that makes them wonder about that. Guide students to read for their question. Discuss whether the text answered their question in detail or not. Give the text a score on a scale of 1-3 for how it addressed their wonder.

Figure 5.18 Compare It! Contrast It!

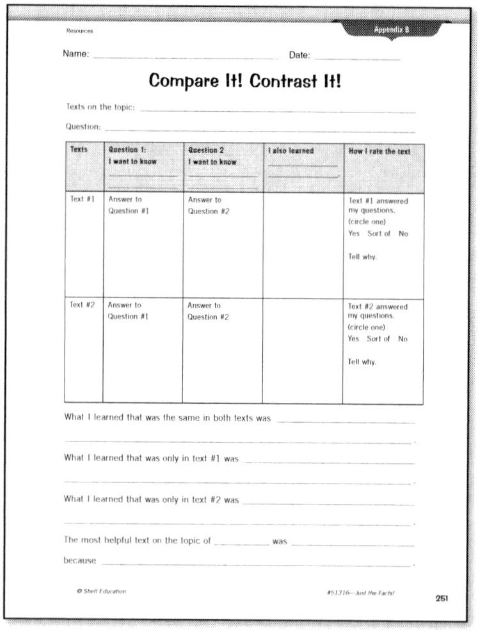
Resources

Appendix B

Name: ______ Date: ______

Compare It! Contrast It!

Texts on the topic: ______

Question: ______

Texts	Question 1: I want to know	Question 2 I want to know	I also learned	How I rate the text
Text #1	Answer to Question #1	Answer to Question #2		Text #1 answered my questions. (circle one) Yes Sort of No Tell why.
Text #2	Answer to Question #1	Answer to Question #2		Text #2 answered my questions. (circle one) Yes Sort of No Tell why.

What I learned that was the same in both texts was ______.

What I learned that was only in text #1 was ______.

What I learned that was only in text #2 was ______.

The most helpful text on the topic of ______ was ______ because ______.

© Shell Education #51316—Just the Facts! 251

Wrap-Up and Reflection

Many schools already strive to teach students to employ the familiar research based on comprehension strategies such as predict/infer, question, monitor/clarify, summarize/synthesize, and evaluate (Dole et al. 1991; Pressley 1997; Keene and Zimmerman 1997). The Common Core State Standards demand a new kind of thinking about comprehension strategies in our classrooms today. By focusing *first* on rich content and *then* using comprehension strategies as proven keys to unlocking informational texts, students are driven to think critically and use their learning to participate in meaningful outcomes such as project-based learning. Comprehension lessons concentrate on guiding students to consider the author's purpose, grasp key ideas and details, study text craft and structure, and integrate knowledge and ideas from a variety of sources.

Here are some key ideas to think about from this chapter:

- Authors of informational text write to inform, persuade, or entertain. Considering author's purpose aides in comprehending informational text.

- The reader's purpose matters, too. Students need to know why they are reading a text, and what they will "do" with the text after reading determines how closely they read.

- Comprehension strategies assist students throughout the reading process (Dole et al. 1991; Pressley 1997; Keene and Zimmerman 1997).

- As students and teachers together ask and answer questions, they consider text evidence in answering their queries.

- Knowledge of text structures helps students to summarize and keep track of the information in texts.

- Teaching students to look "in and around" words teaches them to use decoding and context in figuring out challenging vocabulary in informational texts.

- Visualizing during reading helps students to picture and remember key concepts.

- Summarizing helps students to sort main ideas and details in a logical order.

- Synthesizing across multiple texts guides students in evaluating the value of reading material and coming up with ways to compare and contrast the content.

- Given the wealth of informational text in our world, students need to learn to judge and rate informational texts using a variety of criteria.

Reflect and Discuss

1. How do comprehension strategies help students unlock the content in informational texts? How can you use comprehension strategies as flexible tools during lessons?

2. Why do students need to be aware of the author's purpose? How can you help students to understand the author's purpose?

3. What purposes do readers bring to informational text? How does sharing this information with students help them with their reading?

References Cited

Allington, Richard, L. 2008. *What Really Matters in Response to Intervention: Research-Based Designs.* Upper Saddle River, NJ: Pearson.

———.2011. *What Really Matters for Struggling Readers: Designing Research-Based Programs.* Upper Saddle River, NJ: Pearson.

Allington, Richard L., & Gabriel, R. E. 2012. "Every child, Every day. Educational Leadership" 69 (6): 10-15. Accessed on March 18, 2014. http://www.ascd.org/publications/educational-leadership/mar12/vol69/num06/Every-Child,-Every-Day.aspx.

Allyn, Pam. 2012. *Be Core Ready: Powerful, Effective Steps to Implementing and Achieving the Common Core State Standards.* Upper Saddle River, NJ: Pearson.

Anderson, E. and J.T. Guthrie. 1999 "Motivating Children to Gain Conceptual Knowledge from Text: The Combination of Science Observation and Interesting Texts." Presentation, American Educational Research Association, April.

Anderson, L.W. and D.R. Karthwohl. 2001. *A Taxonomy for Learning, Teaching, and Assessing: A Revision of Bloom's Taxonomy of Educational Objectives.* New York, NY: Longman.

Anderson, Richard C., Paul T. Wilson, and Linda G. Fielding. 1988. "Growth in Reading and How Children Spend Their Time Outside of School." *Reading Research Quarterly* 23: 285–303.

Calkins, Lucy, Mary Ehrenworth, and Christopher Lehman. 2012. *Pathways to the Common Core: Accelerating Achievement.* Portsmouth, NH: Heinemann.

Cappiello, Mary-Ann, and Erika Thulin-Dawes. 2012. *Teaching with Text Sets.* Huntington Beach, CA: Shell Education.

Caswell, Linda J. and Nell K. Duke. 1998. "Non-Narrative as a Catalyst for Literacy Development." *Language Arts* 75: 108–117.

Chall, Jeanne S. 1983. *Stages of Reading Development.* New York, NY: McGraw-Hill.

Cooper, David J., Irene Boschken, Janet McWilliams, and Lynne Pistochini. 2000. *Soar to Success: The Reading Intervention Program.* Boston, MA: Houghton Mifflin.

Dale, Edgar and Jeanne S. Chall. 1948. "A Formula for Predicting Readability." *Educational Research Bulletin* 27 (1): 11–20+28.

Dole, Janice A., Gerald G. Duffy, Laura R. Roehler, and P. David Pearson. 1991. "Moving from the Old to the New: Research on Reading Comprehension Instruction." *Review of Educational Research* 61 (2): 239–264.

Dorfman, L.R. and R. Cappelli. 2009. *Nonfiction Mentor Texts: Teaching Informational Writing Through Children's Literature, K–8.* Portland, ME: Stenhouse.

DRA Level. 2003. Accessed on April 11, 2014. http://www.draoms.com.

Dreher, M. J., and A. Dromsky. 2010 "Increasing the Diversity of Young Children's Independent Reading." Presentation, National Reading Conference.

Duke, Nell K. 2000. "3.6 Minutes per Day: The Scarcity of Informational Texts in First Grade." *Reading Research Quarterly* 35 (2): 202–224.

Duke, Nell K., and V. Susan Bennett-Armistead. 2004. "Nonfiction Reading in the Primary Grades: How and Why It's Good for Young Learners." *Scholastic News Teachers' Edition* 3–4.

Duke, Nell K., V. Susan Bennett-Armistead, and Ebony M. Roberts. 2002. "Incorporating Informational Text in the Primary Grades." In *Comprehensive Reading Instruction Across the Grade Levels* edited by Reading Research Conference and Cathy M. Roller, 40–54. Newark, DE: International Reading Association.

———. 2003. "Bridging the Gap Between Learning to Read and Reading to Learn." In *Literacy and Young Children: Research-Based Practices* edited by Diane M. Barone and Lesley Mandel Morrow, 226–242. New York, NY: Guilford Press.

Duke, Nell K., Samantha Caughlan, Mary Juzwik, and Nicole Martin. 2012. *Reading and Writing Genre with Purpose in K–8 Classrooms.* Portsmouth, NH: Heinemann.

Duke, Nell K. and J. Kays. 1998. "Can I Say 'Once Upon a Time?'": Kindergarten Children Developing Knowledge of Information Book Language. *Early Childhood Research Quarterly.* 13 (2): 295–318.

Emerson, Ralph Waldo. 1901. *In Praise of Books: A Vade Mecum for Book-lovers.* New York, NY: The Perkins Book Company.

Fisher, Douglas, and Nancy Frey. 2007. "Implementing a School Wide Literacy Framework: Improving Achievement in an Urban Elementary School." *The Reading Teacher* 61: 32–45.

———. 2012. "Close Reading In Elementary Schools." *The Reading Teacher* 66 (3): 179–188.

Fisher, Douglas, Nancy Frey, and Diane Lapp. 2012. *Text Complexity: Raising Rigor in Reading.* Newark, DE: International Reading Association.

Flesh-Kincaid. 1975. Accessed March 18, 2014. https://readability-score.com/.

Graves, M.F. 2006. *The Vocabulary Book: Learning and Instruction.* New York, NY: Teachers College Press.

Graves, M.F. and S.M. Watts-Taffe. 2002. *What Research Has To Say About Reading Instruction.* Newark, DE: International Reading Association.

Gurian, Michael. 2001. *Girls and Boys Learn Differently: A Guide for Teachers and Parents*. San Francisco: Jossey-Bass.

Guthrie, John T., Peggy Van Meter, Ann Dacey McCann, Allan Wigfield, Lois Bennett, Carol C. Poundstone, Mary Ellen Rice, Frances M. Faibisch, Brian Hunt, and Ann M. Mitchell. 1996. "Growth in Literacy Engagement: Changes in Motivations and Strategies during Concept-Oriented Reading Instruction." *Reading Research Quarterly* 31 (3): 306–332.

Harvey, Stephanie. 1998. *Nonfiction Matters: Reading, Writing, and Research in Grades 3–8*. Portland, ME: Stenhouse Publishers.

Hattie, John. 2008. *Visible Learning: A Synthesis of Over 800 Meta-Analyses Relating to Achievement*. New York, NY: Routledge.

Heimlich, J.E, and S.D. Pittelman. 1986. *Semantic Mapping: Classroom Applications*. Newark, DE: International Reading Association.

Hess and Harvey. 2010. "Tools for Examing Text Complexity" Accessed on March 18, 2014. http://ndcurriculuminitiative.org/media/common_core/ela/g_ela_3-12_nsd40_text_complex_tool_nciea_3_12_20120629.pdf.

Hoyt, Linda, and Tony Stead 2011. *Explorations in Nonfiction Writing: Grade 2*. Portsmouth, NH: Heinemann.

Jobe, Ron, and Mary Dayton-Sakari. 2002. *Info-Kids: How to Use Nonfiction to Turn Reluctant Readers into Enthusiastic Learners*. Markham, ON: Pembroke.

Kamil, Michael L., and Diane M. Lane. 1998. "Researching the Relation Between Technology and Literacy: An Agenda for the 21st century." In *Handbook of Literacy and Technology: Transformations in a Post-Typographic World* edited by David Reinking, Michael C. McKenna, Linda D. Labbo, and Ronald D. Kieffer, 355–376. Mahwah, NJ: Erlbaum.

Keene, Ellin O., and Susan Zimmerman. 1997. *Mosaic of Thought: Teaching Comprehension in a Reader's Workshop*. Portsmouth, NH: Heinemann.

Kelley, Michelle J., and Nicki Clausen-Grace. 2007. *Comprehension Shouldn't Be Silent: From Strategy Instruction to Student Independence*. Newark, DE: International Reading Association.

Kincaid, Peter J., Robert P. Fishburne, Richard L. Rogers, and Brad S. Chissom. 1975. "Derivation of New Readability Formulas (Automated Readability Index, Fog Count, and Flesch Reading Ease Formula) for Navy Enlisted Personnel." Chief of Naval Technical Training: Naval Air Station Memphis Accessed March 20, 2014. http://www.dtic.mil/dtic/tr/fulltext/u2/a006655. pdf

Krapp, Andreas, Ulrich Schiefele, and Adolf Winteler. 1992. "Interest as a Predictor of Academic Achievement: A Meta-Analysis of Research." In *The Role of Interest in Learning and Development* edited by Ann K. Renninger, Suzanne Hidi, and Andreas Krapp, 183–211. Hillsdale, NJ: Erlbaum.

Lehman, C., and Kate Roberts. 2013. *Falling in Love with Close Reading Lessons for Analyzing Texts and Life*. Portsmouth, NH: Heinemann.

Lexile Framework for Reading. 2014. Accessed on March 18, 2014. http://www.metametricsinc.com/lexile-framework-reading/.

Lipson, M.W. 1996. *Deveploping Skills and Strategies in an Integrated Literature-Based Reading Program*. Boston, MA: Houghton-Mifflin.

Lubliner, Shira. 2001. *A Practical Guide to Reciprocal Teaching*. Bothell, WA: Wright Group/ McGraw-Hill.

Miller, Debbie. 2009. *Reading with Meaning: Teaching Comprehension in the Primary Grades*. Portland, ME: Stenhouse.

Monson, D.L. and S. Sebesta. 1991. *Handbook of Research on the Teaching the English Language*. New York, NY: Macmillan.

Moss, Barbara. 2013. "Ten Essentials for Teaching Informational Texts." *The California Reader* 46 (3): 9–21.

Moss, Barbara, and Terrell A. Young. 2010. *Creating Lifelong Readers Through Independent Reading*. Newark, DE: International Reading Association.

Murphy, Debby. 2009. *You Just Can't Say It Louder: Differentiated Strategies for Comprehending Nonfiction*. Huntington Beach, CA: Shell Education.

National Governors Association Center for Best Practices, Council of Chief State School Officers. 2010. "Common Core State Standards." National Governors Association Center for Best Practices. Accessed on March 18, 2014. http://www.corestandards.org/the-standards.

Ness, Molly. 2011. "Teacher's Uses of and Attitudes Toward Informational Text in K–5 Classrooms." *Reading Psychology* 32 (1): 28–53.

Oczkus, L.D. 2009. *Interactive Think-Aloud Lessons: 25 Surefire Ways to Engage Students and Improve Comprehension*. New York, NY: Scholastic.

———. 2010. *Reciprocal Teaching at Work: Powerful Strategies and Lessons for Improving Reading Comprehension (2nd Edition)*. Newark, DE: International Reading Association.

———. 2012. *Best Ever Literacy Survival Tips: 72 Lessons You Can't Teach Without*. Newark, DE: International Reading Association.

Opitz, Michael. 1998. *Flexible Grouping in Reading: Practical Ways to Help All Students Become Stronger Readers*. New York, NY: Scholastic.

Palincsar, Annemarie Sullivan. 1986. "The Role of Dialogue in Providing Scaffolded Instruction." *Educational Psychologist* 21 (1 and 2): 73–98.

Park, Y. H. "Does Purpose of Reading Matter?" Presentation, American Educational Research Association, 2010.

Partnership for Assessment of Readiness for College and Careers. 2011.

Pearson, David P. 2004. "The Reading Wars." *Educational Policy* 18 (1): 216–252.

———. 2013. "A Close Look at Close Reading." Presentation, California Reading Association, Sonoma State University, November 2.

Pearson, David P., and Nell K. Duke. 2002. "Comprehension Instruction in the Primary Grades." In *Comprehension Instruction: Research-Based Best Practices* edited by Cathy Collins Block and Michael Pressley, 247–258. New York, NY: Guilford.

Pearson, David P., and Margaret C. Gallagher. 1983. "The Instruction of Reading Comprehension." *Contemporary Educational Psychology* 8 (3): 317–344.

Pressley, Michael. 1997. "Imagery and Children's Learning: Putting the Picture in Developmental Perspective." *Review of Educational Research* 47 (4): 586–622.

Purcell-Gates, Victoria, Nell K. Duke, and Joseph A. Martineau. 2007. "Learning to Read and Write Genre-Specific Text: Roles of Authentic Experience and Explicit Teaching." *Reading Research Quarterly* 42 (1): 8–45.

Recht, Donna R., and Lauren Leslie. 1988. "Effect of Prior Knowledge on Good and Poor Readers' Memory of Text." *Journal of Educational Psychology* 80 (1): 16–20.

Reutzel, Ray D., John A. Smith, and Parker C. Fawson. 2005. "An Evaluation of Two Approaches for Teaching Reading Comprehension Strategies in the Primary Years Using Science Information Texts." *Early Childhood Research Quarterly* 20 (3): 276–305.

Rosenshine, Barak, and Carla Meister. 1994. "Reciprocal Teaching: A Review of the Research." *Review of Educational Research* 64 (4): 479–530.

Ross, W. 1860. "Methods of Instruction" *Barnard's American Journal of Education* (9): 367–379

Routman, Regie. 2003. *Reading Essentials*. Portsmouth, NH: Heinemann.

———. 2008. *Teaching Essentials*. Portsmouth, NH: Heinemann.

Schiefele, U., Drapp, A., and A. Winteler. 1992. "Interest as a Predictor of Academic Achievement: A Meta-analysis of Research." *The Role of Interest in Learning and Development.* Hillsdale, NJ: Erlbaum.

Shanahan, Timothy. 2012. "Informational Text: Or How Thick Can You Slice the Salami" *Shanahan on Literacy* (blog), October 3. Accessed March 20, 2014. http://www.shanahanonliteracy. com/2012/10/informational-text-or-how-thinly-can.html

Shanahan, Timothy, Douglas Fisher, and Nancy Frey. 2012. "The Challenge of Challenging Text." *Educational Leadership* 69 (6): 58–62.

Smith, M. Cecil. 2000. "The Real-World Reading Practices of Adults." *Journal of Literacy Research* 32 (1): 25–52.

Snow, C. and C. O'Connor. 2013. "Close Reading and Far-Reaching Classroom Discussion: Fostering a Vital Connection," A Policy Brief from the Literacy Research Panel of the International Reading Association. Newark, DE: International Reading Association.

Swanton, S. 1984. "Minds Alive: What and Why Gifted Students Read for Pleasure." *School Library Journal* (30): 99–102.

Vasquez, A., A. Hansen, and P. Smith. 2013. *Teaching Language Arts to English Language Learners.* New York, NY: Routledge.

Webb, Norman L. 2002. Depth-of-Knowledge Levels for Content Areas. University of Wisconsin Center for Research.

Wilhelm, J. and Smith. 2002. *Reading Don't Fix No Chevys.* Portsmouth, ME: Heinemann.

Wilen, William D. 1991. *Questioning Skills for Teachers, 3rd Edition.* Washington, D.C.: National Education Association.

Venezky, Richard L. 1982. "The Origins of the Present-Day Chasm Between Adult Literacy Needs and School Literacy Instruction." *Visible Language* 16 (2): 112–127.

Wilson, Paul T., Richard C. Anderson. 1986. "What They Don't Know Will Hurt Them: The Role of Prior Knowledge in Comprehension." In *Reading Comprehension from Research to Practice* edited by Judith Oransano, 31–48. Hillside, NJ: Erlbaum.

Literature Cited

Aloian, Molly, and Bobbie Kalman. 2007. *A Rainforest Habitat*. New York, NY: Crab Tree.

Armour, Cy. 2012. *Earthquake*! Huntington Beach, CA: Teacher Created Materials.

Baretta, Gene. 2008. *Now and Ben*. New York, NY: Square Fish.

Bateman, Donna. 2012. *Out on the Prarie*. Watertown, MA: Charlesbridge.

Blazeman, Christopher. 2012. *Snakes Up Close*. Huntington Beach, CA: Teacher Created Materials.

Bradley, Timothy. 2012. *Animal Architects*. Huntington Beach, CA: Teacher Created Materials.

Bradley, Timothy. 2012. *Bug Builders* Huntington Beach, CA: Teacher Created Materials.

Branley, Franklin M. 1986. *Volcanoes*. New York, NY: Harper Trophy

Bunting, Eve. 1988 *How Many Days to America?* New York, NY: Houghton Mifflin Harcourt

Carle, Eric. 1991. *The Very Hungry Caterpillar*. New York, NY: Philomel.

Cash, Roseanne. 2011. *Composed: A Memoir*. New York, NY: Penguin.

Cherry, Lynne. 2000. *The Great Kapok Tree* by Lynne Cherry. Boston, MA. Houghton Mifflin Harcourt.

Cherry, Lynne. 2002. *A River Ran Wild*. Boston, MA: Houghton Mifflin Harcourt.

Cohen, Barbara. 1983. *Molly's Pilgrim*. New York, NY: HarperCollins.

Cohn, Jessica. 2013. *Hand to Earth: Saving the Environment*. Huntington Beach, CA: Teacher Created Materials.

Cohn, Jessica. 2013. *Hand to Heart: Improving Communities*. Huntington Beach, CA: Teacher Created Materials.

Cohn, Jessica. 2013. *Hand to Paw: Protecting Animals*. Huntington Beach, CA: Teacher Created Materials.

David, Jacqueline. 2004. *The Boy Who Drew Birds: A Story of John James Audubon*. New York, NY: Houghton Mifflin Harcourt.

Davies, Nicola. 2005. *Ice Bear: In the Steps of the Polar Bear*. Somerville, MA: Candlewick.

DuTemple, Lesley. 1999. *Whales*. New York, NY: Scholastic.

Florian, Douglas. 2002. *Insectopedia*. New York, NY: Houghton Mifflin Harcourt.

Fowler, Allan. 1997. *Gator or Croc?* New York, NY: Children's Press.

Frank, Anne. 1993. *The Diary of a Young Girl*. New York, NY: Bantam.

French, Vivian. 2012. *Yucky Worms*. Somerville, MA: Candlewick Press.

George, Jean. 1997. *Everglades*. New York, NY: HarperCollins.

Gibbons, Gail. 2000. *Bats*. New York, NY: Holiday House.

Giblin, James C. 2006. *The Amazing Life of Benjamin Franklin*. New York, NY: Scholastic.

Greathouse, Lisa. 2009. *How Toys Work*. Huntington Beach, CA: Teacher Created Materials.

Greathouse, Lisa, and Stephanie Kuligowski. 2012. *Unsolved! Mysterious Events!* Huntington Beach, CA: Teacher Created Materials.

Gregory, Josh. 2013. *Great White Sharks.* New York, NY: Scholastic.

Hemingway, Ernest. 1926. *The Sun Also Rises.* New York, NY: Charles Scribner's Sons.

Hillman, Ben. 2007. *How Big Is It?* New York, NY: Scholastic.

Hughes, Susan. 2012. *Is It Transparent or Opaque?* New York, NY: Crabtree Publishing.

Hunt, Dawson J. 2011. *A Day in Our Lives.* Huntington Beach, CA: Teacher Created Materials.

Isecke, Hariet. 2012. *Women's Suffrage.* Huntington Beach, CA: Teacher Created Materials.

Johnson, Jen Cu. 2010. *Seeds of Change.* New York, NY: Lee and Low Books.

Jenkins, Martin. 2011. *Can We Save the Tiger.* Sommerville, MA: Candlewick Press.

Jenkins, Martin. 2012. *Titanic: Disaster at Sea.* Cambridge, MA: Candlewick Press.

Kuligowski, Stephanie. 2013. *Amazing Americans: Susan B. Anthony* Huntington Beach, CA: Teacher Created Materials.

Larson, Jennifer. 2010. *Do I Need It? or Do I Want It?: Making Budget Choices.* Minneapolis, MN. Lerner Publications.

Lawler, Janet. 2013. *Oceans Counting.* Washington, DC: National Geographic.

Lawton, Caroline. 2011 *Bugs A to Z.* New York, NY: Scholastic.

Levin, Ellen. 1988. *If You Traveled on the Underground Railroad.* New York, NY: Scholastic.

Lollis, Sylvia. 2002. *Should We Have Pets?* New York, NY: Mondo.

Lowry, Lois. 1989. *Number the Stars.* Boston, MA: AMH Books for Young Readers.

Martin, Rafe. 1998. *The Rough Faced Girl.* New York, NY: Puffin.

Matthews, Rupert. 2007. *You Wouldn't Want to Be A Mayan Soothsayer*! New York: Children's Press.

Murphy, Jim. 2006. *The Great Fire.* Huntington Beach, CA: Teacher Created Materials.

Nelson, Robin. 2013. *From Wax to Crayon.* Minneapolis, MN: Lerner Publications.

Ofill, Jenny. 2011. *11 Experiments That Failed.* New York, NY: Schwartz and Wade

Paris, Stephanie. 2013. *Straight Talk: The Truth about Food.* Huntington Beach, CA: Teacher Created Materials.

Peterson, Casey. 2012. *Games Around the World.* Huntington Beach, CA: Teacher Created Materials.

Preus, M. 2013. *Celebritrees: Historic and Famous Trees of the World.* New York, NY: Holt.

Raum, E. 2010. *The Dreadful Smelly Colonies: The Disgusting Details About Life in Colonial America.* Manheto: Fact Finders.

Rice, Dona Herweck. 2012. *A Bee's Life.* Huntington Beach, CA: Teacher Created Materials.

———. 2012a. *A Frog's Life.* Huntington Beach, CA: Teacher Created Materials.

———. 2012b. *Animal Eyes.* Huntington Beach, CA: Teacher Created Materials.

———. 2012c. *Histories Mysteries.* Huntington Beach, CA: Teacher Created Materials.

———. 2012d. *Hit It! History of Tools.* Huntington Beach, CA: Teacher Created Materials.

———. 2012e. *Staying Healthy.* Huntington Beach, CA: Teacher Created Materials.

Rose, Deborah Lee. 2000. *Into the A, B, Sea.* New York, NY: Scholastic.

Rice, William B. 2007. *Inside the Water Cycle.* Huntington Beach, CA: Teacher Created Materials.

Rice, William B. 2007. *Water Scientists* Huntington Beach, CA: Teacher Created Materials.

Rice, William B. 2012. *Jane Goodall.* Huntington Beach, CA: Teacher Created Materials.

Rotner, Shelley. 2010. *Senses at the Seashore.* Minneapolis, MN: Millbrook Press.

Rusch, Elizabeth. 2013. *Volcano Rising.* San Francisco, CA: Charlesbridge.

Say, Allen. 1993. *Grandfather's Journey.* New York, NY: Houghton Mifflin.

Selsam, Millicent E. 1973. *How Kittens Grow.* New York, NY: Scholastic.

Simon, Seymour. 2001. *Animals Nobody Loves.* New York, NY: Chronicle.

Simon, Seymour. 1989. *Whales.* New York, NY: HarperCollins.

Spetgang, Tilly. 2009. *Kids' Solar Energy Book.* Watertown, MA: Imagine.

Strayed, Cheryl. 2013. *Wild: From Lost to Found on the Pacific Trail.* New York, NY: Vintage.

Spier, Peter 1992. *The Star-Spangled Banner.* New York, NY: Dragon Fly.

White, E. B. 1952. *Charlotte's Web.* New York, NY: Harper and Row.

Talbott, Hudson. 2009. *River of Dreams.* New York, NY: G. P. Putnam's Sons.

Wilcox, Charlotte. 1993. *Mummies and Their Mysteries.* Minneapolis, MN: Carolrhoda Books

Winter, Jeanette. 2006. *The Librarian of Basra: A True Story from Iraq.* New York, NY: Harcourt.

Yep, Laurence, and Kathleen Yep. 2008. *The Dragon's Child.* New York, NY: Harper Collins.

Adult Literature

Sandberg, Sheryl. 2013. *Lean In: Women, Work, and the Will to Lead.* New York, NY: Knopf.

Seinfeld, Jessica. 2013. *The Can't Cookbook: 100+Recipes for the Absolutely Terrified.* New York, NY: Atria.

Steinbeck, John. 2006. *The Grapes of Wrath.* New York, NY: Penguin.

Tolstoy, Leo. 2008. *War and Peace.* New York, NY: Vintage.

Thinking Deeply!

Directions: Use the learning action words and tasks at a variety of levels to ask questions, invite students to ask questions, and to create tasks for students to complete.

<table>
<tr><td>

Thinking Deeply!
With Bloom's Revised Taxonomy/Webb's Depth of Knowledge
(Anderson and Krathwohl 2001; Webb 2002; Hess 2006)

</td></tr>
<tr><td>

Remembering/Understanding (Bloom's)
Recall and Reproduction (DOK)
(Recall a fact, information, or procedure)

Learning Action Words and Tasks:

arrange, collect, identify, show, label, illustrate, repeat, tell, who, what, when, where, why, name, classify, describe, discuss, distinguish, explain, indicate, locate, recognize, report, restate, summarize

</td></tr>
<tr><td>

Applying (Bloom)
Application of Skill Concept (DOK)
(Utilize information in two or more steps in new situations)

Learning Action Words and Tasks:

apply, define, compare, classify, complete, demonstrate, discover, dramatize, examine, interpret, modify, operate, practice, relate, show, sketch, use

</td></tr>
<tr><td>

Analyzing (Bloom)
Strategic Thinking (DOK)
(Develop a plan with more than one answer)

Learning Action Words and Tasks:

analyze, cite evidence, infer, arrange, compare, calculate, categorize, classify, connect, contrast, criticize, differentiate, discriminate, distinguish, divide, infer, question, order

</td></tr>
<tr><td>

Evaluating/Creating (Bloom)
Extended Thinking (DOK)
(Investigate, plan something new, and judge the process)

Learning Action Words and Tasks:

argue, prove, assess, convince, defend, recommend, estimate, judge, predict, rate, support, value, evaluate, rank, test, measure, combine, compose, construct, create, design, develop, formulate, generalize, suppose, imagine, organize, plan, prepare, propose, rearrange, rewrite, set up, substitute, what if?

</td></tr>
</table>

(Adapted from Hess 2006)

Digging Deeper Thinking Bookmark

Digging Deeper Thinking Bookmark

Remember/Understand

Who _____? What _____? When _____?
Where _____? Why _____? How _____?
Explain _____.
What is _____?
Retell in your own words.
The main idea is _____. The details are _____.
Choose other words to show what you learned.
label, show, repeat, name, explain, summarize
Reflect: What did I learn? What is important to remember?

Apply

How is _____ and example of _____? Show evidence from the text.
How is _____ like _____? Show evidence from the text.
Give another example of _____.
Choose other words to use what you learned.
apply, classify, complete, demonstrate, draw, dramatize, give another example, state the rule for
Reflect: What are other examples in this text and other texts? What information can I use again?

Analyze/ Strategic Thinking

How does _____ compare/contrast with _____?
What evidence can you use to show _____?
Choose other words to take apart and study what you learned.
analyze, cite evidence, arrange, compare, contrast, calculate, connect, criticize, infer, question, order
Reflect: *What patterns do I see? What do I think now? Why?*

Evaluate/Create/Extend Thinking

Use text evidence to show
Do you agree with _____? Why?
What do you think about _____? Why?
I rate _____ because _____.
What do you predict/infer about _____? Why?
What solutions do you suggest for _____? Explain.
How would you design a new _____? Explain.
Choose other words to evaluate or create a new idea.
argue, prove, assess, convince, defend, recommend, judge, predict, rate, support, evaluate, rank, combine, construct, create, design, develop, generalize, imagine, rewrite, what if?
Reflect: How did I do as a learner? What can I do with this information now? What can I create? How do I rate this?

Digging Deeper Thinking Bookmark

Remember/Understand

Who _____? What _____? When _____?
Where _____? Why _____? How _____?
Explain _____.
What is _____?
Retell in your own words.
The main idea is _____. The details are _____.
Choose other words to show what you learned.
label, show, repeat, name, explain, summarize
Reflect: What did I learn? What is important to remember?

Apply

How is _____ an example of _____? Show evidence from the text.
How is _____ like _____? Show evidence from the text.
Give another example of _____.
Choose other words to use what you learned.
apply, classify, complete, demonstrate, draw, dramatize, give another example, state the rule for
Reflect: What are other examples in this text and other texts? What information can I use again?

Analyze/ Strategic Thinking

How does _____ compare/contrast with _____?
What evidence can you use to show _____?
Choose other words to take apart and study what you learned.
analyze, cite evidence, arrange, compare, contrast, calculate, connect, criticize, infer, question, order
Reflect: *What patterns do I see? What do I think now? Why?*

Evaluate/Create/Extend Thinking

Use text evidence to show
Do you agree with _____? Why?
What do you think about _____? Why?
I rate _____ because _____.
What do you predict/infer about _____? Why?
What solutions do you suggest for _____? Explain.
How would you design a new _____? Explain.
Choose other words to evaluate or create a new idea.
argue, prove, assess, convince, defend, recommend, judge, predict, rate, support, evaluate, rank, combine, construct, create, design, develop, generalize, imagine, rewrite, what if?
Reflect: How did I do as a learner? What can I do with this information now? What can I create? How do I rate this?

© Shell Education

Name: _____ Date: _____

Informational Text Reading Interviews

Directions: Interview classmates and adults to find out what informational texts they are reading and what they will do with the information.

Name of Reader	Job of Reader (nurse, teacher, lawyer, etc.)	Informational Text(s) Read	Reading Strategies the Reader Used	What will reader do with the information? (Why is the reader reading this text?) because... *he or she wants to.* *he or she needs to.* *he or she is interested in...*
1.			Check those that apply __ rereading __ skimming __ reading closely __ clarifying words __ using glossary __ using headings __ using photos, maps, charts __ highlighting __ other	_____ reads, because...
2.			__ rereading __ skimming __ reading closely __ clarifying words __ using glossary __ using headings __ using photos, maps, charts __ highlighting __ other	_____ reads, because...
3.			__ rereading __ skimming __ reading closely __ clarifying words __ using glossary __ using headings __ using photos, maps, charts __ highlighting __ other	_____ reads, because...
4.			__ rereading __ skimming __ reading closely __ clarifying words __ using glossary __ using headings __ using photos, maps, charts __ highlighting __ other	_____ reads, because...

Name: _____ Date: _____

Informational Text Recording Sheet

Informational Texts I Read	Reason for Reading	Strategies Used

Name: _____   Date: _____

Informational Text Checklist

I read _____ .

I used these strategies to understand the text.

☐ I studied the visuals. Example _____

☐ I reread confusing parts. Example _____

☐ I reread confusing words. Example _____

☐ I slowed down on _____ because _____ .

☐ I read the headings. Example _____

☐ I was amazed by _____ .

☐ I wondered _____ .

☐ I flipped through the pages to see _____ .

☐ I went back to _____ because _____ .

☐ I used the glossary to figure out _____ .

☐ I used the table of contents.

☐ I skipped around in the book to find out or see

_____ .

☐ I read slowly to understand _____ .

☐ I marked the text with sticky notes or by writing or highlighting to show my thoughts.

Name: _____ Date: _____

Text Feature Organizer

Text Feature	Page #	Purpose of the Text Feature
Table of Contents		
Headings		
Subheadings		
Photos		
Drawings		
Maps		
Graphs		
Charts		
Diagram		
Table		
Graph		
Index		
Glossary		
Highlighted Words		
Other Text Features		
Write about your favorite feature.	Which text feature was the most helpful to you today? _____ What did you learn by using it? _____ _____	

Text Feature Game Cards

Title	Table of Contents	Index	Glossary
Heading	Subheading	Photo	Caption and Photo
Diagram	Table	Chart	Map
Highlighted Words	Graph	Sidebar	Cut-Away

© Shell Education

Name: _____ Date: _____

Text-Tac-Toe

Directions: Choose nine text feature cards and place them face up on the card.

When the leader shows a text feature and it matches one of yours, flip your card over, keeping it in the same place. When you get three in a row in any direction turned over, you have a Text-Tac-Toe!

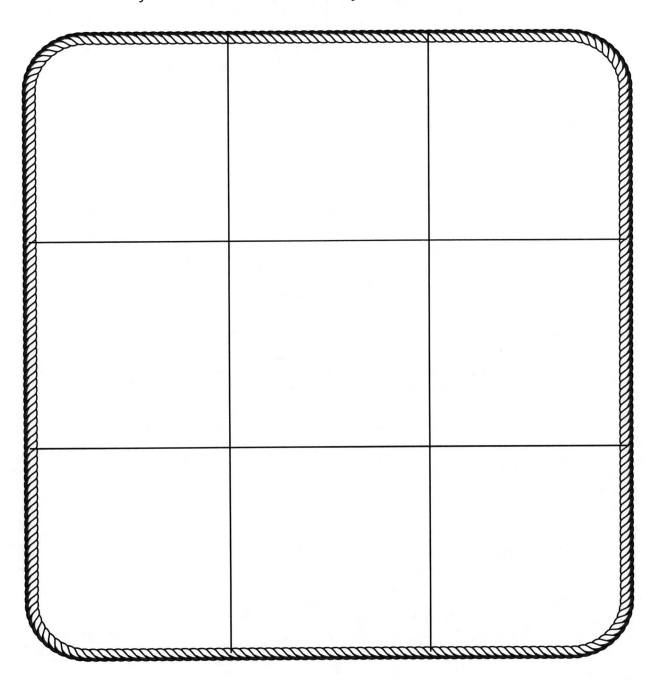

Reciprocal Teaching Bookmark

Reciprocal Teaching Bookmark (adapted from Oczkus 2010)	Reciprocal Teaching Bookmark (adapted from Oczkus 2010)
Predict Look at the headings, illustrations, and text. What do you think you will learn? Talk to your partner or team. **I think I will learn** _____ **because** _____.	**Predict** Look at the headings, illustrations, and text. What do you think you will learn? Talk to your partner or team. **I think I will learn** _____ **because** _____.
Question Ask questions before, during, and after reading. Use who, what, when, where, why, and how. Share with partners or your team. **My question before reading** _____ **My question during reading** _____ **My question after reading** _____	**Question** Ask questions before, during, and after reading. Use who, what, when, where, why, and how. Share with partners or your team. **My question before reading** _____ **My question during reading** _____ **My question after reading** _____
Clarify Be on the lookout for difficult words or ideas. How did you figure them out? Talk to partners/team. **Difficult words** _____ **Confusing ideas** _____ I used the following strategies __reread __sounded words out __read on __used syllables, prefixes, word parts __talked to a friend __looked up the word	**Clarify** Be on the lookout for difficult words or ideas. How did you figure them out? Talk to partners/team. **Difficult words** _____ **Confusing ideas** _____ I used the following strategies __reread __sounded words out __read on __used syllables, prefixes, word parts __talked to a friend __looked up the word
Summarize In your own words, tell the main ideas from the text. **Sketch your summary.** **This text is about** _____.	**Summarize** In your own words, tell the main ideas from the text. **Sketch your summary.** **This text is about** _____.

Name: _____ Date: _____

My Interest Inventory

1. What topics do you know about? _____.

2. What do you enjoy doing? _____.

3. What are you good at? _____.

4. What do you want to learn about? _____.

Finish these sentences.

5. After school, I like to _____.

6. My hobbies are _____.

7. My favorite movie is _____.

8. My favorite television shows are _____.

9. I have a pet _____ . I wish I had a pet _____.

10. I'd like to travel to _____.

Check all the topics you are interested in.

__ zoo animals	__ rainforest	__ heros	__ how-to books
__ farm animals	__ how things are made	__ travel	__ current news
__ ocean creatures	__ natural disasters	__ scientists	__ sports
__ dogs	__ volcanoes	__ inventions	__ football
__ cats	__ hurricanes	__ astronauts	__ baseball
__ horses	__ earthquakes	__ pilots	__ soccer
__ pigs	__ tornadoes	__ world records	__ basketball
__ snakes	__ rocks	__ firemen	__ wrestling
__ birds	__ weather	__ police men/women	__ other sport _____
__ frogs	__ health	__ immigration	
__ insects	__ solar system	__ wars	
__ butterflies	__ history	__ maps	
__ other _____	__ cars		

(Adapted from Harvey 1998; Moss and Terrell 2010)

Name: _____   Date: _____

Informational Text Reading Log

Title/Author	Text Type	Author's Purpose Why did the author write this? • *to inform* • *to persuade* • *to entertain*	My Purpose to learn about _____ to do something I am interested in	Score 1 Best 2 Good 3 Okay 4 Not great 5 Poor Tell why.
	__ magazine __ article __ online article __ book __ other			I gave it a ___ because…
	__ magazine __ article __ online article __ book __ other			I gave it a ___ because…
	__ magazine __ article __ online article __ book __ other			I gave it a ___ because…
	__ magazine __ article __ online article __ book __ other			I gave it a ___ because…
	__ magazine __ article __ online article __ book __ other			I gave it a ___ because…

Name: _____   Date: _____

Predicting with the Table of Contents

Chapter Title _____ _____ After reading (check one) ___ My prediction was on target. ___ I changed my prediction.	I think I will learn _____ because _____. Sketch your prediction.
Chapter Title _____ _____ After reading (check one) ___ My prediction was on target. ___ I changed my prediction.	I think I will learn _____ because _____. Sketch your prediction.
Chapter Title _____ _____ After reading (check one) ___ My prediction was on target. ___ I changed my prediction.	I think I will learn _____ because _____. Sketch your prediction.
Chapter Title _____ _____ After reading (check one) ___ My prediction was on target. ___ I changed my prediction.	I think I will learn _____ because _____. Sketch your prediction.
Chapter Title _____ _____ After reading (check one) ___ My prediction was on target. ___ I changed my prediction.	I think I will learn _____ because _____. Sketch your prediction.

Name: _____ Date: _____

Table of Contents Wonderings

The title of the book is _____. It has _____ chapters. I think the author organized these chapters this way because _____. I am most interested in reading the chapter titled _____.

Chapter _____

I wonder _____

because _____.

Chapter _____

I wonder _____

because _____.

Chapter _____

I wonder _____

because _____.

Chapter _____

I wonder _____

because _____.

Chapter _____

I wonder _____

because _____.

Name: _____ Date: _____

Symbol Summaries Organizer

Chapter Title _____
_____
Symbol

I chose this symbol because
_____
_____.

Chapter Title _____
_____
Symbol

I chose this symbol because
_____
_____.

Chapter Title _____
_____
Symbol

I chose this symbol because
_____
_____.

Chapter Title _____
_____
Symbol

I chose this symbol because
_____
_____.

Chapter Title _____
_____
Symbol

I chose this symbol because
_____
_____.

Chapter Title _____
_____
Symbol

I chose this symbol because
_____
_____.

Chapter Title _____
_____
Symbol

I chose this symbol because
_____
_____.

Chapter Title _____
_____
Symbol

I chose this symbol because
_____
_____.

© Shell Education

Pause to Predict: Partner Bookmark

Pause to Predict: Partner Bookmark

Look over the headings in an informational text.

Use the headings to tell what you think each part is about.

All of these headings are going to teach us about _____.

Heading #1

Copy the heading.

_____

I think the part under this heading is going to be about _____

because _____

_____.

Heading #2

Copy the heading.

_____

I think the part under this heading is going to be about _____

because _____

_____.

Heading #3

Copy the heading.

_____

I think the part under this heading is going to be about _____

because _____

_____.

Pause to Predict: Partner Bookmark

Look over the headings in an informational text.

Use the headings to tell what you think each part is about.

All of these headings are going to teach us about _____.

Heading #1

Copy the heading.

_____

I think the part under this heading is going to be about _____

because _____

_____.

Heading #2

Copy the heading.

_____

I think the part under this heading is going to be about _____

because _____

_____.

Heading #3

Copy the heading.

_____

I think the part under this heading is going to be about _____

because _____

Name: _____ Date: _____

Presto Change-o Headings to Questions

Copy heading #1

_____

_____

Turn it into a question.

_____

_____

_____?

Draw or write the answer to your question after reading.

Copy heading #2

_____

_____

Turn it into a question.

_____

_____

_____?

Draw or write the answer to your question after reading.

Copy heading #3

_____

_____

Turn it into a question.

_____

_____

_____?

Draw or write the answer to your question after reading.

Copy heading #4

_____

_____

Turn it into a question.

_____

_____

_____?

Draw or write the answer to your question after reading.

Rate the headings. Tell a partner why.

Circle one.   great   ok   poor

Rewrite one of the headings here.

© Shell Education

Name: _____   Date: _____

All Aboard the Heading Train

Directions: Choose two headings from the reading that had confusing ideas or words. Complete the chart below using those headings.

Heading _____ _____ **Confusing word or sentence** _____ _____ **Did the headings help me?** (circle one) Yes Sort of Not this time **How I figured it out:** __ looked at the pictures, maps, visuals __ reread the page __ read on __ broke it into parts __ sounded it out __ looked up words __ substituted words of similar meaning **Rate the heading** (circle one) The heading was Great Okay Not so good Why do you think the author chose this heading? _____ _____ What is another heading that the author could have used? _____ _____	**Heading** _____ _____ **Confusing word or sentence** _____ _____ **Did the headings help me?** (circle one) Yes Sort of Not this time **How I figured it out:** __ looked at the pictures, maps, visuals __ reread the page __ read on __ broke it into parts __ sounded it out __ looked up words __ substituted words of similar meaning **Rate the heading** (circle one) The heading was Great Okay Not so good Why do you think the author chose this heading? _____ _____ What is another heading that the author could have used? _____ _____

What's My Heading? Concentration Game

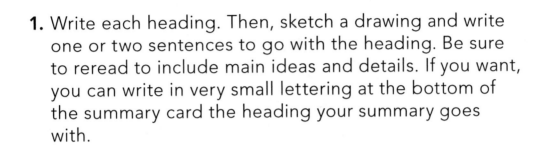

1. Write each heading. Then, sketch a drawing and write one or two sentences to go with the heading. Be sure to reread to include main ideas and details. If you want, you can write in very small lettering at the bottom of the summary card the heading your summary goes with.

2. Cut apart your headings and summaries.

3. Mix them up, turn them over, and play concentration matching with a partner. You may want to use both your and your partner's deck of headings and summaries. Make sure you've both read the texts.

4. Take turns turning over two of the cards. If you have a matching heading and summary, it is a match. If you turn over two cards and they don't match, put the cards back and it is your partner's turn.

5. To make the game more challenging, use headings and summaries from several different chapters or texts.

6. Save your cards in an envelope. Label the envelope with the title of the book.

7. You can glue the envelope into your notebook to save.

© Shell Education

What's My Heading?
Concentration Game (cont.)

Heading	Summary Main ideas 1–2 Details	Heading	Summary Main ideas 1–2 Details
Heading	Summary Main ideas 1–2 Details	Heading	Summary Main idea 1–2 Details
Heading	Summary Main ideas 1–2 Details	Heading	Summary Main ideas 1–2 Details

#51316—Just the Facts!   © Shell Education

Name: _____ Date: _____

Say Cheese!

1. Choose a photo.

I choose the photo on page _____.

The pages around the photo are about

_____.

The caption says _____

_____.

The author included this photo because

_____

_____

_____.

I chose it because _____

_____

_____.

2. Study the photo. Ask questions.

Make up questions to ask a partner about the photo. Use question words: Who, What, Where, When, How, Why, How far..., How long...

Question #1

Question #2

3. Study the photo. Say "cheese" and take a mind photo of it. Cover the photo and sketch what you remember.

*Uncover the photo. Compare it to your drawing. How did you do?

4. Sketch the photo again. This time, look at the photo while you draw it. 📷

5. Was this photo helpful? (circle one) Yes   Sort of   Not Really

Explain why.

Name: _____   Date: _____

Photo Awards

First Prize Photo

The first prize photo award goes to the picture of

_____

I chose this photo because...

(select and ✔ one or more reasons below and explain)

1. ____ It helped me understand why _____
_____.

2. ____ It helped me understand how _____
_____.

3. ____ It adds very important information that is NOT in the text. It shows
_____
_____.

4. ____ It explains the information that was in the text about
_____
_____.

First Prize Page

Second Prize Photo

The second prize photo award goes to the picture of

_____

I chose this photo because...

(select and ✔ one or more reasons below and explain)

1. ____ It helped me understand why _____
_____.

2. ____ It helped me understand how _____
_____.

3. ____ It adds very important information that is NOT in the text. It shows
_____
_____.

4. ____ It explains the information that was in the text about
_____
_____.

Second Prize Page

Third Prize Photo

The third prize photo award goes to the picture of

_____

I chose this photo because...

(select and ✔ one or more reasons below and explain)

1. ____ It helped me understand why _____
_____.

2. ____ It helped me understand how _____
_____.

3. ____ It adds very important information that is NOT in the text. It shows
_____
_____.

4. ____ It explains the information that was in the text about
_____
_____.

Third Prize Page

Name: _____ Date: _____

Sketch It! Diagram It!

1. Choose a diagram.

I chose the photo on page _____ .

The pages around the diagram are about

_____ .

The author included this diagram to teach me about _____

_____

_____ .

I chose it because _____

_____

_____ .

2. Study the diagram. Ask questions.

Write questions to ask a partner about the diagram. Use question words: Who, What, Where, When, How, Why, How far, How long

Question #1

Question #2

3. Study the diagram. Cover the diagram. Sketch what you remember.

*Uncover the diagram. Compare it to your drawing. How did you do?

4. Sketch the diagram again. This time look at the diagram when you draw it.

5. Was this diagram helpful? (circle one)
Yes   Sort of   Not Really

Explain why.

© Shell Education

Name: _____ Date: _____

Thumbs Up, Thumbs On Glossary

Before Reading: Review the text. Look at the glossary and pick one word you know, sort of know, and want to know. Read the definition and sketch the word meaning.

I know this word.	I sort of know this word.	I don't know this word but want to learn it.
_____ Read the definition. Sketch the word.	_____ Read the definition. Sketch the word.	_____ Read the definition. Sketch the word.

During Reading: As you read, what are some tricky or interesting words you find along the way.

I know this word.	I sort of know this word.	I don't know this word but want to learn it.
_____ Read the definition. Sketch the word.	_____ Read the definition. Sketch the word.	_____ Read the definition. Sketch the word.

After Reading: After reading, search through the glossary and choose a new word you know, sort of know, and still want to know.

I know this word.	I sort of know this word.	I don't know this word but want to learn it.
_____ Read the definition. Sketch the word.	_____ Read the definition. Sketch the word.	_____ Read the definition. Sketch the word.

Prize Winning Words

Best Glossary Word: _____ Why? _____

Hardest Glossary Word: _____ Why? _____

Glossary Sensory Bookmark

Glossary Words	Glossary Words

Word I Can See

_____

Clue words in the text or glossary that help are
_____, _____, _____.
_____

Word I Can See

_____

Clue words in the text or glossary that help are
_____, _____, _____.

Clue words in the text or glossary that help are
_____, _____, _____.

Word I Can Hear

_____

Clue words in the text or glossary that help are
_____, _____, _____.
_____

Word I Can Hear

_____

Clue words in the text or glossary that help are
_____, _____, _____.

Clue words in the text or glossary that help are
_____, _____, _____.

Word I Can Touch or Feel

_____

Clue words in the text or glossary that help are
_____, _____, _____.
_____

Word I Can Touch or Feel

_____

Clue words in the text or glossary that help are
_____, _____, _____.

Clue words in the text or glossary that help are
_____, _____, _____.

Word I Can Smell

_____

Clue words in the text or glossary that help are
_____, _____, _____.
_____

Word I Can Smell

_____

Clue words in the text or glossary that help are
_____, _____, _____.

Clue words in the text or glossary that help are
_____, _____, _____.

Words I Can Taste

_____

Clue words in the text or glossary that help are
_____, _____, _____.

Clue words in the text or glossary that help are
_____, _____, _____.

Words I Can Taste

_____

Clue words in the text or glossary that help are
_____, _____, _____.

Clue words in the text or glossary that help are
_____, _____, _____.

© Shell Education

Favorite Words Bookmark

Favorite Words
Choose 5 favorite words from the glossary and the text.

I like the word _____ because
_____
_____ .
It is important because _____
_____ .
The author uses it on page _____ .
The author did a: good job okay job not so great job
(circle one)
explaining this word in the text and glossary.

I like the word _____ because
_____
_____ .
It is important because _____
_____ .
The author uses it on page _____ .
The author did a: good job okay job not so great job
(circle one)
explaining this word in the text and glossary.

I like the word _____ because
_____
_____ .
It is important because _____
_____ .
The author uses it on page _____ .
The author did a: good job okay job not so great job
(circle one)
explaining this word in the text and glossary.

I like the word _____ because
_____
_____ .
It is important because _____
_____ .
The author uses it on page _____ .
The author did a: good job okay job not so great job
(circle one)
explaining this word in the text and glossary.

I like the word _____ because
_____
_____ .
It is important because _____
_____ .
The author uses it on page _____ .
The author did a: good job okay job not so great job
(circle one)
explaining this word in the text and glossary.

Favorite Words
Choose 5 favorite words from the glossary and the text.

I like the word _____ because
_____
_____ .
It is important because _____
_____ .
The author uses it on page _____ .
The author did a: good job okay job not so great job
(circle one)
explaining this word in the text and glossary.

I like the word _____ because
_____
_____ .
It is important because _____
_____ .
The author uses it on page _____ .
The author did a: good job okay job not so great job
(circle one)
explaining this word in the text and glossary.

I like the word _____ because
_____
_____ .
It is important because _____
_____ .
The author uses it on page _____ .
The author did a: good job okay job not so great job
(circle one)
explaining this word in the text and glossary.

I like the word _____ because
_____
_____ .
It is important because _____
_____ .
The author uses it on page _____ .
The author did a: good job okay job not so great job
(circle one)
explaining this word in the text and glossary.

I like the word _____ because
_____
_____ .
It is important because _____
_____ .
The author uses it on page _____ .
The author did a: good job okay job not so great job
(circle one)
explaining this word in the text and glossary.

Name: _____   Date: _____

Glossary Guessing Game

Directions: Choose four glossary words. Sketch each one. Write the definitions and the sentence from the text. Cut them apart, mix them up, and ask your partner to find the drawing, definition, and sentences that go together. Or mix up the cards. Turn them over and take turns making matches and playing concentration!

Sketch the Word	Glossary Definition	Sentence from the Text
		page _____
Sketch the Word	Glossary Definition	Sentence from the Text
		page _____
Sketch the Word	Glossary Definition	Sentence from the Text
		page _____
Sketch the Word	Glossary Definition	Sentence from the Text
		page _____

© Shell Education

Name: _____ Date: _____

Index Hunt

Directions: Work with a partner. Take turns choosing interesting topics to look up in the index. Then, look up the pages with the topic on it. Give a time using a clock with a second hand. Be careful with the pages!

Partner A Name	Partner B Name
_____	_____
Round 1 **Partner A** Turn your back so your partner can't see, and pick an index word. Write it here: _____ Show Partner B so he or she can look up the word and the page numbers that go with it.	**Partner B** Quickly look up the word your partner gives you. Quickly look up the pages listed for the word and read them out loud.

Together A and B	
Write the word _____ Write the pages _____	Sketch a drawing of the word.
Score the word. This word was (check one) ___ Easy to find. ___ Okay to find. ___ Sort of hard to find. ___ Really tricky to find.	Write a sentence about the word.

Index Hunt (cont.)

Round 2	
Partner B	**Partner A**
Turn your back so your partner can't see, and pick an index word. Write it here: _____	Quickly look up the word your partner gives you.
Show Partner A so he or she can look up the word and the page numbers that go with it.	Quickly look up the pages listed for the word and read them out loud.

Together A and B	
Write the word _____ Write the pages _____	Sketch a drawing of the word.
Score the word. This word was (check one) ___ Easy to find. ___ Okay to find. ___ Sort of hard to find. ___ Really tricky to find.	Write a sentence about the word.

Name: _____   Date: _____

Index It!

Directions: Hunt in the index for the main idea, supporting details, and interesting facts to complete the chart below.

+ **Main Idea Index Words**	√ **Supporting Detail Index Words**	* **Interesting Facts Index Words**
Word _____	Word _____	Word _____
Page #s _____	Page #s _____	Page #s _____
Draw it! 	Draw it! 	Draw it!
What I learned about the word. I learned _____ _____ _____ .	What I learned about the word. I learned _____ _____ _____ .	What I learned about the word. I learned _____ _____ _____ .
I also learned _____ _____ _____ _____ .	I also learned _____ _____ _____ _____ .	I also learned _____ _____ _____ _____ .
This is a main idea word because _____ _____ _____ .	This is a supporting detail word because _____ _____ _____ .	This is a fun fact word because _____ _____ _____ .

Name: _____ Date: _____

Favorite Index Word Awards

Directions: Choose your four favorite words from the index to complete the chart below. Put the words in order with #1 as your very favorite.

#1 Word The Favorite Word Award goes to _____ because _____ _____ _____. Draw the word.	**#3 Word** The Favorite Word Award goes to _____ because _____ _____ _____. Draw the word.
#2 Word The Favorite Word Award goes to _____ because _____ _____ _____. Draw the word.	**#4 Word** The Favorite Word Award goes to _____ because _____ _____ _____. Draw the word.

Name: _____   Date: _____

Purpose, Purpose
What's the Author's Purpose?

Before Reading

Skim the text and look at the illustrations.

What do you predict is the author's purpose?

I think the author wrote this to **inform**, **persuade**, or **entertain** the reader. (circle one)

What do you think the author wants us to learn?

I think the author wants to teach us mostly about _____

because I see _____ .

Draw a picture of what you think the author wants us to learn.

After Reading

Answer the questions again.

What is the author's purpose?

I think the author's purpose is to **inform**, **persuade**, or **entertain** the reader. (circle one)

I can tell because the author _____

_____ .

Purpose, Purpose
What's the Author's Purpose? (cont.)

What does the author want us to learn?

I think the author wants to teach us about _____

_____ .

I learned _____ .

Draw a picture of what you will remember most.

Give the author a score.

The words were

1 = great   2 = okay   3 = poor

I gave this score because _____ .

The visuals were

1 = great   2 = okay   3 = poor

I gave this score because _____ .

Name: _____ Date: _____

What's My Purpose?

Title of Text _____ by _____ .

Before Reading:

What is my purpose for reading?

_____ I chose it.

_____ My teacher chose it.

I want (need) to read this text because (check all those that apply):

_____ I need to know the information for a test or project.

_____ I need to read to answer a question.

_____ I need to read to find out more about _____ so I can choose
a detail to learn more about.

_____ I need (want) to read about a different point of view.

_____ I want to read this for fun.

After Reading:

Did I meet my purpose for reading?

_____ The text met my purpose for reading.

4 = great   3 = good   2 = just okay   1 = no

Check all those that apply

_____ I answered my question(s).

_____ I learned some more information for the test or project.

_____ I learned more about _____ and chose the detail
_____ to read more about.

_____ I learned about point of view.

_____ I enjoyed reading this just for fun.

What's My Purpose? *(cont.)*

I learned _____

_____ .

Sketch something important you learned about your purpose for reading.

```




















```

I rate this text:

4 = great   3 = good   2 = okay   1 = not great

because _____

_____ .

What's My Purpose? Bookmark

What's My Purpose? Bookmark	What's My Purpose? Bookmark
Read to learn how to do something. Title _____ By _____ I want/need to read this text to learn how to _____ _____ .	**Read to learn how to do something.** Title _____ By _____ I want/need to read this text to learn how to _____ _____ .
Read to answer questions. Title _____ By _____ I want/need to read this text to answer questions I have about _____ One question I have _____ .	**Read to answer questions.** Title _____ By _____ I want/need to read this text to answer questions I have about _____ One question I have _____ .
Read to narrow a topic. Title _____ By _____ I want/need to read this text to find out more about _____ so I can choose to read more about _____ .	**Read to narrow a topic.** Title _____ By _____ I want/need to read this text to find out more about _____ so I can choose to read more about _____ .
Read to "do" something with the information (report, test, blog, write, project, skit, etc). Title _____ By _____ I want/need to read to use the information when I _____	**Read to "do" something with the information (report, test, blog, write, project, skit, etc).** Title _____ By _____ I want/need to read to use the information when I _____
Read to study a point of view. Title _____ By _____ I want/need to read this to see what _____ says about _____ .	**Read to study a point of view.** Title _____ By _____ I want/need to read this to see what _____ says about _____ .
Read just for fun! Title _____ By _____ I want/need to read this just for fun to learn about _____ .	**Read just for fun!** Title _____ By _____ I want/need to read this just for fun to learn about _____ .

Text Walk This Way: Group Discussion Bookmark

Text Walk This Way: Group Discussion Bookmark

Text Walker #1

Before reading, page/flip through the text with your team.

Ask, *What do you already know about* _____?

Two things our group already knows:

Page _____ What we know about _____.

Page _____ What we know about _____.

Text Walker #2

Before reading, page through the text with your team pausing to study all the text features. Put a check mark for each one you find.

Check all the text features that you see in this text.

_____ heading(s)_____ photo(s) _____ map(s)
_____ diagram(s) _____ chart(s) _____ bold words
_____ table of contents _____ index
_____ glossary

Choose two text features to predict what you will learn.

The _____ on page _____ shows or says _____ so we think we will learn _____.

The _____ on page ____ shows or says _____ so we think we will learn _____.

Text Walker #3

Before reading, page through the book one more time thinking about what you are wondering about the topic.

Choose two things your group is wondering about.

On page _____, we are wondering _____.

On page _____, we are wondering _____.

Tell your group to start reading the text!

Final Text Checker #4

After reading the text, discuss the following:

What is the main idea of the text? _____.

We could tell it was important because the author

_____

We also learned _____

Which text features were most helpful and why? (see list in #2)

1. _____ because _____.

2. _____ because _____.

Text Walk This Way: Group Discussion Bookmark

Text Walker #1

Before reading, page/flip through the text with your team.

Ask, *What do you already know about* _____?

Two things our group already knows:

Page _____ What we know about _____.

Page _____ What we know about _____.

Text Walker #2

Before reading, page through the text with your team pausing to study all the text features. Put a check mark for each one you find.

Check all the text features that you see in this text.

_____ heading(s)_____ photo(s) _____ map(s)
_____ diagram(s) _____ chart(s) _____ bold words
_____ table of contents _____ index
_____ glossary

Choose two text features to predict what you will learn.

The _____ on page _____ shows or says _____ so we think we will learn _____.

The _____ on page ____ shows or says _____ so we think we will learn _____.

Text Walker #3

Before reading, page through the book one more time thinking about what you are wondering about the topic.

Choose two things your group is wondering about.

On page _____, we are wondering _____.

On page _____, we are wondering _____.

Tell your group to start reading the text!

Final Text Checker #4

After reading the text, discuss the following:

What is the main idea of the text? _____.

We could tell it was important because the author.

_____

We also learned _____

Which text features were most helpful and why? (see list in #2)

1. _____ because _____.

2. _____ because _____.

Text Walk This Way: My Own Bookmark

Text Walk This Way: My Own Bookmark

Text Walk #1
Before reading, quickly flip through the text.
What do I already know?
Page _____ I know about _____.
Page _____ I know about _____.

Text Walk #2
Before reading, page through the text pausing to study all the text features.
Check all the text features that you see in this text.
_____ heading(s) _____ photo(s) _____ map(s)
_____ diagram(s) _____ chart(s) _____ bold words _____ table of contents _____ index _____ glossary
Choose two text features to predict what you will learn.
The _____ on page _____ shows or says _____
so I think I will learn _____.
The _____ on page _____ shows or says _____
so I think I will learn _____.

Text Walk #3
Before reading, page through the book one more time thinking about what you are wondering about the topic.
Choose two things you are wondering about.
On page _____, I am wondering _____.
On page _____, I am wondering _____.
Start reading the text!

Final Text Check#4
After reading the text, answer the following:
The main idea was _____.
I could tell it was important because the author
_____.
I also learned _____.
Which text features were most helpful and why? (see list in #2)
1. The _____ on page _____ was helpful because
_____
2. The _____ on page _____ was helpful because
_____

Text Walk This Way: My Own Bookmark

Text Walk #1
Before reading, quickly flip through the text.
What do I already know?
Page _____ I know about _____.
Page _____ I know about _____.

Text Walk #2
Before reading, page through the text pausing to study all the text features.
Check all the text features that you see in this text.
_____ heading(s) _____ photo(s) _____ map(s)
_____ diagram(s) _____ chart(s) _____ bold words _____ table of contents _____ index _____ glossary
Choose two text features to predict what you will learn.
The _____ on page _____ shows or says _____
so I think I will learn _____.
The _____ on page _____ shows or says _____
so I think I will learn _____.

Text Walk #3
Before reading, page through the book one more time thinking about what you are wondering about the topic.
Choose two things you are wondering about.
On page _____, I am wondering _____.
On page _____, I am wondering _____.
Start reading the text!

Final Text Check#4
After reading the text, answer the following:
The main idea was _____.
I could tell it was important because the author
_____.
I also learned _____.
Which text features were most helpful and why? (see list in #2)
1. The _____ on page _____ was helpful because
_____
2. The _____ on page _____ was helpful because
_____

#51316—Just the Facts!

© Shell Education

Name: _____   Date: _____

My Wonders

I wonder what...	I wonder who...	I wonder why...	I wonder how...
I wonder when...	I wonder where...	I wonder if...	

Part I: Wonder walk for the first part of the text.

1. Wonder walk before reading

Skim through the first part of the text. Study the illustrations and headings. Write wonders.

Page _____ I wonder _____

_____ .

Page _____ I wonder _____

_____ .

2. Talk to a partner before reading.

Share your wonders. Add to your wonders.

Now I wonder _____ .

3. Read the text.

Now I wonder _____ .

Now I wonder _____ .

4. Talk to a partner about the reading so far.

Share your wonders. Add to your wonders.

Now I wonder _____

_____ .

Part II: Wonder walk for the rest of the text.

1. Wonder walk before reading

Skim through the rest of the text. Study the illustrations and headings. Write wonders.

Page _____ I wonder _____

_____ .

Page _____ I wonder _____

_____ .

2. Talk to a partner before reading.

Share your wonders. Add to your wonders.

Now I wonder _____ .

3. Read the text.

Now I wonder _____ .

Now I wonder _____ .

4. Talk to a partner about the reading so far.

Share your wonders. Add to your wonders.

Now I wonder _____

_____ .

Name: _____   Date: _____

Interview Show

Character or Object (Sketch and label it.)	Questions Who, what, when, where, why, how, why did you How did you… Why do you think?	
	1. _____ _____ 2. _____ _____	**Draw your answer.** Answer is on page(s) _____
	1. _____ _____ 2. _____ _____	**Draw your answer.** Answer is on page(s) _____
	1. _____ _____ 2. _____ _____	**Draw your answer.** Answer is on page(s) _____

© Shell Education

Name: _____ Date: _____

QBTTT Bookmark

QBTTT Bookmark	**QBTTT Bookmark**

Key ideas and Details

1. What is the author teaching us? Why did the author write this?

The author is teaching us mostly about _____ because _____ .

Give page numbers. _____

2. Choose a sentence. Write a question about it. Page # _____

_____ ?

3. Choose a paragraph. Write a question about it. Page # _____

_____ ?

4. Choose a page. Write a question about it. Page # _____

_____ ?

5. What was confusing about the text? Why?

The confusing part was on page _____. It was hard to understand because _____ .

I _____ to figure it out.

Craft and Structure

Why is the word _____ important to the text?

_____ .

Why did the author choose it?

_____ .

What sentence is the most helpful? Why?

_____ .

Why did the author write this text?

_____ .

What are some of the text features the author used in this text? (map, photo, diagram)

The author used a _____ to show _____ .

This helped me because _____ .

Integration of Knowledge and Ideas

How did the map, photo, diagram (circle one) help you understand the text?

_____ .

I learned _____ .

Ask a quiz question about a (map, photo, diagram).

_____

Compare two texts you've read on the same topic. Which text was more helpful? Why?

The text _____ on the topic _____ was more helpful because it _____ .

Key ideas and Details

1. What is the author teaching us? Why did the author write this?

The author is teaching us mostly about _____ because _____ .

Give page numbers. _____

2. Choose a sentence. Write a question about it. Page # _____

_____ ?

3. Choose a paragraph. Write a question about it. Page # _____

_____ ?

4. Choose a page. Write a question about it. Page # _____

_____ ?

5. What was confusing about the text? Why?

The confusing part was on page _____. It was hard to understand because _____ .

I _____ to figure it out.

Craft and Structure

Why is the word _____ important to the text?

_____ .

Why did the author choose it?

_____ .

What sentence is the most helpful? Why?

_____ .

Why did the author write this text?

_____ .

What are some of the text features the author used in this text? (map, photo, diagram)

The author used a _____ to show _____ .

This helped me because _____ .

Integration of Knowledge and Ideas

How did the map, photo, diagram (circle one) help you understand the text?

_____ .

I learned _____ .

Ask a quiz question about a (map, photo, diagram).

_____

Compare two texts you've read on the same topic. Which text was more helpful? Why?

The text _____ on the topic _____ was more helpful because it _____ .

Name: _____   Date: _____

Building Inspection! Examples of Informational Text Structures

Text Structure	Example (Write an example from the text. Circle the *clue words* in each example.)
Description The author explains a topic and lists examples. **Clue Words:** for example, in addition to, most important, another, such as, has, have, in fact	
Time Order Sequence The author lists events or the topic in order. **Clue Words:** first, next, then, finally, before, after that, not long after	
Problem/Solution The author explains a problem and solutions. **Clue Words:** the problem is, solve, a question is..., one answer is, one reason is, the puzzle is	
Compare/Contrast The author explains how two or more topics are alike/different. **Compare Words** same as, alike, not only but also, either or, similar to, compared with, as well as, likewise **Contrast Words** different from, in contrast to, less than, instead of, however, while	
Cause /Effect The author explains why or how something happens. **Clue Words:** because, since, if, then, so that, for this reason, because of, consequently, in order to	

Name: _____ Date: _____

Bingo Card

Name: _____   Date: _____

Tricky Words

The word _____

on page_____was tricky. I tried

_____

_____

_____ .

The word _____

on page_____was tricky. I tried

_____

_____

_____ .

The word _____

on page_____was tricky. I tried

_____

_____

_____ .

The word _____

on page_____was tricky. I tried

_____

_____

_____ .

Name: _____ Date: _____

Picture This!

I chose the sentence from page _____ to copy. (Write the sentence below.)

_____

_____

Three words that helped me "see" my mind movie or picture in my head the most

My mind movie/picture.

I chose the sentence from page _____ to copy. (Write the sentence below.)

_____

_____

Three words that helped me "see" my mind movie or picture in my head the most

My mind movie/picture

© Shell Education

Name: _____   Date: _____

Presto Change-o

The Text Says...

Copy an important sentence from the book.

_____

_____

This is from page _____.

Draw a picture to go with the sentence.

Presto Change-o

Change the words.

Go back and underline two key words in the sentence you copied.

Copy the words you underlined into this chart and write words that mean the same.

Text Key Word	**Presto Change-o** My Word:
Text Key Word	**Presto Change-o** My Word:

Say the sentence with your words.

The Text Says...

Copy an important sentence from the book.

_____

_____

This is from page _____.

Draw a picture to go with the sentence.

Presto Change-o

Change the words.

Go back and underline two key words in the sentence you copied.

Copy the words you underlined into this chart and write words that mean the same.

Text Key Word	**Presto Change-o** My Word:
Text Key Word	**Presto Change-o** My Word:

Say the sentence with your words.

Name: _____ Date: _____

Presto Combine-o

The Text Says...

Read sentences from page_____.

Read them several times. Cover them with your hand.

Draw a picture to go with the sentences.

Presto Combine-o

Combine sentences.

Cover two or more sentences in the text.

Write a one-sentence summary in your own words below.

_____

_____

_____

_____ .

The Text Says...

Read sentences from page _____.

Read them several times. Cover them with your hand.

Draw a picture to go with the sentences.

Presto Combine-o

Combine sentences.

Cover two or more sentences in the text.

Write a one-sentence summary in your own words below.

_____

_____

_____

_____ .

Show the Evidence Bookmark

Show the Evidence Bookmark

The author says _____

_____

because...

On page _____, it says _____

_____.

An example is _____.

Another example is _____.

The text says _____.

The map shows _____.

The photo shows _____.

The graph/chart/diagram shows

_____.

Show the Evidence Bookmark

The author says _____

_____

because...

On page _____, it says _____

_____.

An example is _____.

Another example is _____.

The text says _____.

The map shows _____.

The photo shows _____.

The graph/chart/diagram shows

_____.

Name: _____ Date: _____

Where'd You Get It—Text or Visuals?

Directions: Choose two pages from the text and tell what you learned from the text and visuals.

Featuring Page _____

On this page, I see (describe visuals, headings):

What I learned from the text	**What I learned from the visuals**
1. I learned _____ .	**1.** From the (map, photo, diagram, chart—circle one) I learned _____ _____ .
2. I learned _____ .	
3. I learned _____ .	**2.** Another visual I learned from was the map, photo, diagram, chart (circle one) I learned _____ _____ .

From both, I learned _____

_____

_____ .

Where'd You Get It—Text or Visuals? *(cont.)*

Featuring Page _____

On this page, I see (describe visuals, headings)

What I learned from the text	What I learned from the visuals
1. I learned _____ .	**1.** From the (map, photo, diagram, chart—circle one) I learned _____ _____ .
2. I learned _____ .	
3. I learned _____ .	**2.** Another visual I learned from was the map, photo, diagram, chart (circle one) I learned _____ _____ .

From both, I learned _____

_____

_____ .

Name: _____ Date: _____

Compare It! Contrast It!

Texts on the topic: _____

Question: _____

Texts	Question 1: I want to know _____ _____	Question 2 I want to know _____ _____	I also learned _____ _____ .	How I rate the text
Text #1	Answer to Question #1	Answer to Question #2		Text #1 answered my questions. (circle one) Yes Sort of No Tell why.
Text #2	Answer to Question #1	Answer to Question #2		Text #2 answered my questions. (circle one) Yes Sort of No Tell why.

What I learned that was the same in both texts was _____

_____ .

What I learned that was only in text #1 was _____

_____ .

What I learned that was only in text #2 was _____

_____ .

The most helpful text on the topic of _____ was _____

because _____ .

Contents of the Digital Resource CD

Page(s)	Lesson	Filename
n/a	Professional Development Guide	pdguide.pdf
202	Thinking Deeply!	thinkingdeeply.pdf
203	Digging Deeper Thinking Bookmark	diggingdeeperbk.pdf
204	Informational Text Reading Interviews	infotextintvw.pdf
205	Informational Text Recording Sheet	infotextsheet.pdf
206	Informational Text Checklist	infotextlist.pdf
207	Text Feature Organizer	textorg.pdf
208	Text Feature Game Cards	textcards.pdf
209	Text-Tac-Toe	texttactoe.pdf
210	Reciprocal Teaching Bookmark	reciprocalbk.pdf
211	My Interest Inventory	interestinv.pdf
212	Informational Text Reading Log	infotextlog.pdf
213	Predicting with the Table of Contents	predictingtoc.pdf
214	Table of Contents Wonderings	tocwonderings.pdf
215	Symbol Summaries Organizer	symsumorg.pdf
216	Pause to Predict: Partner Bookmark	pausebookmark.pdf
217	Presto Change-o Headings to Questions	prestochangeoa.pdf
218	All Aboard the Heading Train	allaboard.pdf
219–220	What's My Heading Concentration Game	whatsmyhead.pdf
221	Say Cheese!	saycheese.pdf
222	Photo Awards	photoawards.pdf
223	Sketch It! Diagram It!	sketchit.pdf
224	Thumbs Up, Thumbs On Glossary	thumbsup.pdf
225	Glossary Sensory Bookmark	glossarybk.pdf
226	Favorite Words Bookmark	favwordbookmark.pdf
227	Glossary Guessing Game	guessinggame.pdf
228–229	Index Hunt	indexhunt.pdf
230	Index It!	indexit.pdf
231	Favorite Index Word Awards	favindexaward.pdf
232–233	Purpose, Purpose What's the Author's Purpose?	authorspurpose.pdf
234–235	What's My Purpose?	whatsmypurpose.pdf
236	What's My Purpose? Bookmark	whatsmypurposbk.pdf
237	Text Walk This Way: Group Discussion Bookmark	textwalkgroup.pdf

Contents of the Digital Resource CD *(cont.)*

Page(s)	Lesson	Filename
238	Text Walk This Way: My Own Bookmark	textwalkmyown.pdf
239	My Wonders	mywonders.pdf
240	Interview Show	interviewshow.pdf
241	QBTTT Bookmark	qbtttbookmark.pdf
242	Building Inspection! Examples of Informational Text Structures	bldginspect.pdf
243	Bingo Card	bingocard.pdf
244	Tricky Words	trickywords.pdf
245	Picture This!	picturethis.pdf
246	Presto Change-o	prestochangeo.pdf
247	Presto Combine-o	prestocombineo.pdf
248	Show the Evidence Bookmark	evidencebkmark.pdf
249–250	Where'd You Get It—Text or Visuals?	wheredyougetit.pdf
251	Compare It! Contrast It!	comparecontrast.pdf

Notes

Notes

Notes

#51316—Just the Facts! © Shell Education